Qlik Sense Cookbook
Second Edition

Over 80 recipes on data analytics to solve business
intelligence challenges

Pablo Labbe
Philip Hand
Neeraj Kharpate

BIRMINGHAM - MUMBAI

Qlik Sense Cookbook
Second Edition

Commissioning Editor: Sunith Shetty
Acquisition Editor: Prachi Bisht
Content Development Editor: Amrita Noronha
Technical Editor: Sneha Hanchate
Copy Editor: Safis Editing
Project Coordinator: Namrata Swetta
Proofreader: Safis Editing
Indexer: Priyanka Dhadke
Graphics: Jisha Chirayil
Production Coordinator: Aparna Bhagat

First published: November 2015
Second edition: August 2018

Production reference: 1280818

Published by Packt Publishing Ltd.
Livery Place
35 Livery Street
Birmingham
B3 2PB, UK.

ISBN 978-1-78899-705-8

www.packtpub.com

`mapt.io`

Mapt is an online digital library that gives you full access to over 5,000 books and videos, as well as industry leading tools to help you plan your personal development and advance your career. For more information, please visit our website.

Why subscribe?

- Spend less time learning and more time coding with practical eBooks and Videos from over 4,000 industry professionals
- Improve your learning with Skill Plans built especially for you
- Get a free eBook or video every month
- Mapt is fully searchable
- Copy and paste, print, and bookmark content

PacktPub.com

Did you know that Packt offers eBook versions of every book published, with PDF and ePub files available? You can upgrade to the eBook version at `www.PacktPub.com` and as a print book customer, you are entitled to a discount on the eBook copy. Get in touch with us at `service@packtpub.com` for more details.

At `www.PacktPub.com`, you can also read a collection of free technical articles, sign up for a range of free newsletters, and receive exclusive discounts and offers on Packt books and eBooks.

Contributors

About the authors

Pablo Labbe is a BI consultant with over 20 years' experience. In 2008 he was introduced to Qlikview, a former product by Qlik and the seed for Qlik Sense. Since then, he has focused on delivering BI solutions in a new way. Now he is the Principal of ANALITIKA Inteligencia, delivering BI projects and training on Qlik products and other technologies that embrace the self-service BI. Pablo is an active member of the Qlik community and other social media sites.

> *I want to thank the people who have been close to me and supported me, especially my wife, Daniela, and my children.*

Philip Hand is a senior BI consultant who has worked with QlikView in the BI space for over 7 years. He has implemented end-to-end solutions in a wide variety of enterprises and for large business customers. He has spent many years consulting on business and QlikView solutions. His belief is that such a role proves invaluable to hone your skills through exposure to many different businesses, problems, technologies, industries, and people.

Neeraj Kharpate works as an independent BI consultant providing services to clients from various industries. Neeraj embarked on his journey with Qlik in mid-2007. He has over 10 years of experience working with clientele from multiple sectors, ranging from banks and insurance to retail. Neeraj has been closely following the developments in Qlik Sense ever since it was launched in 2014 and is actively involved with its enterprise-wide implementations.

About the reviewer

Marcio Lins was born in Guarabira, Brazil, on June 21, 1983. He is the founder of the IMWTI (2012), a Qlik solution provider partner, a Certified Scrum Master, and a Qlik developer leader. He has worked more than 10 ERP and other technologies (PHP, C#, and Clipper). He specializes in the Qlik API, from bots to integration with corporate systems.

Packt is searching for authors like you

If you're interested in becoming an author for Packt, please visit `authors.packtpub.com` and apply today. We have worked with thousands of developers and tech professionals, just like you, to help them share their insight with the global tech community. You can make a general application, apply for a specific hot topic that we are recruiting an author for, or submit your own idea.

Table of Contents

Preface 1

Chapter 1: Getting Started with the Data 7
Introduction 7
Extracting data from databases and data files 8
Getting ready 9
How to do it... 13
How it works... 16
There's more... 16
See also... 16
Extracting data from web files 16
Getting ready 16
How to do it... 17
How it works... 18
There's more... 18
See also... 18
Extracting data from the FTP server 19
Getting ready 19
How to do it... 21
How it works... 22
There's more... 23
See also... 23
Extracting data from web services with REST Connector 23
How to do it... 24
How it works... 26
There's more... 26
See also... 26
Activating the legacy mode in Qlik Sense® desktop 26
How it works... 27
There's more... 27
See also... 28
Previewing data in the Data model viewer 28
Getting ready 29
How to do it... 29
How it works... 29
Viewing the data model 29
Viewing the associations 30
Table metadata 31
There's more... 33
Creating a master library from the Data model viewer 33

Getting ready	33
How to do it…	35
How it works…	39
There's more…	40
Using a master library in Edit mode	**41**
Getting ready	41
How to do it…	41
There's more…	43
Using visual data preparation on the data manager model viewer	**44**
Getting ready	44
How to do it…	45
How it works…	49
There's more…	56
Chapter 2: Visualizations	**57**
Introduction	**57**
Creating snapshots	**58**
Getting ready	58
How to do it…	59
How it works…	60
There's more…	60
See also	60
Creating and adding content to a story	**60**
Getting ready	61
How to do it…	61
How it works…	64
There's more…	64
See also	66
Adding embedded sheets to the story	**66**
Getting ready	66
How to do it…	66
How it works…	67
There's more…	68
Highlighting the performance measure in a bar chart	**68**
Getting ready	68
How to do it…	69
How it works…	71
There's more…	72
See also	72
Associating persistent colors to field values using the script	**72**
Getting ready	72
How to do it…	73
How it works…	74
There's more…	74
See also	74

Using the colormix1 function   75
  Getting ready   75
  How to do it...   75
  How it works...   76
  There's more...   77
  See also   77
Composition   77
  Getting ready   78
  How to do it...   78
  How it works...   79
  There's more...   79
Relationships   80
  Getting ready   81
  How to do it...   81
  How it works...   82
Comparison   83
  Getting ready   83
  How to do it...   83
  How it works...   84
  See also   84
Distribution   85
  Getting ready   85
  How to do it...   85
  How it works...   86
Structuring visualizations   86
  Getting ready   87
  How to do it...   87
  How it works...   89
Measuring statistical data with box plot charts   90
  Getting ready   90
  How to do it...   90
  How it works...   91
Using a waterfall chart to analyze the cumulative effect   91
  Getting ready   92
  How to do it...   92
  How it works...   93

Chapter 3: Scripting   95
 Introduction   95
 Structuring the script   96
  Getting ready   96
  How to do it...   96
  How it works...   97
 Efficiently debugging the script   97
  Getting ready   98

How to do it...	98
How it works...	102
There's more...	102
See also	102
Packaging the code in script files	102
Getting ready	103
How to do it...	103
How it works...	104
See also	105
How to use subroutines in Qlik Sense®	105
Getting ready	105
How to do it...	106
How it works...	108
There's more...	108
See also	109
Optimizing the UI calculation speed	109
Getting ready	109
How to do it...	110
How it works...	111
Optimizing the reload time of the application	111
Getting ready	112
How to do it...	112
How it works...	113
Using a For each loop to load data from multiple files	114
Getting ready	114
How to do it...	114
How it works...	116
There's more...	116
Using the Concat() function to store multiple field values in a single cell	116
Getting ready	116
How to do it...	117
How it works...	117
There's more...	118
See also	118
Executing command-line programs within the script	118
Getting ready	118
How to do it...	119
How it works...	119
There's more...	119
See also	119
Chapter 4: Managing Apps and the User Interface	121
Introduction	122

Publishing a Qlik Sense® application created in Qlik Sense® Desktop   122
Getting ready   122
How to do it…   122
How it works…   123
There's more…   123
Creating private, approved, and community sheets   123
Getting ready   124
How to do it…   124
How it works…   124
There's more…   125
See also   125
Publishing a Qlik Sense® application to Qlik Sense® Cloud   125
Getting ready   125
How to do it…   126
How it works…   127
There's more…   128
Creating geo maps in Qlik Sense®   129
Getting ready   129
How to do it…   130
How it works…   133
There's more…   134
Reference lines in a Sales versus Target gauge chart   135
Getting ready   135
How to do it…   135
How it works…   137
There's more…   137
See also   137
Effectively using the KPI object in Qlik Sense®   138
Getting ready   138
How to do it…   138
How it works…   140
There's more…   141
See also   141
Creating treemaps   142
Getting ready   142
How to do it…   142
How it works…   143
There's more…   144
Creating dimensionless bar charts in Qlik Sense®   145
Getting ready   145
How to do it…   145
How it works…   147
There's more…   147
See also   147

Adding reference lines to trendline charts 147
Getting ready 148
How to do it... 148
How it works... 150
Creating text and images 150
Getting ready 150
How to do it... 151
How it works... 154
Applying limitations to charts 154
Getting ready 154
How to do it... 155
How it works... 156
There's more... 157
Adding thumbnails to a clear environment 157
Getting ready 157
How to do it... 157
How it works... 159
Navigating many data points in a scatter chart 160
Getting ready 160
How to do it... 160
How it works... 162
There's more... 162
Using alternative dimensions and measures 163
Getting ready 163
How to do it... 163
How it works... 165
There's more... 165
Using the visual exploration menu 165
Getting ready 165
How to do it... 165
How it works... 167
There's more... 167
Chapter 5: Useful Functions 169
Introduction 170
Using an extended interval match to handle slowly changing dimensions 170
Getting ready 170
How to do it... 172
How it works... 175
There's more... 175
See also 176
Using the Previous() function to identify the latest record read for a dimensional value 176
Getting ready 176

How to do it...   177
How it works...   179
There's more...   179
See also   179
Using the NetworkDays() function to calculate the working days in a calendar month   179
Getting ready   180
How to do it...   180
How it works...   182
See also   183
Using the Concat() function to display a string of field values as a dimension   183
Getting ready   183
How to do it...   184
How it works...   184
There's more...   185
See also   185
Using the Minstring() function to calculate the age of the oldest case in a queue   185
Getting ready   185
How to do it...   186
How it works...   187
There's more...   187
See also   187
Using the RangeSum() function to plot cumulative figures in trendline charts   188
Getting ready   188
How to do it...   189
How it works...   189
See also   190
Using the Fractile() function to generate quartiles   190
Getting ready   190
How to do it...   191
How it works...   192
There's more...   192
See also   193
Using the FirstSortedValue() function to identify the median in a quartile range   193
Getting ready   193
How to do it...   193
How it works...   194
There's more...   195
See also   195
Using the Declare and Derive functions to generate Calendar fields 195
Getting ready   195

How to do it...   196
How it works...   196
There's more...   197
See also   197
Setting up a moving annual total figure   197
Getting ready   197
How to do it...   199
How it works...   200
There's more...   200
See also   201
Using the For Each loop to extract files from a folder   201
Getting ready   201
How to do it...   202
How it works...   203
**Using the Peek() function to create a currency exchange rate
calendar**   204
Getting ready   204
How to do it...   204
How it works...   207
There's more...   207
See also   208
Using the Peek() function to create a trial balance sheet   208
Getting ready   208
How to do it...   208
How it works...   211
See also   211
Using the subfield() function to split field into multiple records 212
Getting ready   212
How to do it...   212
How it works...   213
There's more...   214
See also   214
Using the dual() function to set the sort order of dimensions   214
Getting ready   214
How to do it...   214
How it works...   216
There's more...   216
See also   216

Chapter 6: Set Analysis   217
Introduction   217
Cracking the syntax for Set Analysis   218
Getting ready   219
How to do it...   219
How it works...   220

There's more…   220
See also   220
Using flags in Set Analysis   221
Getting ready   221
How to do it…   222
How it works…   222
There's more…   223
See also   224
Using the = sign with variables in Set Analysis   224
Getting ready   224
How to do it…   225
How it works…   226
See also   226
Point in Time using Set Analysis   226
Getting ready   227
How to do it…   227
How it works…   229
Using comparison sets in Set Analysis   230
Getting ready   230
How to do it…   231
How it works…   232
Using embedded functions in Set Analysis   233
Getting ready   233
How to do it…   234
How it works…   235
There's more…   235
Creating a multi-measure expression in Set Analysis   236
Getting ready   236
How to do it…   237
How it works…   238
Using search strings inside a set modifier   238
Getting ready   238
How to do it…   239
How it works…   240
There's more…   240
See also   240
Capturing a list of field values using a Cconcat() function in Set Analysis   241
Getting ready   241
How to do it…   241
How it works…   242
Using the element functions P() and E() in Set Analysis   242
Getting ready   243
How to do it…   243
How it works…   245

There's more...   245
See also   246
Using the intersection between sets for Basket Analysis   246
Getting ready   247
How to do it...   247
How it works...   248
There's more...   249
See also   250
Using alternate states   250
Getting ready   250
How to do it...   251
How it works...   252
There's more...   252
See also   252
Chapter 7: Using Extensions in Qlik Sense   253
Introduction   253
Finding extensions on Qlik Branch   254
Getting ready   254
How to do it...   254
How it works...   255
There's more...   255
See also   256
How to import extensions (Desktop and Server)   256
Getting ready   256
How to do it...   256
How it works...   257
There's more...   257
Using the Variable extension   258
Getting ready   258
How to do it...   258
How it works...   261
There's more...   262
Using the Reload button extension   262
Getting ready   262
How to do it...   263
How it works...   263
There's more...   264
Using the simple KPI extension   264
Getting ready   264
How to do it...   265
How it works...   267
There's more...   267
Using the ShowHide Container extension   267
Getting ready   268

How to do it…	268
How it works…	273
There's more…	273
Chapter 8: Advanced Aggregation with AGGR	**275**
Introduction	275
Using nested aggregations	275
Getting ready	276
How to do it…	276
How it works…	277
There's more…	278
See also	278
Using Rank() with Aggr	278
Getting ready	278
How to do it…	278
How it works…	279
There's more…	279
See also	280
Combining set analysis with Aggr	280
Getting ready	281
How to do it…	281
How it works…	282
There's more…	282
See also	282
Creating an ABC analysis	282
Getting ready	283
How to do it…	283
How it works…	285
There's more…	285
See also	285
Chapter 9: Tips and Tricks	**287**
Introduction	287
Working with multiple tabs	287
Getting ready	288
How to do it…	288
How it works…	291
There's more…	291
See also	291
Using the keyboard to navigate and interact	291
Getting ready	291
How to do it…	292
How it works…	292
There's more…	292
Working with the distinct clause	293
Getting ready	293

How it works…   296
There's more…   296
Managing variables in the script and layout   297
Getting ready   297
How to do it…   298
How it works…   300
There's more…   301
Using measure names in object expressions   302
Getting ready   302
How to do it…   303
How it works…   303
There's more…   304
Creating dynamic charts   304
Getting ready   304
How to do it…   305
How it works…   306
There's more…   306

Other Books You May Enjoy   307

Index   311

Preface

Qlik Sense is a powerful, self-servicing business intelligence (BI) tool for data discovery, analytics, and visualization. It allows you to create personalized BI solutions from raw data and get actionable insights from it.

This book is an excellent guide for all aspiring Qlik Sense® developers. It will take you from the basics, right through to the use of more advanced functions. With the recipes in this book, you will be empowered to create fully featured desktop applications in Qlik Sense®.

Starting with a quick refresher on obtaining data from data files and databases, this book moves on to the more refined features of Qlik Sense®, including visualization, scripting, set analysis, advanced aggregation, and useful extensions. The tips and tricks provided will help you to overcome challenging situations while developing your applications in Qlik Sense®. This and more will help you to deliver engaging dashboards and reports efficiently.

By the end of the book, you will be an expert user of Qlik Sense® and will be able to use its features effectively for business intelligence in an enterprise environment.

Who this book is for

The book is for anyone who has been exposed to Qlik Sense® and wants to start using it actively for BI. Anybody with prior knowledge of its sister product, QlikView, will also benefit from this book. Familiarity with the basics of BI is a prerequisite.

What this book covers

Chapter 1, *Getting Started with the Data*, introduces the reader to different methods of loading data into Qlik Sense from various sources, such as relational databases, data files, FTP server, and web services. We will also delve into the creation and usage of Master Library in Qlik Sense and Data Manager for data preparation without code.

Chapter 2, *Visualizations*, focuses on the best design practices in Qlik Sense in order to create engaging applications. It also looks at the concepts of snapshots and stories in Qlik Sense.

Chapter 3, *Scripting*, introduces the reader to the techniques of writing a well-structured script in Qlik Sense. It discusses and explains the benefits of concepts such as subroutines, script files, and loops in scripts, which all form a part of the arsenal of a good Qlik Sense developer.

Chapter 4, *Managing Apps and the User Interface*, introduces the reader to the concept of publishing the Qlik Sense apps on the server and Qlik Sense cloud. We will also look at certain key Qlik Sense objects and using them for the right purpose and to convey the right information.

Chapter 5, *Useful Functions*, deals with some very useful functions that are available in Qlik Sense. We present some challenging scenarios that a Qlik Sense developer faces and provide solutions for them.

Chapter 6, *Set Analysis*, is one of the most powerful concepts in Qlik Sense. This chapter explains the process of writing Set Analysis expressions from scratch. We will also look at some advanced variations in Set Analysis expressions, such as the introduction of flags, defining ranges using the Concat() function in Set Analysis expressions, using P() and E() for indirect selections, set operators, and alternative states.

Chapter 7, *Using Extensions in Qlik Sense*, focuses on managing and using the most useful extensions in your Qlik Sense apps, such as reload app, action buttons, variable input box, KPI visualization, and object containers, which conditionally show and hide objects.

Chapter 8, *Advanced Aggregation with AGGR*, discuss when and how to use AGGR with some useful recipes, such as Ranking and ABC Analysis.

Chapter 9, *Tips and Tricks*, contains recipes to improve your day-to-day productivity using Qlik Sense.

To get the most out of this book

Qlik Sense Cookbook requires you to have at least a basic understanding of Qlik Sense. You should have either already deployed a couple of Qlik Sense apps or have worked extensively with QlikView before if you are now looking to transition to Qlik Sense.

To make the most out of this book, you don't necessarily read it from the beginning until the end (although it's recommended), but you should feel encouraged to start a chapter you're interested in and follow all recipes until the end because some recipe depends on the previous ones. Cross-references between recipes are made to ensure you know where to continue your reading if you wish to deepen your knowledge.

To closely follow the practical examples and to make the most of the code snippets, please ensure you download the latest version of the Qlik Sense Desktop client from the official website, which can be found here `https://www.qlik.com/us/try-or-buy/download-qlik-sense`.

In the time of writing the book, several versions of Qlik Sense were launched introducing new features but also changes to the UI. At the time of writing of the book, we were using Qlik Sense version February/2018. We carefully wrote the recipes to work correctly with the most recent versions, but the recipe about geo map will not work with the current steps presented because the **Map** object was entirely updated in version April/2018 and June/2018.

Download the example code files

You can download the example code files for this book from your account at `www.packtpub.com`. If you purchased this book elsewhere, you can visit `www.packtpub.com/support` and register to have the files emailed directly to you.

You can download the code files by following these steps:

1. Log in or register at `www.packtpub.com`.
2. Select the **SUPPORT** tab.
3. Click on **Code Downloads & Errata**.
4. Enter the name of the book in the **Search** box and follow the onscreen instructions.

Once the file is downloaded, please make sure that you unzip or extract the folder using the latest version of:

- WinRAR/7-Zip for Windows
- Zipeg/iZip/UnRarX for Mac
- 7-Zip/PeaZip for Linux

The code bundle for the book is also hosted on GitHub at `https://github.com/PacktPublishing/Qlik-Sense-Cookbook-Second-Edition`. In case there's an update to the code, it will be updated on the existing GitHub repository.

We also have other code bundles from our rich catalog of books and videos available at `https://github.com/PacktPublishing/`. Check them out!

Download the color images

We also provide a PDF file that has color images of the screenshots/diagrams used in this book. You can download it here: http://www.packtpub.com/sites/default/files/downloads/QlikSenseCookbookSecondEdition_ColorImages.pdf.

Conventions used

There are a number of text conventions used throughout this book.

CodeInText: Indicates code words in text, database table names, folder names, filenames, file extensions, pathnames, dummy URLs, user input, and Twitter handles. Here is an example: "Mount the downloaded WebStorm-10*.dmg disk image file as another disk in your system."

A block of code is set as follows:

```
EmployeeInt:
LOAD *,
if([EmployeeID]= previous([EmployeeID]),'No','Yes') AS
LatestRecordFlag
RESIDENT EmployeeIntTemp
ORDER BY [EmployeeID] ASC, PositionFrom DESC;
DROP TABLE EmployeeIntTemp;
```

When we wish to draw your attention to a particular part of a code block, the relevant lines or items are set in bold:

```
EmployeeInt:
LOAD *,
if([EmployeeID]= previous([EmployeeID]),'No','Yes') AS
LatestRecordFlag
RESIDENT EmployeeIntTemp
ORDER BY [EmployeeID] ASC, PositionFrom DESC;
DROP TABLE EmployeeIntTemp;
```

Bold: Indicates a new term, an important word, or words that you see onscreen. For example, words in menus or dialog boxes appear in the text like this. Here is an example: "Under **Sorting**, make sure that `PositionFrom` is promoted to the top."

Warnings or important notes appear like this.

Tips and tricks appear like this.

Sections

In this book, you will find several headings that appear frequently (*Getting ready*, *How to do it...*, *How it works...*, *There's more...*, and *See also*).

To give clear instructions on how to complete a recipe, use these sections as follows:

Getting ready

This section tells you what to expect in the recipe and describes how to set up any software or any preliminary settings required for the recipe.

How to do it...

This section contains the steps required to follow the recipe.

How it works...

This section usually consists of a detailed explanation of what happened in the previous section.

There's more...

This section consists of additional information about the recipe in order to make you more knowledgeable about the recipe.

See also

This section provides helpful links to other useful information for the recipe.

Get in touch

Feedback from our readers is always welcome.

General feedback: Email feedback@packtpub.com and mention the book title in the subject of your message. If you have questions about any aspect of this book, please email us at questions@packtpub.com.

Errata: Although we have taken every care to ensure the accuracy of our content, mistakes do happen. If you have found a mistake in this book, we would be grateful if you would report this to us. Please visit www.packtpub.com/submit-errata, selecting your book, clicking on the Errata Submission Form link, and entering the details.

Piracy: If you come across any illegal copies of our works in any form on the internet, we would be grateful if you would provide us with the location address or website name. Please contact us at copyright@packtpub.com with a link to the material.

If you are interested in becoming an author: If there is a topic that you have expertise in and you are interested in either writing or contributing to a book, please visit authors.packtpub.com.

Reviews

Please leave a review. Once you have read and used this book, why not leave a review on the site that you purchased it from? Potential readers can then see and use your unbiased opinion to make purchase decisions, we at Packt can understand what you think about our products, and our authors can see your feedback on their book. Thank you!

For more information about Packt, please visit packtpub.com.

Getting Started with the Data 1

In this chapter, we will cover the basic tasks related to importing data into a Qlik Sense application:

- Extracting data from databases and data files
- Extracting data from web files
- Extracting data from the FTP server
- Extracting data from web services with Rest Connector
- Activating the legacy mode in Qlik Sense® desktop
- Previewing data in the Data model viewer
- Creating a master library from the Data model viewer
- Using a master library in Edit mode
- Using visual data preparation on the data manager model viewer

Introduction

Data is the core aspect of any **Business Intelligence (BI)** application. It provides information that helps organizations to make decisions.

A Qlik Sense application is based on the data extracted from various sources, such as relational databases, CRM systems, ERP systems, and data files.

This chapter introduces the user to various methods of extracting data into a Qlik Sense application effectively. It is assumed that the reader is already acquainted with the concepts of ODBC, OLE DB, and relational databases. The chapter also provides essential recipes to extract data from web services with the REST connector and FTP data sources with the native Web File connector.

The latter part of the chapter focuses on a few recipes regarding the creation of a library and content and the new features of visual data transformation available in the data manager.

Extracting data from databases and data files

The data within an organization is usually stored in relational databases and data files. Extracting data is the first step toward creating a data model. This section demonstrates the steps to extract data from an MS Access database and a delimited (.CSV) file. The procedure to extract data from other relational databases is the same as the process for extracting data from MS Access.

The dataset that we will use is available publicly and covers information about routes and fares for various transport systems in Hong Kong. The original data files have been downloaded from the https://data.gov.hk/ website. This dataset can also be obtained from the Packt Publishing website.

The data connections in the Qlik Sense **Data load editor** save shortcuts leading to commonly used data sources, such as databases and data files. The following types of connections exist in Qlik Sense:

- ODBC database connection
- OLE DB database connection
- Folder connection
- Web file connection
- Qlik Essbase Connector
- Qlik ODBC Connector Package
- Qlik REST Connector
- Qlik Salesforce Connector
- Qlik GeoAnalytics Connector
- Web Storage Provider Connector

This recipe deals with the ODBC, OLE DB, and Folder connections. The web file connection and REST Connector will be dealt with in a separate recipe.

For the following connections, here is a short description, but we don't have recipes for them in this book:

- Qlik Essbase Connector allows data extraction from Hyperion Essbase cubes
- Qlik ODBC Connector Package allows data-extraction from several data sources, such as Google Big Query, Amazon Redshift, Hive, Cloudera Impala, IBM DB2, MS SQL Server, My SQL Enterprise Edition, Oracle, PostgreSQL, Sybase ASE, and Teradata

- Qlik Salesforce Connector allows data extraction from Salesforce reports with SOAP or the Bulk API
- Qlik GeoAnalytics Connector is a new service to make geo-analytics calculations, such as calculating the distance between points, clusters, and merging shapes
- Web Storage Provider Connector allows a connection to storage services, such as DropBox, to retrieve data from files, such as XlSX or CSV

With the exception of Qlik GeoAnalytics Connector, all connectors are free to use. GeoAnalytics Connector requires the purchase or subscription of a separate license from Qlik.

Getting ready

The dataset required for this recipe that is downloaded from the Packt Publishing website (https://www.packtpub.com/big-data-and-business-intelligence/qlik-sense-cookbook-second-edition) comes in a zipped folder called QlikSenseData. Extract all the files from this zipped folder and save them on your hard drive at the desired location.

If you are connecting to the database using **Open Database Connectivity (ODBC)**:

1. Install the relevant ODBC drivers on your system.

 For the sake of this exercise, we need the MS Access drivers. The system DSN connection can be set up through the ODBC administrator under **Administrative Tools** in **Control Panel**.

2. While setting up the ODBC connection, select the ROUTE_BUS.mdb file as the data source from the QlikSenseData folder.
3. Name the ODBC DSN connection as HongKong Buses.
4. Create a new Qlik Sense application and open the **Data load editor.**
5. Click on the **Create New Connection** and select **ODBC**.
6. Select **HongKong Buses** under **System DSN.**

7. Name the data connection as `Qlik Sense CookBook ODBC`.
8. The following screenshot shows the details we enter in the **Create new connection (ODBC)** window:

If you are connecting to the database using OLE DB connectivity, we can directly set this up through the editor:

1. Open the **Data load editor** in Qlik Sense.
2. Click on the **Create new connection** and select **OLE DB**.
3. Select the **Microsoft Jet 4.0 OLE DB Provider (32-bit)** driver from the provider drop-down list.
4. Insert the **Data Source** file path, which, in our case, will be the path for the `ROUTE_BUS.mdb` file in the `QlikSenseData` folder.
5. Name the data connection as `QlikSense CookBook OLE DB`.
6. The following screenshot shows the details we enter in the **Create new connection (OLE DB)** window:

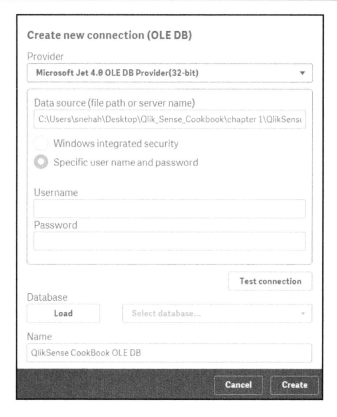

If you are extracting the data from a data file, such as .CSV, perform the following steps:

1. Open the **Data load editor** in Qlik Sense.
2. Click on **Create new connection** and select **Folder**.
3. Select the location of the QlikSenseData folder, which contains our data files. Alternatively, you can enter the path of the source folder directly under **Path**.
4. Name the data connection as Qlik Sense CookBook Data.

5. The following screenshot shows the details we enter in the **Create new connection (folder)** window:

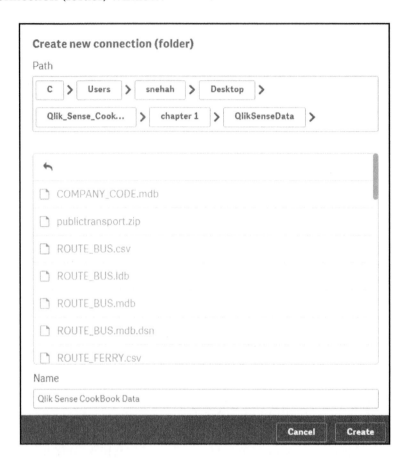

6. Once the connections are created in the Qlik Sense library, they will be seen as a list under **Data connections** in the **Data load editor**, as shown in the following screenshot:

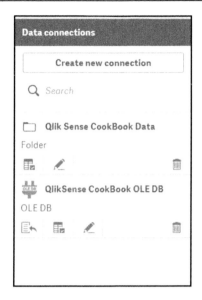

How to do it...

If you are working with an ODBC or an OLE DB data connection, follow these steps:

1. Insert the relevant data connection string to the script by clicking on **Insert connection string**, as shown in the following screenshot:

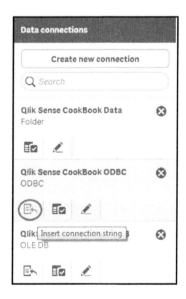

2. Click on Select data under **Data connections** to view and extract data from the ROUTE table in the MS Access database, as shown:

3. The preview of the ROUTE_BUS.mdb table will look like the following. The fields in the table can be excluded or renamed while working in the **Preview** window:

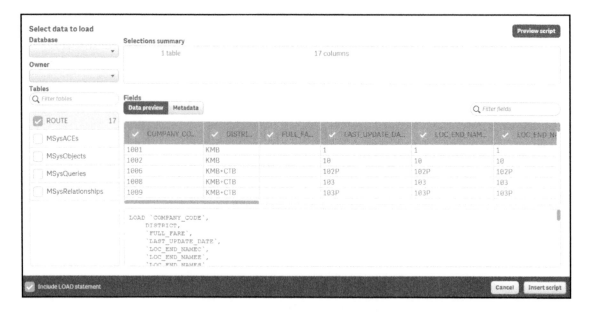

4. Click on **Insert script** in the **Preview** window. This will insert the connection string as well as load the statement to the script. Make sure that you delete the duplicate `LIB CONNECT TO 'Qlik Sense CookBook ODBC';` statement from your script.

5. Load the data in your application by clicking on the button.

Keep the **Close when successfully finished** option checked in the data load progress window. If the data is loaded successfully, the window automatically closes or else the error encountered is highlighted.

On a similar note, in order to test the Qlik Sense data files:

1. Click on the **Select data** option under the **Qlik Sense CookBook Data** connection.

2. Select the `ROUTE_GMB.csv` file from the `QlikSenseData` folder and load it in the application.

3. The preview of the `ROUTE_GMB.csv` table will look like the following screenshot. Make sure that you select **Embedded field names** under **Field names**. Note that the **Delimiter**, in this case, is automatically set to **Comma**:

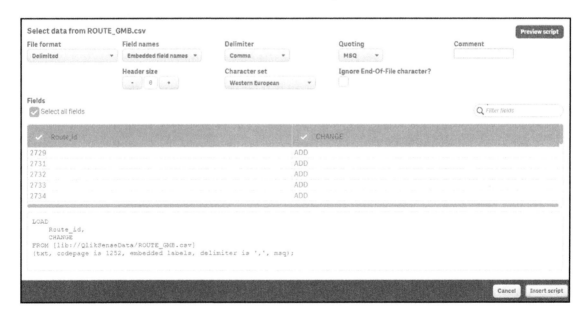

4. Insert the script and then save and load it.

How it works...

The LIB CONNECT TO statement connects to a database using a stored data connection from the Qlik Sense library, thus acting as a bridge between our application and the data source.

There's more...

This recipe aimed to extract data from common data sources, such as RDBMSes and data files. Qlik Sense can also extract data from web files and web services. We will see this in the next section.

See also...

- The *Creating a master library from the Data model viewer* recipe

Extracting data from web files

Often, the data required for the purpose of reporting is not stored in a database, but instead needs to be fetched from a website. For example, customer location information, specifically the geographic coordinates used in mapping analysis, is not available internally within an organization. This information may be available on the web and can be extracted from there.

Getting ready

When extracting the data from a web file:

1. Open an existing Qlik Sense application or create a new one.
2. Open the **Data load editor**.
3. Click on **Create new connection** and select **Web file**.
4. The **Select web file** window will open.
5. Insert the following URL from which you can fetch the data: http://www.csgnetwork.com/llinfotable.html.

6. Name the connection as `QlikSense Cookbook Webfile`, as shown in the following screenshot:

How to do it...

1. In the list under **Data connections**, select **QlikSense Cookbook Webfile** and click on Select data. This will open up a preview window listing all the tables from the web page. When you carefully examine the table contents, you realize that it is the second table, **@2**, that contains the location information.

2. Check the box next to **@2** and ensure that it is selected, so that the correct table is shown in the preview. The user will need to change the value under **Field names** to **Embedded field names**.

3. The preview of the table will look like the following screenshot:

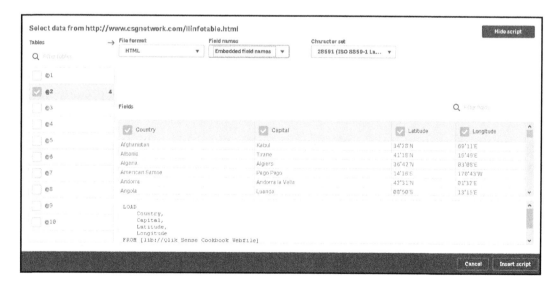

4. Select all the fields from the table in the preview window. Click on **Insert script** to load the web data in the application.

5. Name the table as `Country_Location` and the script will read as follows:

```
Country_Location:
LOAD
Country,
Capital,
Latitude,
Longitude
FROM [lib://QlikSense Cookbook Webfile]
(html, codepage is 1252, embedded labels, table is @2);
```

6. Save and load the data. Once the script is successfully loaded, the **Data model viewer** will show the loaded table.

How it works...

Qlik Sense connects to the web file using the stored data connection. Once connected, it identifies the tables in the HTML source and lists them in the preview window.

Certain external websites require authentication in order to be accessed and Qlik Sense is unable to cope with websites that are secured in this manner. In order to get over this issue, we can use a third-party data-extraction tool. The extracted data can be stored in a data file, such as a QVD. The `.qvd` file can then be used as a data source in the Qlik Sense application.

There's more...

Qlik Sense can also extract data from other data formats, such as XML. The underlying principles remain the same as explained in the preceding recipes.

See also...

- The *Creating a master library from the Data model viewer* recipe
- The *Activating the legacy mode in Qlik Sense® desktop* recipe

Extracting data from the FTP server

In the last recipe, you learned how to fetch data from a website using the web file connection. With the same connection type, we can extract data from files available in an FTP server.

To demonstrate this recipe, I'm using a local FTP server with user authentication. My server is `localhost`, my `userid` is `qlik`, and my `password` is `pwd`.

As a general rule, you must use the following parameters in the URL if the server requires authentication to retrieve data from a file
`ftp://<userid>:<password>@<servername>/path/filename.qvd.`

Getting ready

When extracting the data from the FTP server:

1. Open your web browser to check whether the URL is correct and whether you have access to the server (I prefer Firefox for this task).
2. Insert the following URL from which you can see a list of folders and files from a local FTP server: `ftp://qlik:pwd@localhost` (change the URL with your credentials and server name):

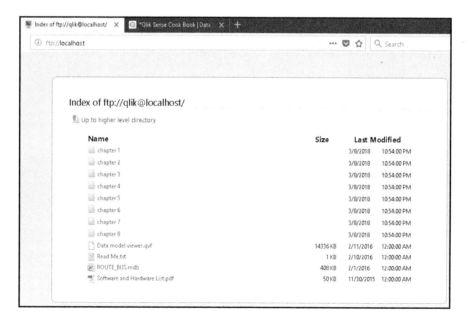

3. Navigate to the folder with the files you need:

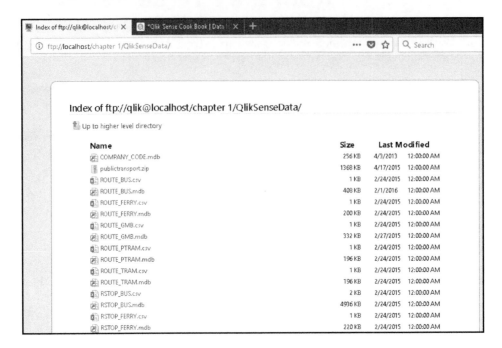

4. Right-click on the file and select **Copy Link Location**:

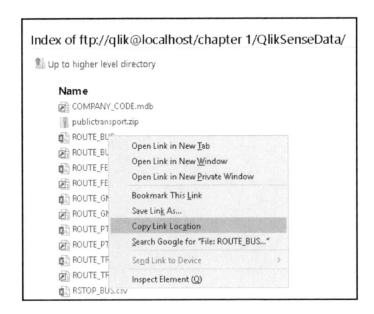

In my example, I chose `ROUTE_BUS.csv`:

1. Open an existing Qlik Sense application or create a new one.
2. Open the **Data load editor**.
3. Click on **Create new connection** and select **Web file**.
4. The **Select web file** window will open.
5. Insert the URL copied from the web page to set a connection with the file to extract data: `ftp://qlik:pwd@localhost/chapter%201/QlikSenseData/ROUTE_BUS.csv`.
6. Name the connection as `QlikSense Cookbook FTP ROUTE_BUS`, as shown in the following screenshot:

How to do it...

1. In the list under **Data connections**, select **QlikSense Cookbook FTP ROUTE_BUS** and click on Select data. This will open up a preview window listing the contents of the file.
2. If the file is large, more than one megabyte, the preview can take a long time to open because of low internet speed and bandwidth when connecting to the remote FTP server.
3. Change the value under **Field names** to **Embedded field names**.

4. The preview of the table will look like the following screenshot:

5. Select all the fields from the table in the preview window. Click on **Insert script** to load the web data in the application.

6. Name the table as ROUTE_BUS and the script will read as follows:

```
ROUTE_BUS:
LOAD
    Route_id,
    CHANGE
FROM [lib://QlikSense Cookbook FTP ROUTE_BUS]
(txt, codepage is 28592, embedded labels, delimiter is ',',
msq);
```

7. Save and load the data. Once the script is successfully loaded, the **Data model viewer** will show the loaded table.

How it works...

Qlik Sense connects to the FTP source file using the stored data connection. Once connected, it identifies the content of the source folders and lists them in the preview window.

If the file is large, the preview will take a long time to open.

For each file, you must create an FTP connection, so this recipe is used in very specific use cases.

If you need to read several files, files that are large in size or both, I recommend using an FTP client to download the files beforehand to a local folder.

You can perform the FTP download using the Windows FTP command. The `LOAD` script can trigger the FTP command using `EXECUTE` if legacy mode is enabled.

There's more...

Qlik Sense can also extract data from other data formats, such as XML, XLSX, XLS, or QVDS. The underlying principles remain the same as explained in the preceding recipes.

See also...

- The *Creating a master library from the Data model viewer* recipe
- The *Activating the legacy mode in Qlik Sense® desktop* recipe

Extracting data from web services with REST Connector

Qlik Sense provides connectivity to several data sources, such as SQL databases, Excel files, and text files, but we also have an increasing need to connect to web services that provide data in the JSON or XML format. This recipe shows you how to configure a REST connection to retrieve data in the JSON format from a public web service with data related to the Star Trek Series.

For this recipe, we will use a URL to extract all the Star Trek movies. When extracting the data from a REST data source:

1. Open an existing Qlik Sense application or create a new one.
2. Open the **Data load editor**.
3. Click on **Create new connection** and select Qlik **REST** Connector.
4. The Qlik **REST** Connector configuration window will open.
5. Insert the following URL from which you can fetch the data: `http://stapi.co/api/v1/rest/movie/search`.
6. Set up **Authentication Schema** as **Anonymous**.

7. Name the connection as `QlikSense Cookbook REST`, as shown:

8. Click **Test Connection** to check whether the parameters are OK.
9. Click **Create** to create the connection and close the configuration panel.

How to do it...

1. In the list under **Data connections**, select **QlikSense Cookbook REST** and click on Select data. This will open a preview window listing the tables found in the JSON response from the web service. When you carefully examine the table contents, you realize that it is a root node, and when you expand the node, you find a movies node.
2. Check the box next to **movies** and ensure that it is selected, so that the correct table is shown in the preview (when working with JSON data sources, we always have to expand the nodes to find the right table to be extracted).

3. The preview of the table will look like the following screenshot:

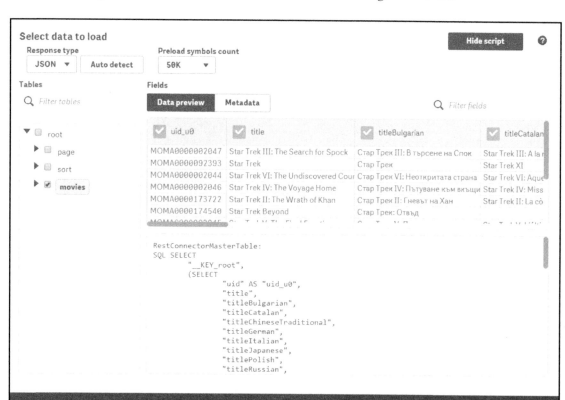

4. Save and load the data. Once the script is successfully loaded, the **Data model viewer** will show the loaded tables.
5. Click on **Insert script** to load the JSON data in the application.
6. Several commands have been inserted in the script.
7. The main one has a name of RestConnectorMasterTable. This table contains the JSON data in a flattened format.
8. Two more tables are created by a resident load from the mainDirector main table and movies. In the end, the RestConnectorMasterTable main table is dropped from memory.

How it works...

Qlik Sense connects to the REST service using the stored data connection. Once connected,

it identifies the source formats and lists them in the preview window.

JSON data sources contains nested data with several children records. Qlik Sense creates a multi-table schema when the source contains nested data.

There's more...

Qlik Sense REST Connector can also extract data from other data formats, such as XML and CSV. The underlying principles remain the same as explained in the preceding recipes. You can also extract data using authentication methods, the POST method for SOAP web services, or the pagination method to retrieve a large amount of data.

See also...

- The *Creating a master library from the Data model viewer* recipe

Activating the legacy mode in Qlik Sense® desktop

Qlik Sense is a developing product; hence, certain features are not active when running the Desktop version in its standard mode. A prime example of this is running Windows command-line statements or external programs, such as the 7zip file compressor. Both these activities are not possible if Qlik Sense runs in its standard mode. In order to get these functionalities to run, we need to activate the legacy mode. However, you must be aware that enabling the legacy mode has security implications, if the application is deployed on the Sense server. You do not have control over the data connections in QMC (if the legacy mode is activated). The library security features may also be lost; moreover, the user has access to the entire filesystem on Qlik Sense Server because the account running the Qlik Sense Engine Service has administrative privileges. Activating the legacy mode requires changing a parameter value in the `settings.ini` file for Qlik Sense Desktop. In the Qlik Sense Server, you must have an Administration Role to access the QMC.

The recipe is only valid for Qlik Sense Desktop:

1. Make sure that Qlik Sense Desktop is closed before opening the `settings.ini` file.
2. Open the `settings.ini` file that is, by default, stored under `C:\Users\{user}\Documents\Qlik\Sense\Settings.ini`, as shown in the following screenshot:

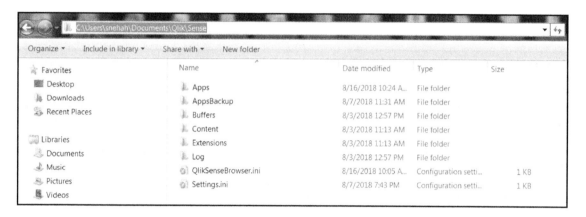

3. Change `StandardReload=1` to `StandardReload=0`.
4. Save the file and start Qlik Sense Desktop in order to run it in a legacy mode.

How it works...

Changing the value for the `StandardReload` parameter in the `settings.ini` file enables the legacy mode in Qlik Sense. When running in legacy mode, any of the scripts in Qlik View can be directly used in Qlik Sense. This will also allow us to use the library connections.

There's more...

Qlik Sense has the ability to use the same script that is found in any QlikView file. You can also use a binary load statement in Qlik Sense in order to load the entire data model from an existing QlikView file. We can also run Windows command-line statements.

See also…

- The *Executing command line programs within the script* recipe in Chapter 3, *Scripting*

Previewing data in the Data model viewer

As any experienced Qlik developer will tell you, the **Data model viewer** is a key component you will undoubtedly use on your Qlik journey. Qlik Sense has brought with it some nice new features. We will also delve into the different insights that can be gleaned from the **Data model viewer**:

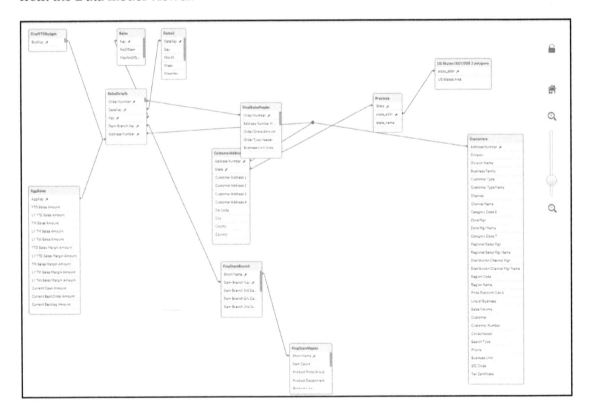

Getting ready

For this recipe, we will make use of the `Data model viewer.qvf` application. This file is available for download on the Packt Publishing website.

How to do it...

1. Open the `Data model viewer.qvf` application that has been downloaded from the resource library.
2. Click on **Data model viewer** in the Navigation drop-down on the toolbar.

How it works...

In this section, we will see how the different types of data are viewed.

Viewing the data model

The data model consists of a number of tables joined by the key fields. The following screenshot contains functions that can be used to manipulate the layout of the data model:

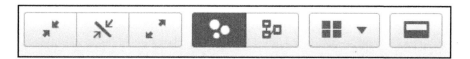

The details of the available keys (from right to left) are given as follows:

- **Collapse all**: This reduces the tables to just their headers, thus hiding all the fields
- **Show linked fields**: Expands the tables enough to only display the key fields in each
- **Expand all**: Displays all the fields for each table
- **Internal table viewer**: Shows the internal representation of the data model
- **Layout**: Provides options to auto-align the table grid or space out across the screen
- **Show preview**: Toggles the data preview screen to either on or off

Viewing the associations

Clicking on a table will highlight its associated tables in orange. The customer's table is selected in the following screenshot and the shared key here is **Address Number**:

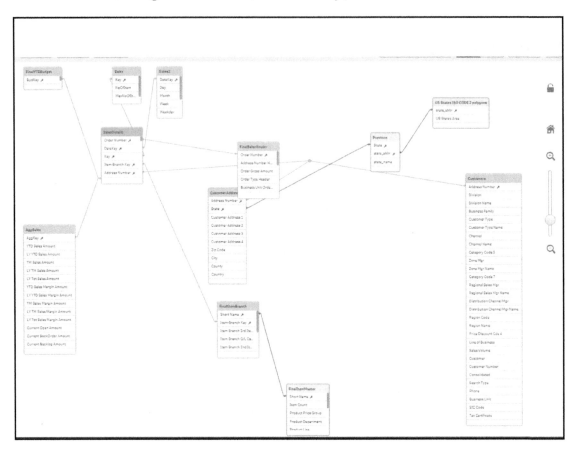

Click on the **CustomerAddress** table to see a highlighted expansion, via the state key, as shown:

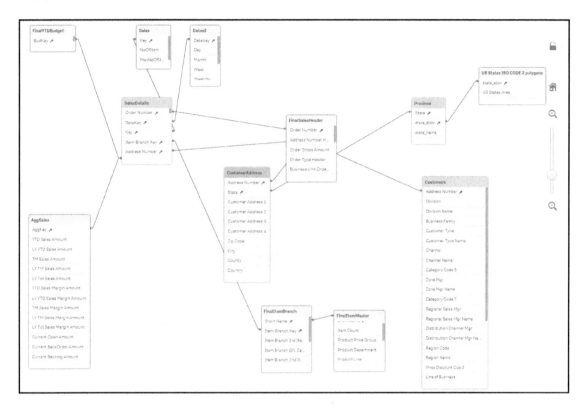

Table metadata

The **Data model viewer** also provides information on the contents of each table.

Click the header of the customer address table, and then open the **Preview** pane by clicking the **Preview** button in the bottom-left corner.

The following preview will be displayed at the bottom of the screen:

CustomerAddress		Preview of data				
		Address Number	**State**	**Customer Address 1**	**Customer Address 2**	**Customer Address 3**
Rows	688	10025919	CA	801 West Artesia Boulevard		
Fields	10	10025249	TN	7221 Highway 64		
Keys	2	10025249	TN	7221 Highway 64		
Tags	$key $ascii $text	10011732	-			
		10011732	-			
		10018644	KS	Attention Accounts Payable Department	PO Box 12990	
		10025242	-	Parts Division	140-2 Kye-Dong	Chongro-Ku

Along with a small snippet of the table's contents, the far-left table also provides some high-level table information about the number of rows, fields, keys, and any tags.

Next, click the **Address Number** field from the `Customers` table in the **Data model viewer**.

You can now see more detailed information about the individual field.

These are:

- Density
- Subset ratio
- Has duplicates
- Total distinct values
- Present distinct values
- Non-null values
- Tags

This information is very helpful when we are debugging issues. If a count does not return the expected result, you may want to ensure that there are no duplicates.

If a selection is not filtered correctly, you may want to check the subset ratio of the key and so on.

There's more…

Double-clicking a table header in the **Data model viewer** will either collapse or expand the table fully.

Creating a master library from the Data model viewer

To help reduce the repetition and developer error, Qlik has introduced a master library where we can store reusable items, such as dimensions, measures, and even whole visualizations. For people experienced with Qlik's other products, such as QlikView, just think, "No more linked objects and storing expressions in variables!"

It is easy to think of library items in a self-service context. Don't get me wrong; ultimately, you will have to decide what will be published – from your data model to the world for their own analysis purposes. Having said that, the secret sauce of this recipe is in saving your own time.

It is a productivity hack that implies, "Automation is to your time what compound interest is to money." While it is not an exact parallel, this is a nice concept to frame the usefulness of time-saving functions in Qlik Sense. The effective use of the library saves time spent on scrolling downfield lists, rewriting expressions over and over, and applying a single change in multiple places.

Once you have saved enough time to eclipse the setup investment, the value of taking this approach can only compound with continuous development.

Getting ready

1. Create a new Qlik Sense application and name it `Master Library`.
2. Open the **Data load editor**.

3. Enter the following script and load the data by clicking on the button (the script is available in a separate text file that can be downloaded from the Packt Publishing website):

```
Data:
LOAD * INLINE [
    Name, Region, Country, City, OrderId, Sales, Company,
    OrderDate
    Wooten, C, Mozambique, Carmen, 1, 45.55, Est Nunc
    Laoreet LLC, 22/12/14
    Blankenship, Delta, Cayman Islands, Sapele, 2, 95.76,
    Lorem Donec Inc., 17/01/15
    Sheppard, Wyoming, Vatican City State, Cheyenne, 3,
    38.31, Lobortis, 07/08/14
    Goddard, H, Curaçao, San Francisco, 4, 86.33, Non Inc.,
    07/09/14
    Galloway, Aragón, Trinidad & Tobago, Zaragoza, 5,
    85.80, Diam Proin., 21/01/15
    Kirsten, Tamil Nadu, Wallis & Futuna, Neyveli, 6,
    28.47, Mollis Non Limited, 03/05/14
    Holland, Cartago, Falkland Islands, San Diego, 7, 1.34,
    Ullamcorper Inc., 17/07/14
    Thaddeus, BC, Canada, Oliver, 8, 59.04, Ante Nunc
    Mauris Ltd, 17/02/15
    Lareina, CA, Spain, San Diego, 9, 4.55, Pellentesque
    Tincidunt Limited, 29/07/14
    Jescie, Vienna, Monaco, Vienna, 10, 54.20, Ultricies
    Ligula Consulting, 16/06/14
    Logan, IL, Saint Barthélemy, Paris, 11, 91.31, Mi
    Foundation, 13/12/14
    Shannon, CG, Nepal, Aberystwyth, 12, 80.86, Auctor Non
    LLC, 03/05/14
    Andrew, SO, Argentina, Sokoto, 13, 88.78, Scelerisque
    Mollis Associates, 12/12/14
    Jocelyn, WP, Tanzania, Konin, 14, 15.91, Ligula Tortor
    Dictum Ltd, 22/08/14
    Gordon, FL, Hong Kong, Miami, 15, 93.97, Suscipit Inc.,
    12/05/14
];
```

How to do it...

Once the data has been loaded, you can check the results by opening the **Data model viewer** through the Navigation dropdown () in the top corner on the left-hand side of the toolbar, as shown in the following screenshot:

You can find the **Preview** button at the bottom-left of the screen. There are several other places in Qlik Sense where you can create master library items, but the data model preview screen is the best, as it also lets you see the data first. Take a minute to browse the data you have loaded in the **Data model viewer**:

1. In the **Data model viewer**, select the Data table by clicking on its header and then click the **Preview** button to view the fields and the field values loaded from the Data table.

2. The **Preview** window will appear, as shown in the following screenshot:

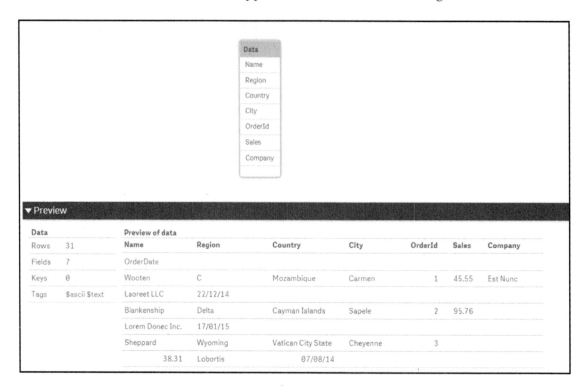

Data						
Rows	31					
Fields	7					
Keys	0					
Tags	$ascii $text					

Preview of data

Name	Region	Country	City	OrderId	Sales	Company
OrderDate						
Wooten	C	Mozambique	Carmen	1	45.55	Est Nunc
Laoreet LLC	22/12/14					
Blankenship	Delta	Cayman Islands	Sapele	2	95.76	
Lorem Donec Inc.	17/01/15					
Sheppard	Wyoming	Vatican City State	Cheyenne	3		
38.31	Lobortis	07/08/14				

3. Select the **Region** field from the table to get the preview, as shown in the following screenshot:

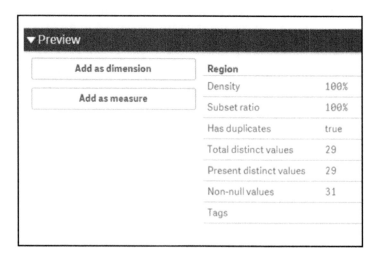

Region	
Density	100%
Subset ratio	100%
Has duplicates	true
Total distinct values	29
Present distinct values	29
Non-null values	31
Tags	

4. Click the **Add as dimension** button.
5. The following window appears. If you are likely to publish this dimension for consumption by users, you can enter a description here:

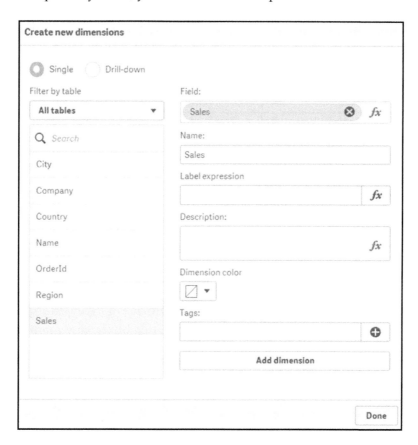

6. It is advised to use tags to make our life easier. Add the **Geo** tag and click on ⊕
7. Click on the **Add dimension** button to create a master dimension in the library.
8. Repeat this process for the **Country** and **City** fields.

9. Click on **Done** to go back to the **Data model viewer**.

10. It's time to create a measure. Select the **Sales** field from the **Data** table in the **Data model viewer**.

11. Click the **Add as measure** button. When we create a Master measure, we need to make sure we use an aggregation function, such as Sum or Avg, along with the selected field.

12. In the **Create new measure** window, type SUM in front of (**Sales**), as shown in the following screenshot:

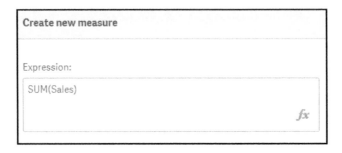

13. Click on **Create**.

14. Save the changes made in the master library by clicking on the button on the toolbar in the table preview. Exit the table preview by going to **App overview**.

15. Open (or create) a sheet and enter the edit mode by clicking on the Edit sheet button.

16. Once you are in edit mode, click the chain ([&]) icon on the left-hand side of the asset panel to open the **Master items** menu.

17. To add visualizations, first create them in the user interface and then drag them into the library.

While the **Master items** menu panel is very useful to speed up the development when defining the content, it is easier to do it from the filters pane. In short, you can browse the entire content of your data model and right-click on the most important fields to add the ones that will be frequently used.

How it works...

1. Right-click on a field from the field's pane that you want to add to the master library:

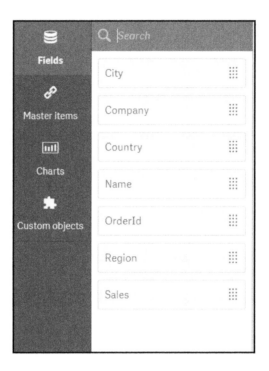

2. Click on **Create Dimension**, enter a **Description** and any relevant **Tags**, and click **Done** once finished:

There's more...

We can also create Master dimensions and measures through the GUI. In order to do this:

1. Open an existing sheet or create a new one.

2. Click on the Master items (🔗) icon.

3. Click on either **Dimensions** or **Measures**. This will enable an option to create new library items.

Using a master library in Edit mode

As mentioned in the *Creating a master library from the Data model viewer* recipe, a great benefit of creating a master library is to save you time and reduce the complexity by applying global changes to your visualizations.

There are three main areas in the asset panel when editing a Qlik Sense sheet (**Charts, Custom objects, Master items**, and **Fields**). Clicking the chain button (🔗) opens the **Master items** pane.

From here, you can manage every aspect of the **Master items**, such as renaming, replacing, deleting, and editing.

Getting ready

You can continue to use the application from the *Creating a Master Library from the Data model viewer* recipe:

1. If you have not completed the *Creating a Master Library from the Data model viewer* recipe, load the following in your **Data load editor**:

   ```
   LOAD * INLINE [
   Country, Area, Quantity
   USA, North, 1000
   USA, North, 1200
   USA, South, 2500
   USA, South, 2500
   UK, North, 1000
   UK, North, 2500
   UK, South, 2000
   UK, South, 1900
     ];
   ```

2. Add **Country** and **Area** as Master dimensions, both with the **Geo** tag.
3. Add **Quantity** as a Master measure.

How to do it...

1. Open the **App overview** screen by clicking on the navigation dropdown on the toolbar at the top.
2. Create a new sheet or open an existing one.

3. Enter the edit mode by clicking on the 🖉 **Edit** button.

4. Click on the object pane button (📊) and double-click on the 📊 Bar chart button. The chart will be added to the main content area automatically.

5. Type Geo in the search box of the asset panel on the left of your screen. While there are no charts called Geo, the search has flagged up our two tagged dimensions in the master library pane with a yellow circle.

6. Drag the **Area** field to where it says **Add dimension**. Repeat the steps where the **Country** field selects **Add "Country"** when prompted, as shown in the following screenshot:

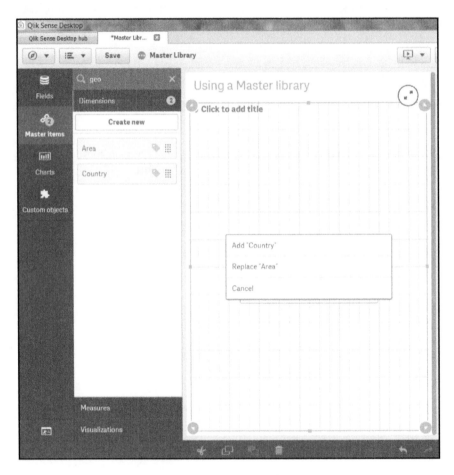

7. Clear your search on **Geo** by pressing the ⊗ button.

8. Click on **Measures**.

9. Drag the **Sales** measure from the asset panel over to the add measure area of the chart. Voila! You have created your first visualization using Master dimensions and measures:

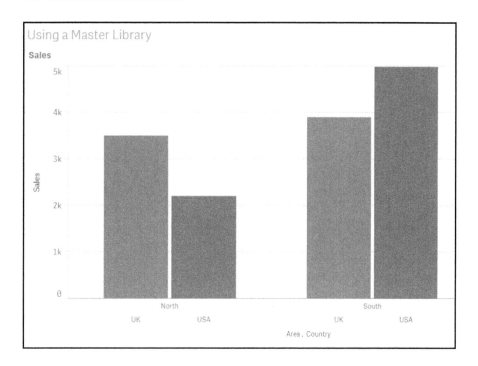

10. You can now drag this chart into the asset panel and it will become a master visualization.

There's more...

If you delete a Master dimension or Master measure, the visualizations that use the deleted Master item will not work unless you replace it with a new dimension or measure. The same applies to delete a field from the data model; the reference will remain part of the Master item pane until it's updated from the edit screen.

Creating master measures replaces the need to write expressions as variables for reuse. Another piece of QlikView functionality that has been replicated and expanded upon is the concept of linked objects. Any updates you make in the Master visualization area will be applied globally.

If you rename a field in your script without moving the position, it will be applied automatically to all the objects.

Using visual data preparation on the data manager model viewer

If you are a QlikView developer beginning to use Qlik Sense, you are very familiar with the load-script editor and the powerful commands available there, but most business users are not familiar with coding, so Qlik Sense provides **Data manager**, a visual data preparation tool tailored for non-technical users. It's a great tool even for experienced QlikView developers.

With data manager, you can create table associations using drag and drop, concatenate tables, and synchronize scripted tables within the data manager.

You can also create table fields that calculate values, create calendar fields, use the data profiling cards to create numeric buckets, and handle string fields with the **Replace**, **Set nulls**, **Order**, and **Split** functions.

The data manager can detect geographical data in your table if it have columns with country and city names. It can detect geopoint data (latitude, longitude) for a single location, such as a city or a customer site. It can also detect area data (polygons) to represent regions or countries when loading this information from flat files like TXT or XLS.

Our recipe focuses on some of these functionalities, such as visual data association, concatenation, calculated field, and string replace.

Getting ready

The dataset required for this recipe that is downloaded from the Packt Publishing website (https://www.packtpub.com/big-data-and-business-intelligence/qlik-sense-cookbook-second-edition) comes in a zipped folder called QlikSenseData. Extract all the files from this zipped folder and save them on your hard drive at the desired location.

The files used in this recipe are Sales Data.xlsx and Sales Data 2017.xlsx.

How to do it...

1. Create a new Qlik Sense application and name it `Qlik Sense Cookbook Visual Data Peparation`.

2. When starting a new application, Qlik Sense always asks to choose between the **Data manager** and the load script editor. Choose **Add data from files and other sources**:

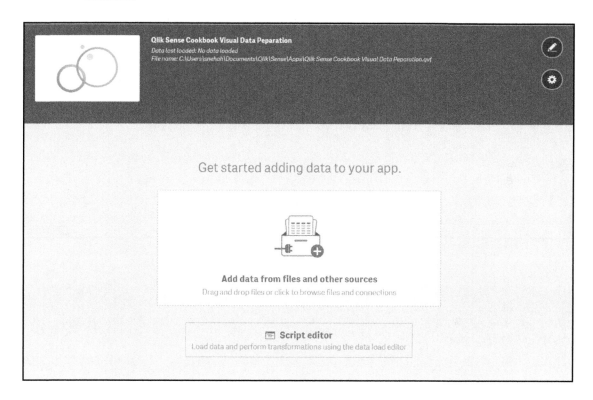

3. Click on **My computer** in the file location section on the left, and navigate to the folder with the `Sales Data.xlsx`file and click in the file:

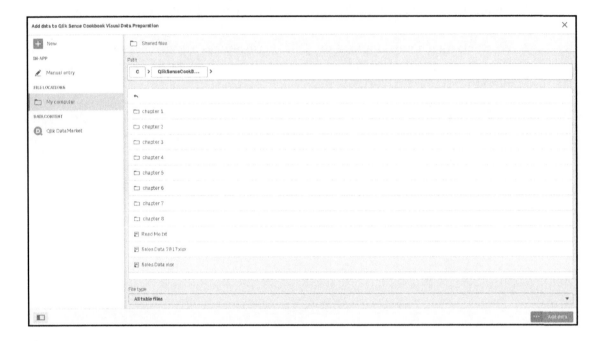

4. After selecting the file, we can see a list with all sheets in the Excel file. Select all sheets, as in the following screenshot:

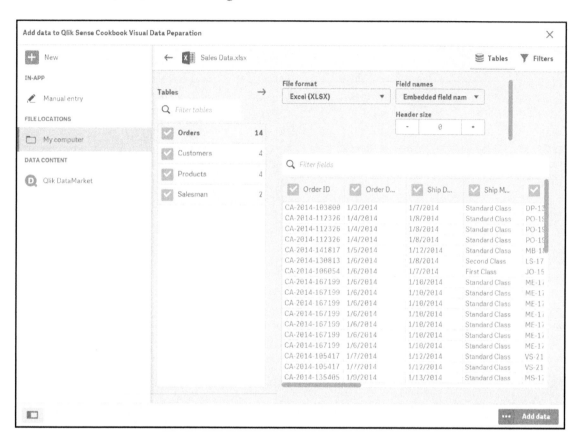

5. Before proceeding to the next step, check whether the data profiling is active. Click on the button with the three dots to check:

07/01/2014	First Class	JO-15145	Athens	Georgia	30605
10/01/2014	Standard Class	ME-17320	Henderson	Kentucky	42420
10/01/2014	Standard Class	ME-17320	Henderson	Kentucky	42420
10/01/2014	Standard Class	ME-17320	Henderson	Kentucky	42420
10/01/2014	Standard Class	ME-17320	Henderson	Kentucky	42420
10/01/2014	Standard Class	ME-17320	Henderson	Kentucky	42420
10/01/2014	Standard Class	ME-17320	Henderson	Kentucky	42420
10/01/2014	Standard Class	ME-17320	Henderson	Kentucky	42420
12/01/2014	Standard Class	VS-21820	Huntsville	Texas	77340
12/01/2014	Standard Class	VS-21820	Huntsville	Texas	77340
13/01/2014	Standard Class	MS-17830	Laredo	Texas	78041
13/01/2014	Standard Class	MS-17830	Laredo		
15/01/2014	Standard Class	AJ-10780	Springfield		
15/01/2014	Standard Class	AJ-10780	Springfield		

Data profiling
Enabled
Prepare the data in the data manager.

••• Add data

6. Click on **Add data**:

We also have a fourth table with data from 2017, so we need to import that too.

7. Click on the Plus circle in the top-left corner to insert another table:

    - Open **My computer** and select `Sales Data 2017.xlsx`. It only has one sheet with data related to 2017.
    - In the preview windows, select the **Orders** sheet and click on **Add Data**.
    - Once the connection is created, we can start to model and prepare our data with the associations and table editors:

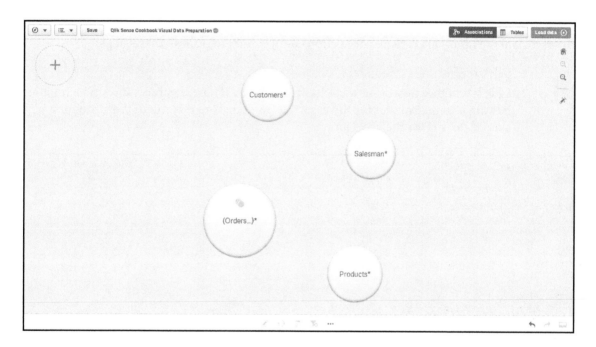

How it works...

When we added the data, Qlik sense created a bubble for each table. After inserting a new table with data from 2017, it automatically created a table concatenation between the `Orders` table from `Sales Data.xlsx` and `Sales Data 2017.xlsx`. Note the multi-circle at the top of the table name; it's an indicator for a table created by file concatenation:

To associate the tables and create connections between them, follow these steps:

1. Click on the `Customers` table.
2. Check whether any other table has a green bar. The green bar shows which table has the stronger match for the association. The more it is filled, the stronger a candidate it is for the association:

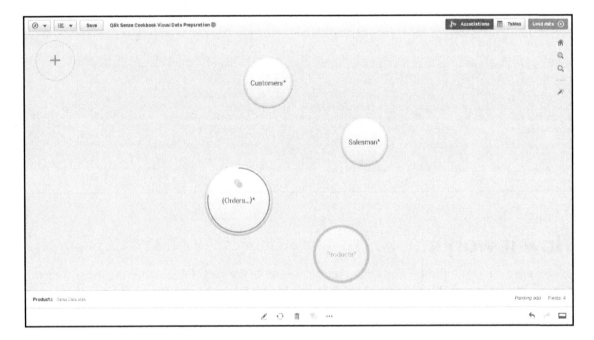

3. Drag the `Customer` table over the `Orders` table to create the association between them.

4. Click on the association to review which field was used:

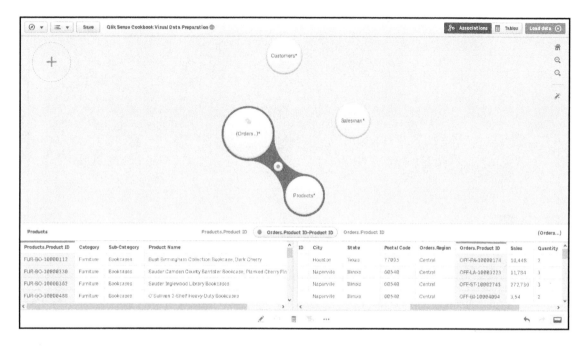

5. The field is `Customer ID`.

6. Repeat steps *1* through *5* for the `Products` and `Salesman` tables.

7. At the end, the tables' connections will look like the following screenshot:

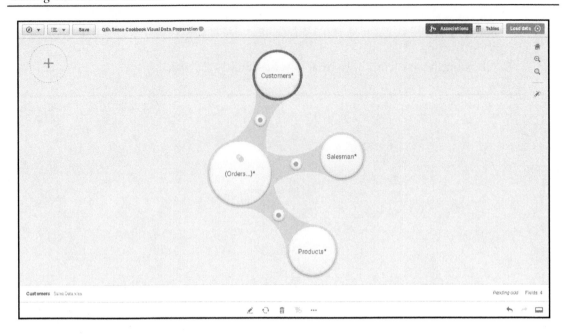

Now we must review the data in the `Sales` table. Perform the following steps:

1. Click on the **Tables** button at the top-right of the screen to open the table editor. You will see the following screen:

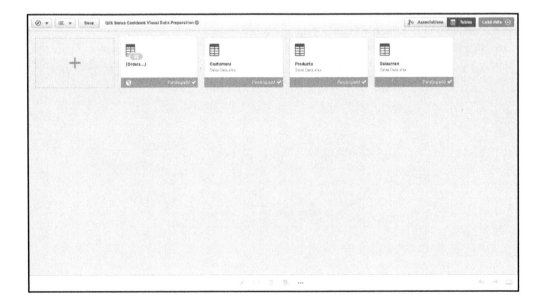

2. Move the mouse pointer over the Order box and click on the pencil to edit the table:

3. In the table editor, click on the **Ship Mode** column header to select the field. A profiler window at the bottom shows the distribution of values for each category of data, and the data profiling card on the left. It looks like the following screenshot:

4. There are some data mismatches in the column that we need to fix using the replace card. Select **Standard Class** and **Std Class** (note that the replacement value is the first value selected).

5. Click on **Replace**. The card will be updated and show only the replaced value merging **Std Class** with **Standard Class**.

6. Repeat the steps to merge **First Class** and **1st Class** as **First Class**.

7. Repeat the steps to merge **Second Class**, **2nd Class**, and **Second Clas** as **Second Class**.

8. We have replaced several values to keep with only four distinct values, as in the following screenshot:

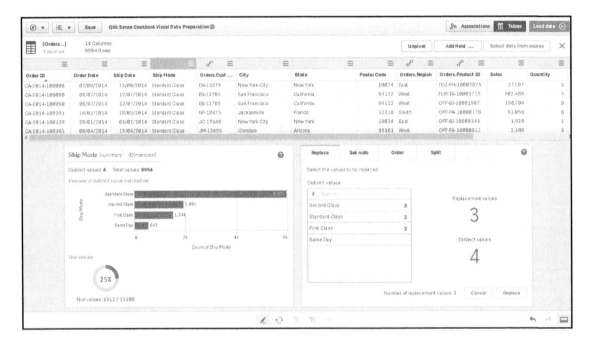

Add a calculated field:

1. In the same table, click on **Add field** and select **Calculated field**. It will show the calculated field panel editor on the right of the screen.

2. In the **Name** field, write `Discount Value`.

3. In the **Expression** box, write `Sales * Discount`. The panel provides a preview box showing the result of the expression for each line of the table.

4. Click on **Create**. Now you see a new column at the end of the table with the calculated field. An example is shown in the following screenshot:

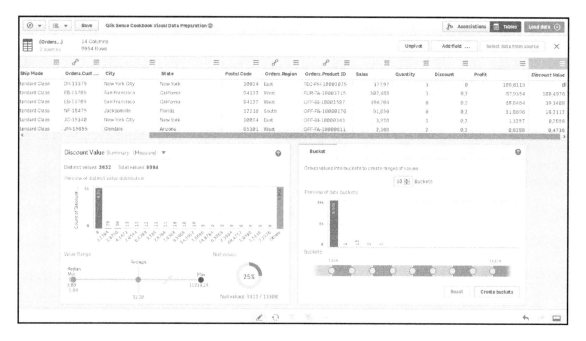

5. Click on **Load data** to reload data in the application.

When we create a table association, Qlik Sense profiles your data help you create associations between tables, irrespective of the name of the column on each table. When adding several tables with the same name and column, the data manager creates an automatic concatenation. In all fields of the table, it's possible to transform the data: if the data is a numeric value, you can create buckets. If the column contains string data, you can perform **Replace**, **Set Nulls**, **Order**, or **Split** operations. You can create calculated columns as well, but the calculation can only reference columns in the same table.

When doing all this data preparation, the data doesn't load in the memory; you need to click on Load data (the green button) to reload the app with all changes into memory and to start creating visualizations with new tables and fields.

There's more...

If you are aware of the data you are loading, you can disable data profiling to speed up the load processing in the data manager, especially if you have memory constraints and huge datasets with millions of rows.

When disabling data profiling, Qlik Sense can't recognize location data using city and country names, so you will not be able to visualize data with maps in your app.

The editor also can handle tables with different columns, and you can force the concatenation during column pairing. To do this, click on More options (the button with three dots) at the bottom of the screen in the associations or table editor, and select **Concatenate Tables**.

2
Visualizations

In this chapter, we will cover some visualization tips and tricks to create a compelling dashboard in Qlik Sense:

- Creating snapshots
- Creating and adding content to a story
- Adding embedded sheets to the story
- Highlighting the performance measure in a bar chart
- Associating persistent colors to field values using the script
- Using the colormix1 function
- Composition
- Relationships
- Comparison
- Distribution
- Structuring visualizations
- Measuring statistical data with box plot charts
- Using a waterfall chart to analyze the cumulative effect

Introduction

A typical Qlik Sense application should always follow the **Dashboard Analysis Reporting (DAR)** methodology. This methodology focuses on developing a dashboard sheet followed by an analysis sheet and then a reports sheet. The dashboard projects the high-level figures of the business; the analysis sheet gives more control to the end user to filter the data, while the reports sheet has the detailed information at a granular level.

For more information on the DAR concept, visit `https://community.` `qlik.com/blogs/qlikviewdesignblog/2013/11/08/dar-methodology.`

While this concept can be easily implemented within the application, it is easy to forget the best design practices that help in making the applications more engaging for users. An optimal design will convey the right information to the right people at the right time. This will elevate the decision-making process within the organization.

This chapter focuses on some of the key concepts in data visualization that will help the users take their Qlik Sense design capabilities to the next level.

It also discusses the importance of choosing the right visualization for the right purpose. Some useful blogs written by the experts in data visualization can be accessed by users to enhance their knowledge:

- `http://www.perceptualedge.com/blog/`
- `http://global.qlik.com/uk/blog/authors/patrik-lundblad`

Creating snapshots

Snapshots are an exciting feature in Qlik Sense that enable users to capture the point-in-time state of the data object. Snapshots work as insights for a story, which will be discussed in later recipes.

Getting ready

For the sake of this exercise, we will make use of the `Automotive.qvf` Qlik Sense application. This application is downloaded as a sample file with the default Qlik Sense desktop installation and can be accessed through the Qlik Sense hub.

The sample files may differ by region. If the `Automotive.qvf` application is not available in the Qlik Sense hub, it can be downloaded from the Packt Publishing website.

Perform the following steps once you download the application from the Packt Publishing website (`https://www.packtpub.com/big-data-and-business-intelligence/qlik-sense-cookbook-second-edition`):

1. Copy the `.qvf` file to the `C:\Users\<user>\Documents\Qlik\Sense\Apps` folder

2. Open the Qlik Sense desktop and the app will appear in the hub

How to do it...

Qlik Sense provides you with the opportunity to take a single snapshot of a selected object, or to take several snapshots of multiple objects at the same time.

In order to take snapshots, perform the following steps:

1. Open the `Automotive.qvf` application from the Qlik Sense Desktop hub:

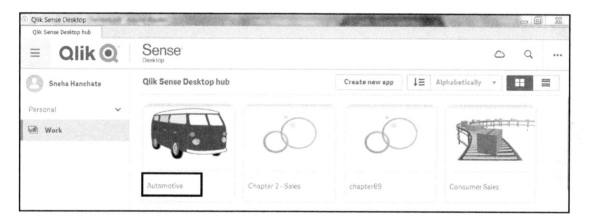

2. Open the **Sales overview** sheet and select the trendline chart **Vehicle sales by year**. Right-click on the object to display the options and select **Take snapshot** on the menu. You can also hover the mouse over the object and click on the

   snapshot icon 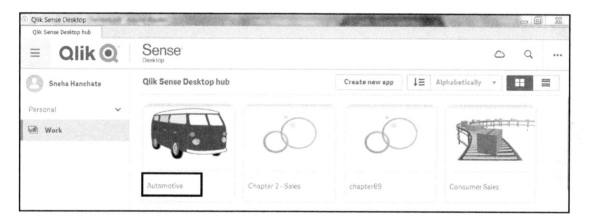 .

3. The snapshot is saved within the snapshot library and is titled with the same name as the object. You can add a description on each snapshot as an annotation.
4. Repeat the previous step for the **Car sales by territory** and **Vehicle sales by region** objects.
5. Right-click on any object whose snapshot you have taken and select **Open snapshot library** to see a list with previous snapshots.

How it works...

Snapshots are usually taken by the users when they want to store the point-in-time picture of an object corresponding to any selections. Snapshots are synonymous with taking a static picture of the object on the screen. As this is a static picture, it does not get updated with the change in data or with the change in state of the individual Qlik Sense object. The state and selections within a snapshot will not be updated after a data reload.

There's more...

A snapshot can be called a sibling of another Qlik Sense feature called **Bookmarks**, the difference being that bookmarks capture the state of selections within an application, while snapshots store the state of objects as it was at a particular point in time. The data projected by a bookmark gets updated on data reload.

See also

- *Creating and adding content to a story*

Creating and adding content to a story

Qlik Sense introduces the concept of storytelling within the application. The data story interface helps the user to collate all the important observations and insights from the application to create a convincing narrative and present it to the intended audience in the form of a slideshow.

Getting ready

As in the previous recipe, we will again make use of the `Automotive.qvf` Qlik Sense application.

How to do it...

To create a story, perform the following steps:

1. Open the `Automotive.qvf` application

2. While you are still on the **App overview** page, click 📺 **Stories** on the toolbar

3. Click on the ＋ sign to create a new story

4. Add the story name as `Sales Overview` and description as `A narrative of the overall sales for the company`

5. Click outside the description window to save the story

To add content to a storyboard, perform the following steps:

1. Open the storyboard for `Sales Overview` by clicking on the thumbnail.

2. The right-side pane of the storyboard represents six libraries that serve as the source for the content which we can use for our storyline:

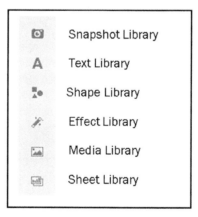

3. Click on the Snapshot library icon. This will display the list of snapshots we took in the earlier recipe:

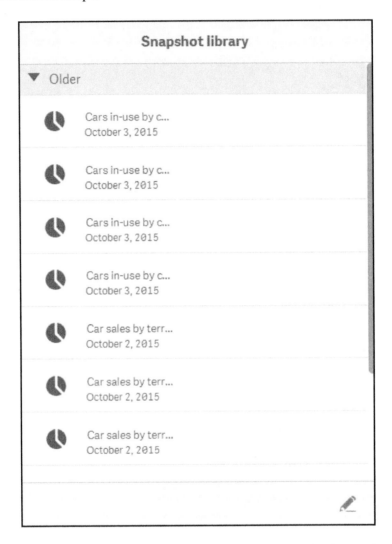

4. Drag and drop the **Vehicle sales by region** and **Car sales by territory** snapshot on the sheet.
5. Click on the Text objects. Drag and drop the **Title** box on the sheet.
6. Double-click the **Title** box and add the title `Sales by Region and Territory`.
7. Click on the Text objects. Drag and drop the **Paragraph** box on the sheet.

8. Double-click on the **Paragraph** box and add the following text:

   - AOME region has the highest number of total car sales while if we consider commercial vehicles, Americas leads the way.
   - China is the biggest market for cars followed by United States. There is very little comparison amongst the volume of sales for european nations Italy France and United Kingdom.

9. Click on the **Shapes library**. Drag and drop the ◀ and ▼ shapes on the sheet.

10. Save the story by clicking on the **Save** toolbar.

11. The effective story interface should look like this:

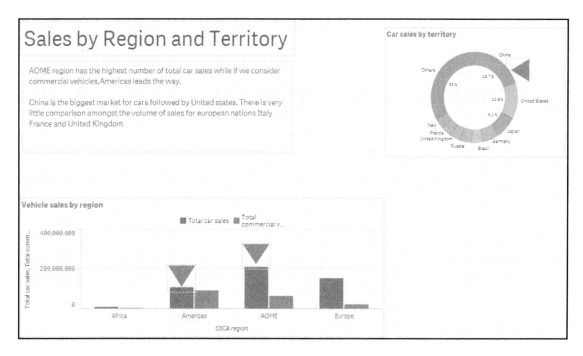

12. The story can be played as a presentation by clicking on the button on the left-hand side vertical pane.

How it works...

The story with all the essential elements, namely the snapshots, commentary, and the highlighters, conveys the essence of the data to the audience. The data added through the snapshots contain static point-in-time information. Since stories are native to Qlik Sense, there is no need to create separate PowerPoint files for presentations, although, with Qlik Sense version 2.1.1, you have the option to export the stories to PowerPoint so that they can be shared offline.

There's more...

While working in the story Edit mode, click on any individual object. Upon clicking the object, we will find two options highlighted in the top right-hand corner. The first one is for **Replace snapshot** and the other one is for **Unlock the snapshot**. Use the following steps to explore the **Replace snapshot** and **Unlock the snapshot** functionalities:

1. Click on **Replace snapshot**.
2. The following dropdown appears, which lists all the snapshots captured for the original visualization. The snapshot in use is marked with a tick mark at right:

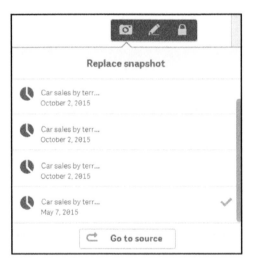

3. The user can replace the existing snapshot with a new one.

4. Alternatively, the user can click on the ⟳ **Go to source** button in the dropdown that opens the original sheet where the visualization resides. New snapshots can then be created using the live data.

5. Click on the ↩ **Return** button on the original sheet to return to the story.

6. Next, click on the 🔒 button for visualization. This will unlock the snapshot and activate the edit ✎ option.

7. Click on ✎ to change the basic properties of the object. The modified properties for the object are specific to the story. The object on the Qlik Sense sheet still has the original properties, as shown in the following screenshot:

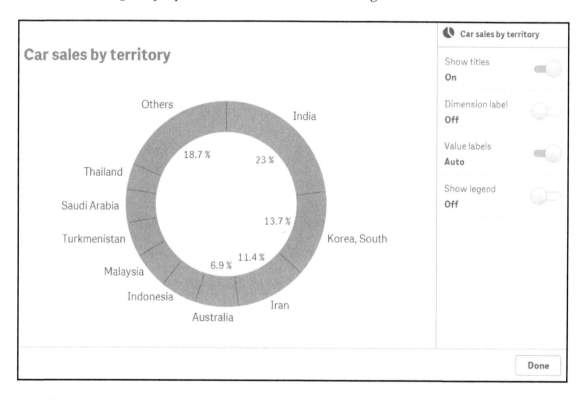

A Qlik Sense storyline can also have embedded sheets. This is particularly useful if we want to showcase the entire content of the sheet on the slide.

See also

- *Adding embedded sheets to the story*

Adding embedded sheets to the story

Multiple sheets can be added to the story and the following section deals with the steps involved.

Getting ready

As in the previous recipe, we will again make use of the `Automotive.qvf` Qlik Sense application:

1. Open the `Automotive.qvf` application from the Qlik Sense hub.
2. Next, open the **Sales Overview** story, which was created in the previous recipe, by clicking ⊡ **Stories** on the toolbar.

How to do it...

Please follow the steps for adding embedded sheets to the story:

1. In the story view, click on the ＋ icon in the bottom-left corner of the storyboard to add a new slide.
2. On the panel at the right, click on ⊞ to insert a sheet.
3. Select the **In-use overview** sheet from the dialog box, and set the alignment on the slide (left, center, right), as shown in the following screenshot:

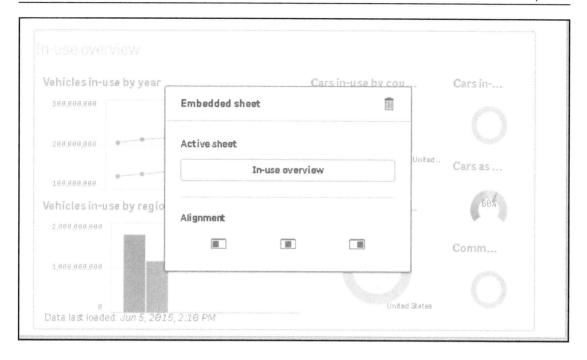

4. Click on the **In-Use overview** button to select another sheet for the slide.

5. Save the file by clicking on the Save button.

The story can be played as a presentation by clicking on the ▶ button on the left-hand side vertical pane.

How it works...

When we embed a sheet into our story, it places all the content of the desired sheet on the slide. The embedded sheet always has the same set of selections as the sheet in the sheet view.

There's more...

When we play the story, you will observe that we have two buttons at the top of the embedded sheet slide, namely Reset selections and Go to sheet . Selections can be made on the embedded sheet by clicking on each individual object. The **Reset selections** button clears the selections and the **Go to sheet** option takes the user back to the original sheet where new snapshots of objects can be taken. The **Go to sheet** button is also available in the Edit mode of the embedded sheet.

We can add effects and images to the story using **Effects** and **Media library**, which is available in the storytelling view.

Highlighting the performance measure in a bar chart

One of the essential components of a Qlik Sense dashboard is the **Key Performance Indicators (KPIs)**. The KPIs indicate the health of the company based on specific measures. The information displayed in the KPI should stand out distinctly and demand attention. For example, one of the key KPIs that a CEO of the company may like to have on his dashboard is **Actuals vs Budget**. A CEO is mostly interested in knowing whether the company is below or above the budgeted figures. So, it makes sense to highlight the required information inside the visualization object. The following recipe explains and shows you how to do this in a bar chart.

Getting ready

A "Dial Gauge" is quite commonly used to display the key KPIs in Qlik Sense. However, the best design practices say that the "bar chart" is the most effective way of conveying the information to the user. The following example makes use of a bar chart to strengthen this thought.

Perform the following steps to get started:

1. Create a new Qlik Sense application. Name it `Performance Measure_Bar Chart`.
2. Open the **Data load editor**.

3. Load the following script, which contains information on the actuals and budget for four products. The script can be downloaded from the Packt Publishing website:

```
Products:
LOAD * INLINE [
Product, Actuals, Budget
Footwear, 100000, 120000
Tyres, 180000, 150000
Mountain Bikes, 250000, 195000
Road Bikes, 200000, 225000
];
```

How to do it...

To highlight the performance measure in a bar chart, perform the following steps:

1. Open the **App overview** and create a new sheet.
2. Create a **Bar chart** on the sheet.
3. Add **Product** as the first dimension.
4. Under the **Properties** panel present on the right-hand side, click on the **Data** section and click on the **Add** button under **Dimensions**.
5. Open the expression editor by clicking on fx.
6. Add the following calculation as the second dimension and name it `Performance Type`:

```
=ValueList ('Actuals Up To Budget','Actuals Below
    Budget','Actuals Above Budget')
```

7. Click on the **Add** button under **Measures** and add the following measure to the object and call it **Performance**:

```
if(ValueList ('Actuals Up To Budget','Actuals Below
    Budget','Actuals Above Budget')='Actuals Up To Budget',
    RangeMin(Sum(Budget),Sum(Actuals)))/Sum(Budget) ,
    if(ValueList ('Actuals Up To Budget','Actuals Below
    Budget','Actuals Above Budget')='Actuals Below Budget' ,
    num((RangeMax(Sum(Budget)-
    Sum(Actuals),0))/Sum(Budget),'$#,##0.00;-$#,##0.00') ,
    (RangeMax(Sum(Actuals)-Sum(Budget),0))/Sum(Budget) ) )
```

8. Once we define the **Performance** measure, we will notice that just following the expression box for the measure, we get a dropdown for **Number formatting**. Under this dropdown, change the number format to **Number**. Next, we define the exact format of the number. To do this, switch off **Custom Formatting** and then, under the dropdown below that, select the **Formatting** representation as **12%**.

9. Under **Appearance**, click on **General** and add the `Product Performance` as the **title**.

10. Under **Sorting**, set the sort order for Performance type as alphabetically and **Descending**.

11. Under **Appearance**, click on **Presentation** and pick the style for the chart as **Stacked** and **Horizontal**.

12. Under **Colors and legend**, switch off **Auto** colors to activate **Custom** colors.

13. Along with the **Custom** colors, a dropdown to define the colors is also activated. This is situated right below the colors switch. Under this dropdown, select **By expression**.

14. Add the following expression under the color expression:

```
if(ValueList('Actuals Up To Budget','Actuals Below
  Budget','Actuals Above Budget')='Actuals Up To
  Budget',rgb(234,234,234),
if(ValueList('Actuals Up To Budget','Actuals Below
  Budget','Actuals Above     Budget')='Actuals Below
  Budget',rgb(255,0,0),rgb(0,255,0) )
  )
```

15. Make sure that **The expression is a color code** is checked.

16. The resulting chart will look like the following screenshot:

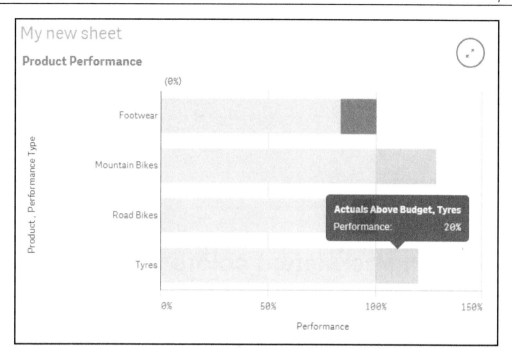

How it works...

The chart in this recipe shows the user the relative performance of each product. The colored segments highlight the extent by which a product has exceeded or failed to reach the budgeted value. The green segment indicates that the product has fared well, while the red segment indicates that the product is below the budgeted figure.

The preceding example makes use of the `ValueList` function in both the dimension and the measure. For the dimension, this results in three string values, namely `'Actuals Up To Budget'`, `'Actuals Below Budget'`, and `'Actuals Above Budget'` as row labels, which are further referenced in the measure.

The measure takes the values from the dimension and references them in a nested `if` statement as an input to three aggregated calculations.

We use the `ValueList` function in this recipe as Qlik Sense doesn't allow you to have custom colors for each measure, which we need in order to do the highlighting.

There's more…

The same information can be conveyed using a CapVentis Redmond Pie Gauge, the credit for which goes to Stephen Redmond, former CTO of Capventis. The Redmond Pie Gauge chart can be accessed on Qlik Branch at `http://branch.qlik.com/projects/showthread.php?159-CapVentis-Redmond-Pie-Gauge-for-Qlik-Sensehighlight=redmond+pie+gauge`.

See also

* *Using the colormix1 function*

Associating persistent colors to field values using the script

The best practices say that a designer should avoid using bar charts with multi-colored bars or avoid having too many colors in any of your chart objects. But, at times, we need to cater to the demands of the organization and take an uncalled for approach to designing. The following recipe explains how to associate a distinct field value with different colors in the Qlik Sense script.

Getting ready

This recipe serves as a good example to demonstrate the use of the `pick` function in the script. Perform the following steps to get started:

1. Create a new Qlik Sense application and name it `Persistent Colors`.
2. Open the **Data load editor**.
3. Load the following script that contains information about the actuals and budget of four products. The script is available for download on the Packt Publishing website:

```
ProductsTemp:
LOAD * INLINE [
Product, Actuals, Budget
Footwear, 100000, 120000
Tyres, 180000, 150000
Mountain Bikes, 250000, 195000
Road Bikes, 200000, 225000
```

```
];

Products:
LOAD *,
pick(match("Product", 'Footwear', 'Tyres', 'Mountain
    Bikes', 'Road Bikes'), RGB(236,129,0),RGB(250,185,0),
    RGB(70,137,164), RGB(141,25,8)) as "Product color"

RESIDENT ProductsTemp;

Drop table ProductsTemp;
```

How to do it...

1. Open the **App overview** and create a new sheet.
2. Create a **Bar chart** on the sheet.
3. Use **Product** as the dimension.
4. Use **Sum (Actuals)** as the measure. Label it as **Actuals**.
5. Under **Colors and legend**, switch off **Auto** colors to activate **Custom** colors.
6. Along with the **Custom** colors, a dropdown to define the colors is also activated. This is situated right below the colors switch. Under this dropdown, select **By expression**.
7. Add the following expression under the color expression:

    ```
    =[Product color]
    ```

8. Make sure that **The expression is a color code** is checked.

9. The result should be as follows:

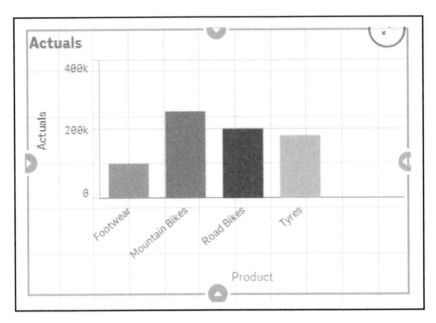

How it works...

The `pick` function used in the script links values in the Product field to distinct RGB values. Each product is displayed in a different color bar when the Product color field is used in the color expression of the chart.

There's more...

Persistent colors can also be defined in a master dimension. This ensures that a dimension value will have the same color in different charts. Colors assigned to a dimension value are available through the chart properties when we select the colors by dimension. You can set the colors through the value colors section in the edit dimension panel.

See also

- *Using the colormix1 function*

Using the colormix1 function

Heat maps are a common requirement in most of the BI implementations. A `colormix1` function helps to create a gradient between two colors. Look at the following recipe to understand the use of this function.

Getting ready

We will make use of a simple inline load for this recipe. Perform the following steps to get started:

1. Create a new Qlik Sense application. Name it `HeatMaps_Colormix1`.
2. Open the **Data load editor**.
3. Load the following script that gives you information about actuals and budget for products:

```
Products:
LOAD * INLINE [
Product, Actuals, Budget
Footwear, 100000, 120000
Tyres, 180000, 150000
Mountain Bikes, 250000, 195000
Road Bikes, 200000, 225000
Chains, 80000, 90000
Helmets, 240000,160001
Gloves, 56000,125000
Pedals, 45000,100000
Rucksacks, 300000,450000
];
```

How to do it...

1. Open the **App overview** and create a new sheet.
2. Create a **Bar chart** on the sheet
3. Use **Product** as the dimension.
4. Use **Sum (Actuals)** as the measure and label it as **Actuals**.
5. Switch off **Auto** colors to activate **Custom** colors under **Colors and legend**.
6. Along with the **Custom** colors, a dropdown to define the colors is also activated. This is situated right below the colors switch. Under this dropdown, select **By expression**.

7. Add the following expression under the color expression:

```
colormix1(sum(Actuals) / $(=max(aggr(sum(Actuals),
    Product))), white(), RGB(0, 70, 140))
```

8. Under **Sorting**, promote sales above the product in the order of priority. This can be done by holding the button and dragging it to sales above priority.
9. Set the sort order for sales as **Sort numerically** and **Descending**.
10. Make sure that **The expression is a color code** is checked.
11. The result will be as follows:

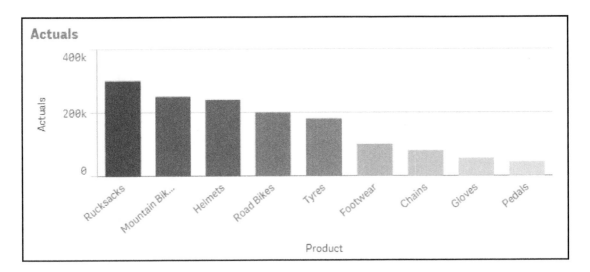

How it works...

The `colormix1` function creates a gradient between two colors using a number that varies from 0 to 1.

We know that the bar for the product with the highest value of actuals will be the most intense. So, to achieve a value between 0 and 1, we calculate the relative shares of each actual value against the highest actual value from the entire product range, that is, "Actuals for each product"/"The highest Actuals value from the entire product range".

In our expression, the `colormix1` function helps to establish a gradient from white to RGB (0, 70, 140).

There's more...

A sequential color gradient across the chart can be obtained through the chart properties if we select the color by measure. However, we can't have custom colors if we use this approach and we will have to depend on the color scheme in Qlik Sense.

See also

Similar to `colormix1` function, we can also use the `colormix2` function, which gives us an option to have an intermediate color between the lower and upper limit color.

Composition

Composition can be defined as looking at a particular measure compared to the whole.

For example, in a "Sales by Region" chart, the sales for each singular region would be a discrete value, while the total sales across all countries would be the "Whole".

Total sales can be divided into "Relative shares" for each region. Having information on "Relative Sales Percentages," as compared to total sales, has a greater impact rather than viewing just the plain sales figures. Eureka moments are much more likely when people use a tool to answer their own questions, which is a core belief behind the design of Qlik Sense.

As with everything else, data composition can be visualized in multiple ways. Understanding what you are trying to achieve will eventually dictate the best choice of visualization.

For example, depending on what matters, each of the following points will favor a different form of visualization:

- Relative differences
- Relative and absolute differences
- Share of the total
- Accumulation to the total (or subtraction)
- Breaking down components of components

As such, each example in the next four recipes will be supported by a goal, questions, and an analysis description, as follows:

- **Goal**: As a business analyst, I want to report on the best regions for focusing our marketing strategy
- **Question**: I want to see how our total revenue is shared this year across the various regions
- **Analysis**: I want to see how the total revenue is divided per region and whether it is performing positively

Getting ready

Downloading the example code

You can download the example source files from your account at `http://www.packtpub.com`, for all Packt books that you have purchased. If you have purchased the book elsewhere, you can visit `http://www.packtpub.com/support` and register to have the files emailed directly to you.

Perform the following steps to get started:

1. Download the `Chapter 2 - Sales.qvf`, application from the Packt Publishing website
2. Save the application at the following location: `C:\Users\<user>\Documents\Qlik\Sense\Apps`
3. Open the application through the Qlik Sense hub

How to do it...

1. Click the button in the top right-hand corner in the application overview, and click the **Create new sheet** button. Name this sheet as `Composition`.
2. Go to the **Charts** asset pane and double-click the **Line chart** button .
3. Add the following measure (m) and dimensions (d) in the same order as follows:

```
(m)  Sum(Sales)
(d)   Month
(d)   Region
```

4. Select **Area** from the properties pane under the **Appearance** | **Presentation** menu.
5. Finally, tick the stacked area box. The following screenshot is an example of the final visualization:

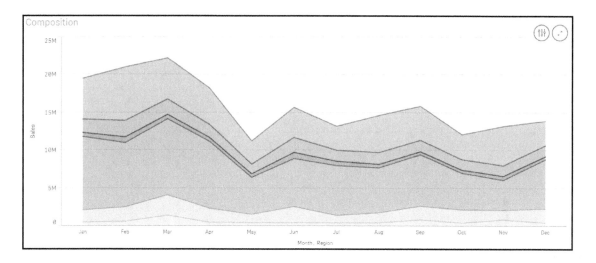

How it works...

Enabling the right property settings can turn a line chart into a stacked area chart. This clearly shows the differences when we analyze the relative and absolute composition of many time periods, as shown in the preceding example. If you had less time, say the last three years, then you would use the same approach; however, you will change the chart type to **Bar chart** instead of **Line chart**, as the magnitude of change is more important than the change trend.

There's more...

When looking at the composition in terms of accumulation or subtraction from the TOTAL, a good option for representation is the waterfall chart. If the only important differences are the relative differences, then write your calculation as a percentage of TOTAL.

To achieve this, perform the following steps:

1. Replace the `Sales` expression from the preceding recipe with the following:

   ```
   Sum(Sales) / sum( TOTAL <Month> Sales).
   ```

2. Once we define the preceding measure, we will notice that just below the expression box for the measure, we get a dropdown for **Number formatting**. Under this dropdown, change the number format to **Number.** Next, we define the exact format of the number. To do this, switch off **Custom formatting** and then, under the dropdown below that, select the **Formatting** representation as **12%**. This will produce the following 100 percent stacked area chart:

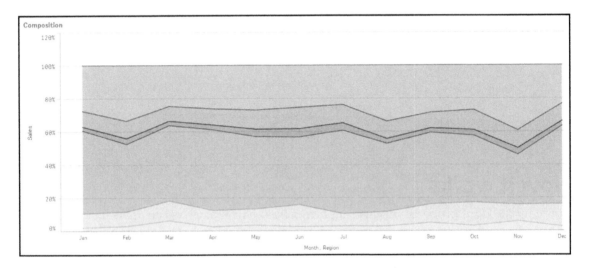

Relationships

Seeing relationships in data is something that is very difficult to achieve when we view data numerically. The following visualizations are the key to uncovering correlations, outliers, and clusters in the data:

- **Goal**: Increase product subscriptions
- **Question**: Are there any differences in the relationship between the revenue and the sales quantity by product sub-group?
- **Analysis**: Here, we will use a scatter graph to plot product sales that are grouped by product sub-group

Getting ready

We will make use of the same `Chapter 2 - Sales.qvf` application used in the *Composition* recipe.

How to do it...

1. In the application overview, click on the button in the top right-hand corner in order to create a new sheet and then click on the **Create new sheet** button. Name this sheet `Relationships`.

2. Once inside the newly created sheet, go to the **Charts** asset pane and double-click on the **Scatter plot** chart button.

3. Add the following measure (m) and dimension (d) in exactly the same order as shown here:

```
(m)  Sum(Sales)
(m)  Sum([Sales Qty])
(m)  Sum(Margin)
(d)  Product Sub Group
```

4. In the properties pane, under **Appearance** | **Colors and legend**, switch off the **Auto** colors. Then select **By expression** from the drop-down menu.

5. Finally, add the following expression to the area provided below the drop-down menu:

```
IF([Product
   Line]='Drink',ARGB(100,255,0,0),ARGB(100,0,0,255))
```

6. The final visualization should resemble the following screenshot:

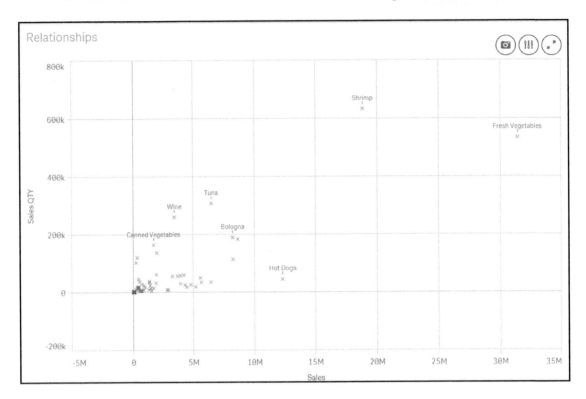

How it works...

Since the nature of the product sub-group dimension is hierarchical, we can actually show two relationships. The first is between the different measures, whereas the second looks at the relationships between different product sub-group categories by coloring them separately.

Comparison

The bar graph is one of the most common data visualizations. This is because it is simply the best way of comparing the difference in value across a single item.

- **Goal**: Increase product subscriptions
- **Question**: Why does a subset of similar products not respond as positively as others in the same market?
- **Analysis**: Combo chart

Getting ready

We will make use of the same `Chapter 2 - Sales.qvf` application used in the *Relationships* recipe.

How to do it...

1. From the application overview, click the button in the top right-hand corner and click the **Create new sheet** button. Name this sheet `Comparison`.
2. Once inside the newly created sheet, go to the **Charts** asset pane and double-click the **Combo chart** button.
3. Add **Product Group** as a dimension.
4. Next, add `Sum (Sales)` as the first measure. Label it **Sales**.
5. Add `sum ([Sales Qty])` as the second measure. Label it **Sales Qty**.
6. For the **Sales Qty** measure:
    - Change the default display format for the expression from **Bars** to **Marker**
    - Right below the display format options, there is a dropdown to define the axis
    - Set the axis to secondary. Just below the axis formats, there is a markers style dropdown. Select the style as **Line**
7. Under **Sorting**, promote **Sales** to the top of the list.

8. The visualization should resemble the following diagram:

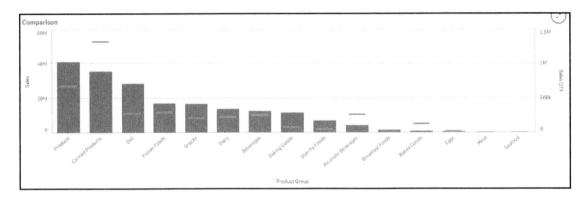

How it works...

When it comes to comparing the magnitude of change of the values against each other, you really cannot beat a bar chart. When you need to compare multiple dimensions in the same visualization, a common approach is to stack them on top of each other. This option is available in the properties of the bar chart object.

However, this removes the length comparison we are so good at, thus making the view not as effective.

The preceding method of using symbols instead of additional bars still leaves a good focus on the comparative length to determine the magnitude of change. This is also a more efficient use of space than creating separate visualizations to cover additional analysis.

See also

- *Highlighting the performance measure in a bar chart*

Distribution

Distribution analysis takes a look at how quantitative values are distributed along an axis, from the lowest to the highest. The characteristics emerge while looking at the shape of the data, such as central tendency, shape, and outliers:

- **Goal**: To understand which demographics should be focused on for our marking approach for a specific product group
- **Question**: The suitable age range to target our new marketing campaign toward
- **Analysis**: Use a histogram to see a useful range from the mean age

Getting ready

We will make use of the same `Chapter 2 - Sales.qvf` application used in the *Comparison* recipe.

How to do it...

1. In the application overview, click on the button in the top right-hand corner and click on the **Create new sheet** button. Name this sheet `Distribution`.
2. Once inside the newly created sheet, go to the **Charts** asset pane and double-click on the **Bar chart** button.
3. In the properties pane to the right of your screen, click on **Add** data and select **Dimension**.
4. Click on the *fx* button for the input box of **Add dimension** and enter the following pre-calculated dimension. Label the dimension as `Age`:

    ```
    =Aggr(Class(Age/19,1),Order)
    ```

5. Add the following line as the measure and label it `Order Count`:

    ```
    Count(Order)
    ```

6. In the properties panel, select `Age` under **Sorting** and check **Sort numerically**. In the dropdown located right below the **Sort numerically** check box, select the order as **Ascending**.

7. The final distribution chart should look like the following screenshot:

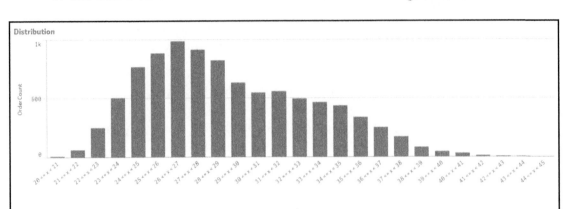

How it works...

Distribution visualizations help you to analyze one or two variables spread along an axis starting from the lowest to the highest. The shape of the data will tell you about characteristics, such as the central tendency, shape, and outliers.

Structuring visualizations

As discussed in the introduction, when choosing visualizations, you should start with knowing if you are looking at a comparison, composition, distribution, or relationship.

While this helps in answering a single question effectively, this is often to fulfill the goal that you want to see the information from different angles. Structuring visualizations to easily answer "the next question" keeps consistency in analysis.

While in QlikView, it is common to design a user interface with more interaction than simply filtering the data. Qlik Sense is built with a large focus on the business user and analyst. This recipe involves little practical work and instead, it carries the torch for the expert designers in the product team at Qlik. Here is an example of how and why you should make use of a screen and not just an object.

Getting ready

We will make use of the same `Chapter 2 - Sales.qvf` application used in the *Distribution* recipe.

How to do it...

The charts that were built in the previous visualization category recipe are available as master visualizations in the `Chapter 2 - Sales.qvf` application. As mentioned during the introduction, the reason behind the structure of the previous four recipes was to think of the business question first. If you can answer someone's question about the business with each page (tab), you have a book of gold:

1. From the application overview, click the button in the top right-hand corner in order to the **Create new sheet** button. Name this sheet as `Structuring Visualization`.

2. Open the **Master items** pane.

3. Under **Visualizations,** drag the **Composition** chart into the top left-hand corner:

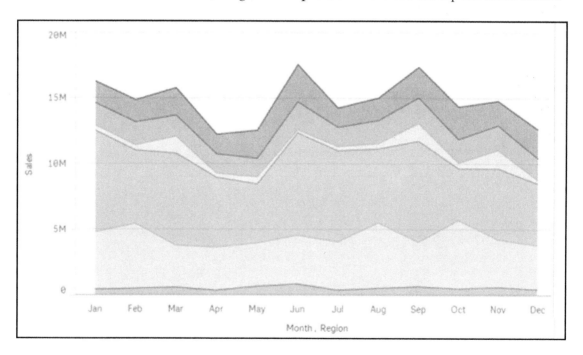

4. Next, drag the **Relationship** chart into the top right-hand corner:

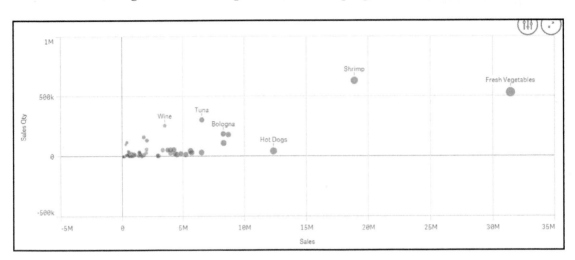

5. Drag the **Comparison** chart into the bottom left-hand corner:

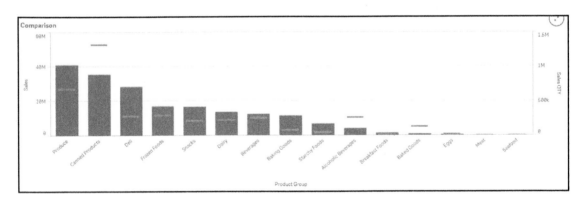

6. Finally, drag the **Distribution** chart into the bottom right-hand corner:

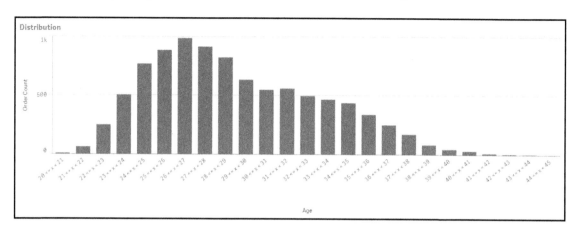

How it works...

Each of the four preceding recipes has a question to answer for a shared or similar goal. Placing complementary visualizations near each other is good page design. Each chart adds context to the others and helps to build up a clearer analysis picture. The final result should look like the following screenshot. Selecting a point of interest in any of the four charts will show you that the dataset from other angles gives you a greater insight with a single click:

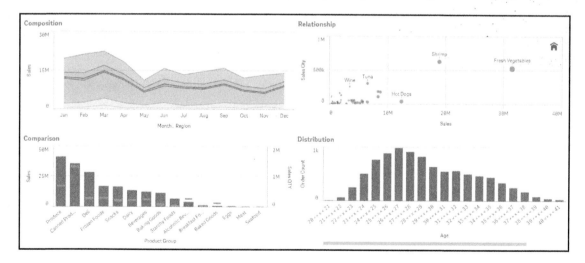

Measuring statistical data with box plot charts

If you need to compare a range and distribution of numerical data, the box plot is the best choice. With the box plot, you can easily see the ranges and outliers using one of the three presets:

- Standard (J Tukey method)
- Percentile based
- Standard deviation

Each preset leads to different results in the box plot graph.

Getting ready

We will make use of the same `Chapter 2 - Sales.qvf` application that we used in the *Comparison* recipe.

How to do it...

1. In the application overview, click on the button in the top right-hand corner and click on the **Create new sheet** button. Name this sheet `Boxplot`.
2. Once inside the newly created sheet, go to the **Charts** asset pane and double-click on the **Box plot** chart button ⊣☐⊢ Box plot .
3. In the properties pane to the right of your screen, click on **Dimensions** and click **Add**.
4. Select **Field capital city** as the first dimension.
5. Add **OICA region** as the second dimension.
6. Add the following line as the measure and label it `Total Car Sales`:

```
Sum([Car sales])
```

7. In the properties panel, select **Box plot elements** and change the preset to **Standard deviation**.

8. The final box plot chart should look like the following screenshot:

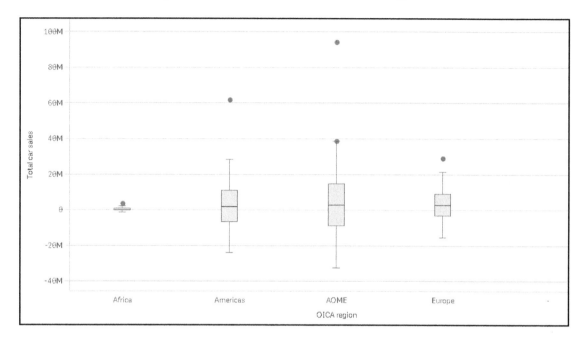

How it works...

Box plot visualizations help you to analyze the numeric distribution and find outliers shown as dots outside the wiskers limits.

You can play with the presets and see the change affect the chart presentation.

Using a waterfall chart to analyze the cumulative effect

A waterfall chart helps you understand the cumulative effect of sequentially positive or negative values impacting a subtotal or total value. It's often used to visualize financial statements.

Getting ready

We will make use of the same Chapter 2 - Sales.qvf application used in the *Comparison* recipe.

How to do it...

1. In the application overview, click on the button in the top right-hand corner and click on the **Create new sheet** button. Name this sheet Waterfall.

2. Once inside the newly created sheet, go to the **Charts** asset pane and double-click on the **Waterfall chart** button I'.'I .

3. In the properties pane to the right of your screen, click on **Measures** and click **Add**.

4. Add the following line as the measure and label it Total Commercial vehicle Sales:

   ```
   sum([Commercial vehicle sales])
   ```

5. Add another line as the measure and label it Total Non Commercial vehicle Sales:

   ```
   sum([Car sales])- sum([Commercial vehicle sales])
   ```

6. Add another line as the measure and label it Total car sales:

   ```
   Sum([Car sales])
   ```

7. In the measure properties of Total car sales, select **Subtotals** in **Measure operation**.

8. The final waterfall chart should look like the following screenshot:

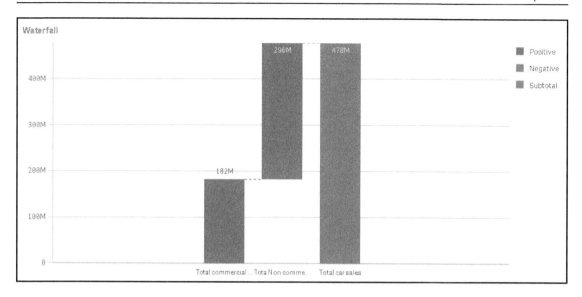

How it works...

Waterfall visualizations help you to evaluate the cumulative effect of individual categories or compare them with a total or subtotal. The bar is displaced with add or subtract over the previous measure following the order in measures.

3
Scripting

In this chapter, we will discuss the creation of optimized and well-structured scripts for a Qlik Sense application. We are going to cover the following topics:

- Structuring the script
- Efficiently debugging the script
- Packaging the code in script files
- How to use subroutines in Qlik Sense®
- Optimizing the UI calculation speed
- Optimizing the reload time of the application
- Using a `For each` loop to load data from multiple files
- Using the `Concat()` function to store multiple field values in a single cell
- Executing command-line programs within the script

Introduction

What is a script in Qlik Sense? In layman's terms, a script instructs the Qlik Sense engine on how to extract the data from the data source and what to do with it.

It forms an essential component of the ETL process. Hence, it is important to have a well-structured script in order to load the data efficiently. A good understanding of how to optimize an ETL process leads to a better data model. A good data model is one of the core components alongside well-written expressions to realize a good user interface performance.

Structuring the script

The techniques for adding structure to the script is something that comes naturally to experienced developers. This is because they have often learned it the hard way, through other people's work, and spent additional time understanding that the script can be made easier with a couple of simple additions. Again, this is something that won't be covered in user guides, but it is a very important skill for new developers to have under their belt.

Getting ready

In this example, we will generate the required data automatically in the script.

How to do it...

1. Create a new Qlik Sense application and name it Structuring Scripts.
2. Create a new section in the **Data load editor** called Change Log.
3. Add the following code:

```
/*
This application demonstrates the importance of adding
    structure to the back end script of your applications

Change Log:

[10/06/2015] Philip Hand: Initial build

*/
```

4. Create another section called `Calendar` and add the following script:

```
/*=========================================================
Section: Calendar Tab; DESCRIPTION: Generates every date
between the periods
 vMinDate & vMaxDate; DEVELOPERS: Philip Hand, Neeraj Kharpate;
//=======================================================*/
TRACE START:~~~~Loading Calendar Tab~~~~; Let
vMinDate=DATE(Floor(MakeDate(2009,1,1)),'DD/MM/YYYY'); Let
vMaxDate=DATE(Floor(Today())); TRACE Calendar date range set to
$(vMinDate) & $(vMaxDate); Let vDiff=vMaxDate-vMinDate+1;
Calendar: Load DateID,
Year(DateID) As Year,
Month(DateID) As Month,
Date(DateID) As Date,
Day(DateID) As Day,
Week(DateID) As Week;
Load
RecNo()-1+$(vMinDate)
As DateID AutoGenerate($(vDiff));
TRACE END:~~~~Loading Calendar Tab~~~~;
```

5. Finally, save the data and load the script.

How it works...

The first tab gives an overview of the application and calls out any key information that a new developer who is seeing the script for the first time will find useful. It also includes a change log to track the changes.

The second tab has a high-level description of the contained code and the developers who have worked on it. Finally, we can make use of the TRACE statements to write information into the execution window. This allows you to see each action being performed during script execution and is a useful tool to debug errors.

Efficiently debugging the script

It is good script practice to debug the script in your data load editor before its full execution. This way, the developer minimizes the risk of script failures and also saves on valuable time. The process of debugging makes it possible to monitor every script statement and examine the variable values while the script is being executed. The following recipe explains how to debug the Qlik Sense script efficiently.

Getting ready

Load the following script, which gives information about the Products and Customers in the Qlik Sense **Data load editor**. The sample code is available for download from the Packt Publishing website:

```
Products Temp:
LOAD * INLINE [
Product, ProductID, Sales
Footwear, F21Lon, 120000
Tyres, T21Man, 150000
Mountain Bikes, MB32Lon, 195000
Road Bikes, RB12Bir, 225000
];

Customers:
LOAD * INLINE [
Customer, ProductID, City
Hero, F21Lon, London
Avon, T21Man, Manchester
Force1, MB32Lon, London
Ferrari, RB12Bir, Birmingham
];
```

How to do it...

1. Save the preceding script.
2. When you save the script, Qlik Sense automatically detects syntax issues present in the script, if any. The syntax issues are highlighted in red, as shown in the following screenshot. Also, make a note of the ⊕ mark beside the section name in the section panel. This indicates that there is an issue with the script on the tab:

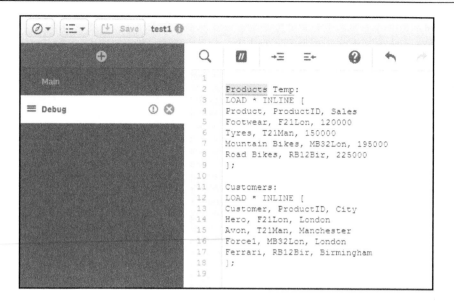

3. Next, click on the Show debug panel 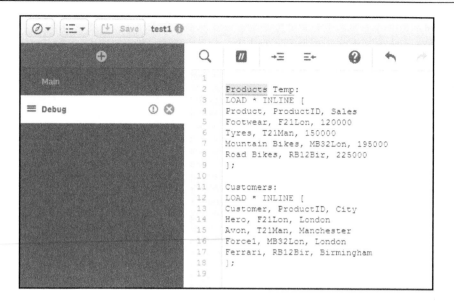 button in the top-right corner.

4. A debug panel pops up from the bottom of the screen with three toggles, **Output**, **Variables**, and **Breakpoints**.

5. In order to debug the script, load only the limited records, as this will speed up the process of debugging. Keep in mind that when you load limited records from a number of tables in your Qlik Sense script, there may be no records that associate the tables. However, you don't need to worry, as the main concern here is checking the accuracy of the script. Once it is confirmed, the script will run through without errors and you may go ahead and do a full reload.

6. Take a limited load of 10 records by ticking the box for **Limited load** and entering 10 in the input box. Click on the Run button.

7. On running the debugger, Qlik Sense checks the entire script line by line and looks for any errors. If the script has an error, the execution stops at that point and the issue is highlighted in the amber-colored box, as shown in the following screenshot. The line at which the execution has stopped is highlighted in red:

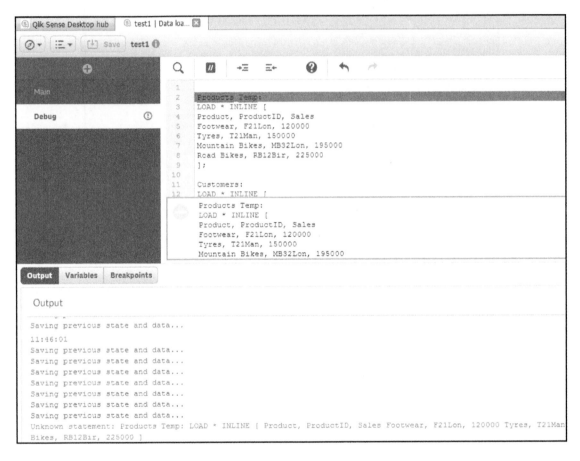

8. The **Output** window gives us the details of the error encountered. Click on the Run button again to complete the script execution. Once the script execution is complete, you will notice that the Customers table has loaded fine but that the Products Temp table has not loaded at all. We can verify the same by checking the **Data model viewer**.

9. Check the **Variables** tab. The **ScriptErrorCount** variable gives the count of errors, and the **ScriptErrorList** shows the type of error, which in our case is a **Syntax Error**:

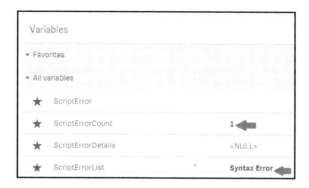

10. At this point, the user can remove the space between the words `Products` and `temp` in the label for the `Products` table to rectify the script error.

11. We can also define breakpoints in our script by clicking on the area beside the line number in the script window. The breakpoints are denoted by ⊖ .

12. The script execution stops at the breakpoint.

13. The breakpoints can be enabled, disabled, and deleted at will by selecting and deselecting them under the **Breakpoints** list, or by re-clicking on the ⊖ icon on the number line. The **Breakpoints** are ignored at the blank lines and inside the LOAD statement in the middle of the field list:

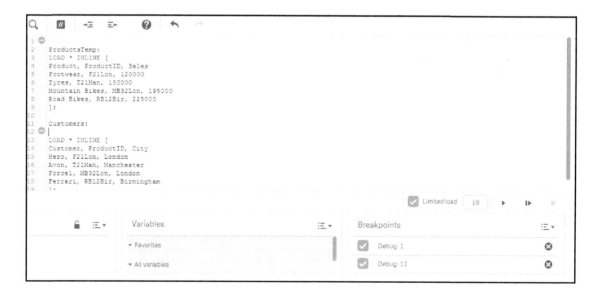

14. Alternatively, the user can step through each statement of code in the script by clicking on the Step ▐▶ button.

How it works...

The Debug panel in Qlik Sense checks through the entire script for errors and makes sure that it is accurate. One major benefit of using a debugger is that the user can load only a few records into the data model for the test. The debugger also allows the user to check the output of the executed script and make sure that it is as desired.

There's more...

The Debug panel also helps you to identify issues related to variables and fields in the files defined under the $(include) statement. We can also inspect the variables during the script execution. The variables can be accessed by clicking on the **Variables** toggle. You can set any of the variables as favorites by clicking on the ★ button next to the variable.

See also

* *Packaging the code in script files*

Packaging the code in script files

Script files are complete blocks of code that are stored in external files such as .qvs or .txt, and they can be included in your application with a single reference. They are conceptually similar to the subroutines that are covered in *How to use subroutines in Qlik Sense®* recipe in this chapter. However, there is a subtle difference in the usage. **QVS** simply stands for **QlikView Script File**.

Everything from data sources, expressions, and visualizations can be governed centrally and the script files can be leveraged in a similar way to help build standards in backend data preparation across multiple applications.

Getting ready

Open a new QlikSense application and create a data connection in a folder where you want to store your script files, as shown in the following example:

How to do it...

1. Open a Notepad document.
2. Copy the following subroutine script (a simplified version of the calendar code from the previous recipe) into the Notepad document:

```
SUB Calendar(vMinDate,vMaxDate) Let vDiff=vMaxDate-vMinDate+1;
Calendar: Load DateID, Year(DateID) As Year, Month(DateID) As
Month, Date(DateID) As Date, Day(DateID) As Day, Week(DateID)
As Week; Load RecNo()-1+$(vMinDate) As DateID
AutoGenerate($(vDiff)); END SUB
```

3. Save the Notepad file as `Calendar.qvs` in the folder for which you created the data connection. Remember to change the **Save as type** to **All Files**, as shown:

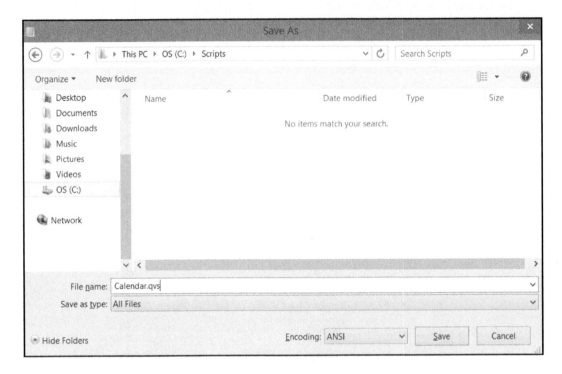

4. Add the following line of code to your application:

```
$(Include=[lib://Scripts/calendar.qvs]);
```

5. You can now call the same subroutine without seeing the code, as in the previous example. In order to generate a calendar, use the following CALL statement in the script:

```
CALL Calendar(makedate(2010,01,01),Floor(Today())) ;
```

How it works...

We have replaced a page of code with just one line using a script file. If you have a code that can be packaged and reused across applications, it makes sense to store this code in a script file for others to use. Doing this reduces the complexity and keeps the focus of new developers on the backend code and on the matter that is relevant to that application.

It's worth pointing out that you could copy the code in the preceding point directly into the script editor and it will still get created and be ready for use. We save this code as a QVS file so that we can load the code using the $(Include...) statement. Loading the script from external files using the $(Include...) statement is a good method of reusing blocks of script across applications or using them for source control.

See also

- *How to use subroutines in Qlik Sense®*

How to use subroutines in Qlik Sense®

At times, it is mandatory to use the same set of code at different places in the script. To achieve this, developers will sometimes use a copy and paste approach. However, this makes it difficult to maintain and read the script. It is always advised to create subroutines and then simply call them as and when needed.

In the following recipe, we use subroutines to create **QlikView Data** (**QVDs**) file and store them in a specific folder. We also generate fields using various functions within the subroutines, which also helps in auditing the QVD files.

Getting ready

1. This recipe makes use of certain functions such as QVDTablename, QVDNoOfFields, and QVDNoOfRecords, which don't work in the normal script mode in Qlik Sense. Hence, we need to activate the legacy mode by following the steps given in the recipe entitled *How to activate legacy mode in Qlik sense* in Chapter 1, *Getting Started with the Data*.

2. Once the legacy mode is activated, open Qlik Sense Desktop and create a new application called Subroutines in Qlik Sense.

3. Create a folder called QVD at a desired location on the hard drive. For the sake of this recipe, we are creating the QVD folder at the following location:

   ```
   C:\Qliksense cookbook\Chapters\3\QVD
   ```

4. This folder will store the QVDs generated in the subroutines.

How to do it...

1. Open the **Data load editor**.
2. Create a new data connection called QVDFolder. This data connection should create a folder connection to the QVD folder created in Step 1.
3. In the **Data load editor**, create a new section, Variable Setting, and add the following code to it:

```
LET vFileName = subfield(DocumentName(),'.',1);

SET vTable1 =1; //Product

SET vTable2 =1; //Customer

LET vQVD='QVDFolder';
```

4. Create a new section, Data, and add the following code to it:

```
SUB Create_T_Product

  $(vTable):
  LOAD * INLINE [
  Product, ProductID, Sales
  Footwear, F21Lon, 120000
  Tyres, T21Man, 150000
  Mountain Bikes, MB32Lon, 195000
  Road Bikes, RB12Bir, 225000
];
END SUB

SUB Create_T_Customer

  $(vTable):
  LOAD * INLINE [
  Customer, ProductID, City
  Hero, F21Lon, London
  Avon, T21Man, Manchester
  Force1, MB32Lon, London
  Ferrari, RB12Bir, Birmingham
];
END SUB
```

5. Create a new section called `Store_Drop`, and add the following code to it:

```
SUB Create_QVD_Standard(vTable,vSub)

  LET vQVDStartTime = timestamp(now(),'DD MMM YY hh:mm:ss');
  CALL $(vSub)

  STORE '$(vTable)' INTO [lib://$(vQVD)\$(vTable).qvd(qvd);

  DROP TABLE $(vTable);

  LET vFieldType = 'QVD_Standard';

  LET vQVDEndTime = timestamp(now(),'DD MMM YY hh:mm:ss');

  LET vQVDTimeTaken = Interval(vQVDEndTime - vQVDStartTime,
'hh:mm:ss');

  LET vTableFullPath = DocumentPath();

  TablesLoaded:
  LOAD
  QVDTableName('lib://$(vQVD)\$(vTable).qvd') AS [STDQVD Name],
  Timestamp($(vQVDStartTime),'DD MMM YY hh:mm') AS [STDQVD
Start Time],
  Timestamp($(vQVDEndTime),'DD MMM YY hh:mm') AS [STDQVD End
Time],
  Interval($(vQVDTimeTaken),'hh mm ss') AS [STDQVD Time Taken
(hh mm ss)],
  QVDNoOfFields('lib://$(vQVD)\$(vTable).qvd') AS [STDQVD No of
Fields],
  QVDNoOfRecords('lib://$(vQVD)\$(vTable).qvd')AS [STDQVD No of
Records]
  AUTOGENERATE (1);

END SUB
```

6. Create a new section called `Create qvd`, and add the following code to it:

```
LET vRunStart = timestamp(now(),'DD MMM YYYY hh:mm:ss');
If $(vTable1) = 1 Then
   CALL Create_QVD_Standard('T_Product','Create_T_Product')
ENDIF;
If $(vTable2) = 1 Then
   CALL Create_QVD_Standard('T_Customer','Create_T_Customer')
ENDIF;
LET vRunFinish = timestamp(now(),'DD MMM YYYY hh:mm:ss');
LET vRunTime = Interval(num(timestamp#('$(vRunFinish)','DD MMM
```

```
YY hh:mm:ss')) -num(timestamp#('$(vRunStart)','DD MMM YY
hh:mm:ss')),'hh:mm:ss');
```

7. Save and reload the document.
8. On the frontend, click on Edit sheet icon at the top right-hand corner and create a new `Table` object by dragging it across the sheet from the left-hand side panel.
9. Add all the available dimensions in the table to get the following output:

QVD Audit					
STDQVD Name	STDQVD No of Fields	STDQVD No of Records	STDQVD Start Time	STDQVD End Time	STDQVD Time Taken (hh mm ss)
T_Customer	3	4	09 Jun 15 10:53	09 Jun 15 10:53	00 00 00
T_Product	3	4	09 Jun 15 10:53	09 Jun 15 10:53	00 00 00

How it works...

The first two subroutines, named `SUB Create_T_Product` and `SUB Create_T_Customer`, create the tables called `Product` and `Customer`, and then store the data in these tables.

The third subroutine, `SUB Create_QVD_Standard(vTable,vSub)`, passes the values of the respective table names and the subroutines. Within this subroutine, we also create a number of fields using the load script functions, which are used for our QVD audit purposes.

Further, the `CALL` statements call the subroutines and create QVDs to store them in specified folders.

Along with creating and storing the QVDs, we also get valuable information, such as the number of fields in each QVD, the time it takes to create the QVDs, and so on. This is especially helpful while loading a large dataset.

There's more...

The subroutines can be stored in an external file and further used in the script using an `include` statement.

See also

- *Packaging the code in script files*

Optimizing the UI calculation speed

The following recipe discusses the creation of flags in the script and the use of these flags in the chart expressions to optimize the calculation speeds.

A flag can be described as a binary status indicator that is used to indicate certain states of data; for example, creating a new field in the table called `MonthToDate Flag`. This field can be used to flag records with the number 1 if the record was created in the last month, else we mark the record with a 0.

Using this approach, we can now count the number of records in the table that were created in the last month using the expression `SUM([Month To Date Flag])`.

A flag is often used to code complex decision logic into the load script so that the binary "yes" or "no" decisions can be quickly identified from the calculations.

Getting ready

For this recipe, we will generate sales data in the script, as defined in the following. Load the following script into the **Data load editor**:

```
Calendar:
Load
    DateID,
    RowNo()                             AS ID,
    Year(DateID)                        As Year,
    Year(DateID)&''&NUM(Month(DateID),'00')  AS YearMonth,
    Month(DateID)                       As Month,
    Date(DateID)                        As Date,
    Day(DateID)                         As Day,
    Week(DateID)                        As Week,
    Floor(2000 * rand())                AS Sales;
Load
RecNo()-1+makedate(2014) As DateID
AutoGenerate(730);
```

How to do it...

1. In the preceding `Load` statement, add the following line of code just below the `DateID` field:

```
if(Year(DateID)=2015,1,0) AS YearFlag_2015,
```

2. Reload the script.
3. Create a **Line chart** with `YearMonth` as the dimension.
4. Add the following measure and label it as `Sales`:

```
sum({<YearFlag_2015={1}>}Sales)
```

5. Make sure that the sort order for the months is maintained as `Numeric` and `Ascending` for the `YearMonth` field.
6. The graph should appear as follows:

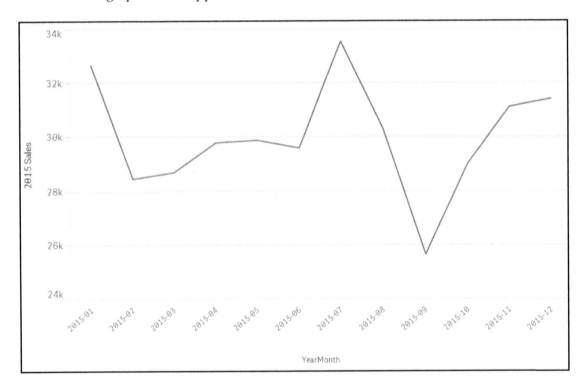

How it works...

The flag field that we set up simply adds an indicator against the records that fall within the rules we established. Now that we have identified the records from 2015, we can use this flag in the expression to calculate across those records.

The real-world difference between using a flag to identify the records in 2015 and just using set analysis to identify the record directly will be almost nothing. The preceding code is a very simplified example of turning business logic into a flag indicator to be used later on. Once you have a grip on the concept and implementation, the same method can be used to add a level of complex and detailed business logic to a binary yes or no flag. Instead of writing the complex If-then-Else logic in the chart expressions, it is always advised to move it to the backend script and create flags. The flags are then used in the frontend expressions, thus making them more efficient.

Adding as much of the business logic to the script as possible makes everything much quicker and simpler to read. This way, you don't have to look at each chart before making a change; you can make it in one place only and the change will propagate through the whole application.

Optimizing the reload time of the application

There are two methods of loading data from QVDs: optimized and non-optimized. The key point here is that the optimized loads can be up to 100 times quicker than the non-optimized loads.

This speed increase is a result of the data passing directly from the disk (QVD) into the memory (RAM) without being unpacked from its compressed QVD format.

As you may have guessed, the reason every load is not optimized is that we often want to change the data coming out of the QVD. This requires it to be uncompressed before going into memory; hence, it is significantly slower. Just about any change to the data will cause the load to be non-optimized; however, there are a few things that we can do.

Getting ready

1. Open a new QlikSense application and go straight to the **Data load editor**
2. Create a folder library connection to any location where you want to save example data files, and call that connection QVDs

How to do it...

1. Copy the following code into the **Data load editor**. Please note that if you are using a very low-specification machine, you can reduce the 20 million number on the third line to something smaller, like 1 million:

```
ExampleData:
Load RecNo() AS TransID
Autogenerate 20000000;

Store ExampleData into [lib://QVDs/Data1.qvd](qvd);
Drop Table ExampleData;

OptimizedLoad:
LOAD
TransID
FROM [lib://QVDs/Data1.qvd](qvd);


Store OptimizedLoad Into [lib://QVDs/Data2.qvd](qvd);
Drop Table OptimizedLoad;

UnoptimizedLoad:
LOAD
    'Example Text' AS NewField,
    TransID
FROM [lib://QVDs/Data2.qvd](qvd)
Where Not IsNull(TransID);
```

2. Reload the application and make a note of the time it takes to load the records in each table:

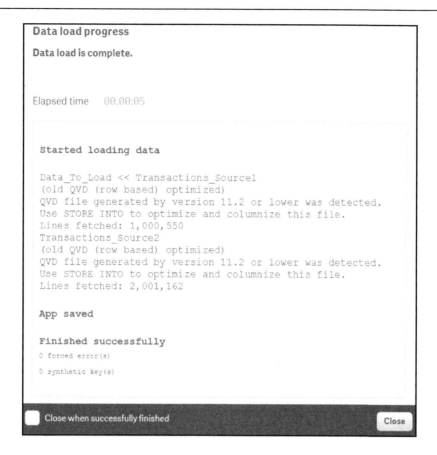

How it works...

The first 20 million records loaded are simply auto-generated data records that we store in a Data1.qvd file to use later on. Now, we have a QVD available to read from, which we can use to demonstrate the difference between an optimized load and an un-optimized load. As a rule of thumb, any data transformations on the QVD data in the script will cause the load to be un-optimized.

The second load of 20 million records simply reads the data from the Data1.qvd file (created in the preceding step) directly into memory and no further transformations take place. As no transformations take place in the Load statement, the load is an optimized load as stated in the **Data progress** window. We store the data loaded from this step into another QVD file called Data2.qvd.

The third load is from the `Data2.qvd` file, the difference being that this time, the script adds a `Where` clause and a new calculated field. Either of these transformations will cause Qlik Sense to use the un-optimized load method. Notice that the **Data progress** window does not specify "optimized load," even though we are loading the data from a QVD file.

You can think of optimized versus un-optimized loads as data being directly loaded into RAM for reading versus the unpacked data that is read line by line. A good exception to a `Where` clause that breaks the optimization rule is the `Exists()` function. Using `Where Exists(<Field>)` at the end of a load is a good method of loading the data that's relevant to what has been loaded previously.

Using a For each loop to load data from multiple files

Often in a Qlik Sense application, we need to load data from a directory that contains an identical set of data files; for example, sales for each country come in different files for each month. In such a case, we use a wildcard load, in order to fetch the data for our application. The following recipe discusses the data modeling issues encountered when using the wildcard load and how we make use of the `For each` loop structure in the script to overcome this issue.

Getting ready

For this exercise, we will make use of two sample XLSX files, namely, `Apr2015.xlsx` and `May2015.xlsx`, that contain mock sales data for six countries. These files can be downloaded from the Packt Publishing website.

How to do it...

1. Once the source files are downloaded, store them in a folder called `ForEachLoadData`.
2. Create a folder connection as explained in `Chapter 1`, *Getting Started with the Data*, that points to the `ForEachLoadData` folder. Name the connection as `QlikSenseCookBookForEachLoadData`.
3. Select any file from the folder and extract its content to the Qlik Sense application.

4. Next, modify the script as the following example, to get the data from all files that reside in the `ForEachLoadData` folder. Note that we are using a wildcard `*` in place of the filename in the `from` statement. The `Filebasename()` function gets the filename so that we can identify the origin of the data:

```
CountrySales:
  Load
  Filebasename () AS Source, Country, Sales
FROM [lib://QlikSenseCookBookForEachLoadData/*.xlsx]
(ooxml, embedded labels, table is Sheet1);
```

5. Add the preceding load to the script (the preceding `Load` is placed directly above the `Load` statement of the `CountrySales` table:

```
LOAD*,
  Left(Source,3) as Month;
```

6. Upon loading, we observe that a synthetic key has been created in the data model.

7. In order to avoid the synthetic key, we will make use of the `For each` loop along with the wildcard load.

8. Modify the block of code to start with a `For each` loop statement and end with a `Next`, as shown in the following code:

```
For each vFile in FileList
    ('lib://QlikSenseCookBookForEachLoadData/*.xlsx')
    CountrySales:
    LOAD *, Left(Source,3) as Month;

    Load
    Country,
    Sales,
    Filebasename() as Source
    from [$(vFile)]
    (ooxml, embedded labels, table is Sheet1);
Next vFile
```

9. Once the script is in place, save and reload the application again.

10. We observe that all the files from the folder have been reloaded properly and there is no synthetic key in the data model.

How it works...

The * wildcard character loads all the files from the ForEachLoadData folder into the Qlik Sense application. When we use a preceding load statement to generate the Month field, the load is only applied to the first file loaded from the folder; hence, the Month field is created only for the first file. This is the reason why a synthetic key is created between the two tables.

When we use the For loop, every file is sequentially loaded from the source folder and then a preceding load is applied; thus, creating a month field in each created table. The two tables are then auto-concatenated, as they contain the same number of fields with the same name. As a result, a synthetic key is avoided and we get a clean data model.

There's more...

We used iteration or the For Each loop in the preceding recipe outside the Load statement. We can also have iterations inside the Load statement using the Where clause or the Subfield function. Iterations are also possible using the Peek() function. A useful article from Henric Cronstrom on iterations can be accessed using the following URL: https://community.qlik.com/blogs/qlikviewdesignblog/2013/09/02/loops-in-the-script.

Using the Concat() function to store multiple field values in a single cell

The information in orders and invoices is typically stored at the header or line level in the database. However, when we display the sales value for a particular order on the UI, it is sometimes desired that all the products for an order are displayed in a single cell rather than on a separate line. The Concat() function is helpful in such a case.

Getting ready

For this recipe, we will make use of an inline data load that gives sales information for orders. Load the following order line information in Qlik Sense:

```
Orders:
LOAD * INLINE [
OrderID,Product, ProductID, Sales
```

```
101,Footwear, F21Lon, 120000
101,Tyres, T21Man, 150000
101,Mountain Bikes, MB32Lon, 195000
102,Road Bikes, RB12Bir, 225000
102,Chains, F21Lon, 140000
103,lubricant, T21Man, 56869
103,Mountain Bikes, MB32Lon, 195000
104,Road Bikes, RB12Bir, 65233
];
LEFT JOIN
LOAD OrderID, CONCAT(Product,',') as Products
Resident
Orders
GROUP BY OrderID;
```

How to do it...

1. Create a **Table** chart.
2. Add `OrderID` as the first dimension.
3. Add `Products` as the second dimension.
4. Add `Sum(Sales)` as the measure. Label it `Sales`.
5. The resultant table should look like the following:

Orders		
OrderID Q	Products Q	Sales
Totals		1147102
101	Footwear,Mountain Bikes,Tyres	465000
102	Chains,Road Bikes	365000
103	Mountain Bikes,lubricant	251869
104	Road Bikes	65233

How it works...

The `Concat()` function in the script is used to string together multiple product values in a single string separated by a specified delimiter. The `Concat()` function is an aggregation function, and would require a `Group By` clause after the `from` statement.

There's more...

The `Concat()` function can also be used in the frontend instead of the script. In this case, we will have to create a calculated dimension, as follows:

```
=AGGR(Concat(DISTINCT Product,','),OrderID)
```

Call it `Products`. As mentioned earlier, being an aggregation function, `Concat()` requires an `AGGR` that is a substitute of `Group By` used in the script.

See also

- `Chapter 5`, *Useful Functions*, discusses some cool utilization of functions within Qlik Sense.

Executing command-line programs within the script

In `Chapter 1`, *Getting Started with the Data*, we learned how to activate the legacy mode and leverage the use of the `EXECUTE` statement to run a windows command-line statement to create a copy of a file. The following recipe explains the steps to run a command line using load script variables as a parameter.

Getting ready

The files required for this recipe that are downloaded from the Packt Publishing website come in a zipped folder called `QlikSenseData`. Extract all the files from this zipped folder, and save them on the hard drive at the desired location if you haven't done this for the previous recipes.

How to do it...

Once we have the files saved on the hard drive, go to the Qlik Sense app you have created to apply this recipe.

In order to run a windows command line, perform the following steps:

1. Activate the legacy mode as described in Chapter 1, *Getting Started with the Data*.
2. Open Qlik Sense **Data load editor**.
3. Write the following commands, assuming you have saved the Qlik Sense CookBook files on C:\QlikSenseCookBookData:

```
Let vpath = 'C:\QlikSenseCookBookData'; Let vtimestamp =
timestamp (Now() ,'YYYY-MM-DD hh:mm:ss'); Execute cmd.exe /c
copy "$(vpath)ROUTE_BUS.csv"
"$(vpath)ROUTE_BUS_$(vtimestamp).csv"
```

How it works...

When using the EXECUTE statement, we can use variables to set several parameters to dynamically build the command line. It is worth noting that, by default, this command won't work in Qlik Sense, unless it is running in a legacy mode. It's an inheritance from QlikView and must be used carefully.

There's more...

Qlik Sense can execute batch files from command-line and external programs such as 7zip to compress files as well. Just write the executable along with the path where it is installed.

See also

- *Activating the Legacy Mode in Qlik Sense® desktop*

4
Managing Apps and the User Interface

In this chapter, we will be dealing with the user interface in Qlik Sense. We will cover the following topics:

- Publishing a Qlik Sense® application created in Qlik Sense® Desktop
- Creating private, approved, and community sheets
- Publishing a Qlik Sense® application to Qlik Sense® Cloud
- Creating geo maps in Qlik Sense®
- Reference lines in a Sales versus Target gauge chart
- Effectively using the KPI object in Qlik Sense®
- Creating treemaps
- Creating dimensionless bar charts in Qlik Sense®
- Adding reference lines to trendline charts
- Creating text and images
- Applying limitations to charts
- Adding thumbnails to a clear environment
- Navigating many data points in a scatter chart
- Using alternative dimensions and measures
- Using the visual exploration menu

Introduction

The information required for analysis and decision-making within an organization is communicated via the user interface in Qlik Sense. We discussed the best design practices in Chapter 2, *Visualizations*. We will take this discussion a step further and learn how to implement a few key objects found in Qlik Sense in our applications, which will help the business convey the desired information to the end user in an effective manner. The chapter starts with important concepts for managing Qlik Sense applications, such as publishing apps on the server and on Qlik Sense Cloud. In later parts, the chapter deals with topics such as the use of reference lines and navigating data points in scatter charts in a Qlik Sense application.

Publishing a Qlik Sense® application created in Qlik Sense® Desktop

The licensing model of Qlik would not be very useful if everyone used Qlik Sense Desktop only for themselves. In a published BI environment, simply creating an application in Qlik Sense Desktop will not suffice; it has to be made available to the end user. The application needs to be published via the Qlik Sense Management Console.

Getting ready

To accomplish this recipe, you need access to Qlik Sense Enterprise Server. You need some administration rights, such as content admin or root admin, to execute the following steps as well.

How to do it...

Any Qlik Sense application that is created in Qlik Sense Desktop needs to be imported using the Qlik Sense management console prior to publishing it:

1. To do this, open the Qlik Sense **Qlik Management Console** (**QMC**) through the Windows shortcut or use the following URL:

   ```
   https://<Qlik Sense Server Hostname>/QMC
   ```

2. In the QMC, click on **Apps** in the left pane and go to the **Apps** section.

3. Click on the **Import** button in the bottom pane.

4. Click on **Choose File**, select the application to be uploaded from your local folder, and press **Import**. Once imported, select the app and click **Publish** in the action bar.

5. You will be prompted to specify a stream for the application. Choose a stream from the defined streams in the drop-down menu.

6. Click on **OK** to publish.

How it works...

Publishing an application is the first step toward sharing the application with a wider set of end users. Once published, the layout of the application cannot be changed. Also, the publication of the application cannot be undone and you will have to delete the application to remove it from the stream. A better approach to handling such a situation is to duplicate the application without publishing it and make the desired changes to the duplicate application. We can then use the **Replace existing app** option to replace a published app.

There's more...

Sheets and bookmarks can be published and categorized as Private, Approved, or Community. This will be discussed in the next recipe.

Creating private, approved, and community sheets

Sheets are the key components of a Qlik Sense application. They contain all the objects that carry information and provide a framework for analysis. There are three types of sheet that can be defined in a Qlik Sense application. These are private, approved, and community sheets:

- Approved sheets are all sheets that are defined by the author of the application. These cannot be changed by the user and are defined as read-only.

- Private sheets can be viewed only by the author of the application. These are not yet published for access by the end user.

- Community sheets are also private sheets but are defined and published by a user other than the author, who has been granted access to the application on the hub.

Getting ready

Sheets can be defined as private, approved, or community once the application has been imported into the Qlik Sense Management Console to be published and made available to end users.

How to do it...

1. Once the application is published, all the sheets in the application become "Approved" sheets; approved sheets are read-only.
2. An "Approved" sheet cannot be modified unless duplicated as a "Private" sheet. As the name suggests, "Private" sheets are private to the author. In order to duplicate a sheet, right-click on the sheet and select the **Duplicate Sheet** option.
3. Once the sheet is made "Private", modifications can be made to the relevant sheet if required. The sheet can then be published by right-clicking and selecting **Publish Sheet**.
4. "Private" sheets can also be created by clicking **Create a new sheet** in the published application.
5. Sheets can be created by other users and published to the hub. Sheets published in such a way are categorized as "Community" sheets.

How it works...

Only published sheets can be accessed by end users. Sheets kept as private or approved are not shared until published, so they add a layer of security. The concept of community sheets brings in collaborative features, where other users can contribute and share objects and reports created by themselves.

There's more...

On a similar note, you can create private, approved, and community bookmarks in Qlik Sense. The idea and approach remain the same.

See also

- *Publishing a Qlik Sense® application created in Qlik Sense® Desktop*

Publishing a Qlik Sense® application to Qlik Sense® Cloud

Qlik has come up with this wonderful concept of sharing Qlik Sense applications in the cloud. The author can share applications on the cloud with up to five people by sending an email invitation. These applications can be viewed on any mobile device and on any web browser. In a small implementation, Qlik Sense Cloud can be particularly helpful, as you can share applications over the web without installing the Sense Server. If you need more users, more space, and more functionality, such as schedule refreshing and user access management, you can subscribe to Qlik Sense Cloud Business.

Getting ready

Create a Qlik Sense Cloud account at `https://qlikcloud.com/login`.

How to do it...

1. The Qlik Sense Cloud web page looks like the following screenshot:

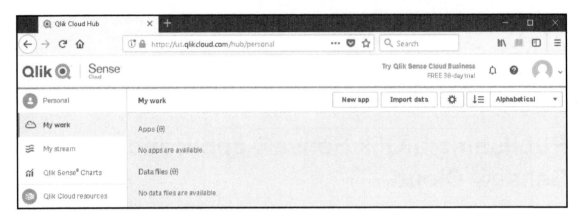

2. Under **My work**, click on the **New app** button to import the desired Qlik Sense application into the cloud:

3. Click on the **Upload an app** button, then click on the **Choose file** button to select the Qlik Sense application. Qlik Sense applications are stored in the following location by default:

   ```
   'C:\Users\<\*your own user folder*>\Documents\Qlik\Sense\Apps'
   ```

4. Select the desired application and click on the **Open** button. This will trigger the app upload.

5. The application will appear in **My workspace** on successful upload.

6. To share an application with other users, it needs to be published in **My stream**.
7. Right-click on the app icon and select **Publish** in the floating menu to share the app.
8. Click on **My stream**. Here, you will find recently published Qlik Sense applications.
9. Click on the button at the right of the window and the following window will pop up:

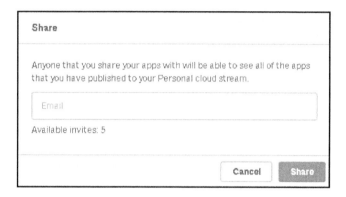

10. Enter the email address of the recipient. The recipient will receive an email with a link to create a Qlik Sense Cloud account.
11. You can open Qlik Sense Cloud while working on Qlik Sense Desktop by clicking on the cloud button in the Qlik Sense Desktop Hub toolbar:

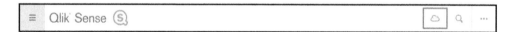

How it works...

Applications that are published to the cloud can be viewed by any recipient who has been provided with the shareable link. Once the recipient registers on Qlik Sense, the author of the application will receive a notification that they have a new follower. As the information is shared with different users, both within the organization and outside it, it provides the user with a great collaboration feature. Any application in the **My stream** area is considered to be shared and can be seen by all followers. It is not possible to share only one application with a particular user. Applications can be unpublished and can be moved to the personal cloud by right-clicking and selecting the **Unpublish** option.

At the time of writing there are certain restrictions on using the cloud:

- The maximum size of the application to be uploaded is 25 MB
- Images and extensions cannot be uploaded to the cloud
- While creating new applications directly in the cloud, we can load data only through files uploaded to the **Data files** section in **My work** or through DataMarket
- Followers are not notified if a new application is published to the shared stream
- Applications on the cloud can be shared with a maximum of five followers

Qlik Sense offers Qlik Cloud Business as a subscription service per user. It offers more space for apps and data, and several interesting features, such as direct data connectivity, up to 50 users, co-development of content, group administration, scheduled data refresh, and more.

There's more...

Qlik Cloud has the functionality of a personal cloud, where the author can keep his or her own private applications, which are not published to outside recipients. Personal data files can be added under the **Data files** section in **My work**. Once the files are added under personal data, they can be used to create a new Qlik Sense application in the cloud. The process to create a new Qlik Sense application directly in the cloud is as follows:

1. Select **My work** and then click on the **New app** button.
2. Add a title to the new application.
3. Click on the **Create app** button. This will open the Qlik Sense application in a browser.
4. Open the **Data load editor** to enter the script. If personal data files are uploaded to the cloud, you will notice that a data connection to these files is automatically created within the **Data load editor**, with a folder connection named as your `qlikid`.
5. You can also make use of DataMarket to upload data to the application.
6. Add the required data to the script and reload the application.

Creating geo maps in Qlik Sense®

Geographical information can be plotted in Qlik Sense by making use of the **Map** object. In order to create geo maps in Qlik Sense, we need to load the location information, also called point or area data. The location information can be loaded either from a **Keyhole Markup Language** (**KML**) file, if available, or a database, web service, or simple Excel file. Data can also be loaded inline, which is what we are going to do in the following recipe.

Getting ready

For the purpose of this recipe, we will make use of inline data loading, which gives us the location information for different countries in the form of latitudes and longitudes:

1. Create a new Qlik Sense file and name it `Geolocations`.

2. Add the following `Inline`, which that contains the location information for countries:

```
Country:
Load RowNo() As CountryID, *,GeoMakePoint(Latitude,
    Longitude) As CountryGeoPoint Inline [
    Country, Latitude, Longitude
    Australia, -25.274398,133.775136
    Argentina, -38.416097,-63.616672
    India, 20.593684,78.962880
    China, 35.861660,104.195397
    Colombia, 4.570868,-74.297333
    Great Britain,55.378051,-3.435973
    Switzerland ,46.8181887,8.227512
    Netherlands,52.132633,5.291266
    Salvador,13.794185,-88.896530
    Italy,41.871940,12.567380
    Peru,-9.189967,-75.015152
];
```

3. Next, add the following `Inline` table, which contains the `Sales` information for each country:

```
Sales:
Load * Inline [
    Country, Region, Sales
    Australia,Australia,133775
    Argentina, Latam,6361672
    India, APAC,7896880
    China, APAC,10419397
```

```
            Colombia, Latam,742333
            Great Britain,EMEA,3590073
            Switzerland ,EMEA,8227512
            Netherlands,EMEA,521266
            Salvador,Latam,8886530
            Italy,EMEA,12567807
            Peru,Latam,750152
    ];
```

Load the data and save the file. Open the **App overview** by clicking on the **Navigation** dropdown in the top-left corner.

How to do it...

1. Create a new sheet in the Qlik Sense application.
2. Enter Edit sheet mode and drag the Map object from the left-hand side Assets panel onto the sheet. Name it `Sales by Country`.
3. Click on **Add dimension** and then select **CountryGeoPoint**. Select **Country** to represent the point name:

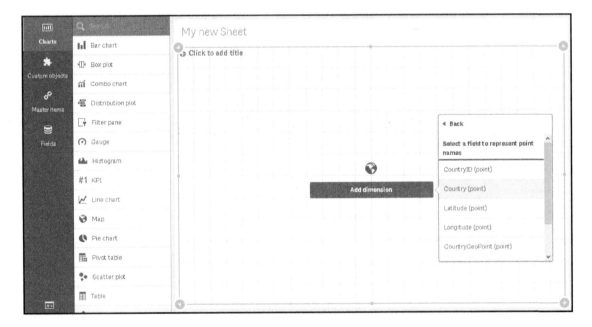

4. In the Properties panel to the right of your screen, add **Sum(Sales)** as your expression under data.

5. The resulting map on the screen will look like the following. The map automatically picks up the CartoDB background in its point layer. The only available image type is a slippy map:

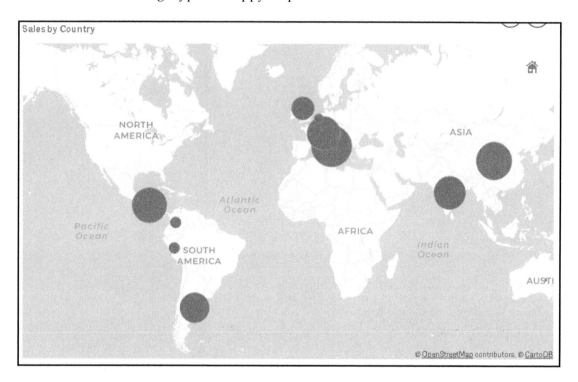

6. Next, we will change the background of the map.

7. To do this, open the Properties panel and click on **Background**. The **Background** window's **Show** property is set to **On** by default. The URL and **Attribution** boxes get activated when you switch the **Map service** from **Auto** to **Custom**.

8. Click on the **URLs and attributions** hyperlink at the bottom of the **Background** window to see documentation about the URL syntax:

9. There are many tile image providers but most of them require registration and an API key to generate images.

10. For the sake of our exercise, we will use the **URL** and **Attribution** string from Stamen. Stamen is a custom tile generator that provides some custom tiles for free. One of the styles is watercolor, which shows a map painted in watercolors. You can find the attribution HTML code here: `http://maps.stamen.com/#watercolor/12/37.7706/-122.3782`.

11. Paste `http://tile.stamen.com/watercolor/${z}/${x}/${y}.jpg` into the **URL** text field.

12. Next, copy the attribution HTML string for the chosen URL and paste the string into the **Attribution** text field.

13. Click on . The final map will look like the following screenshot:

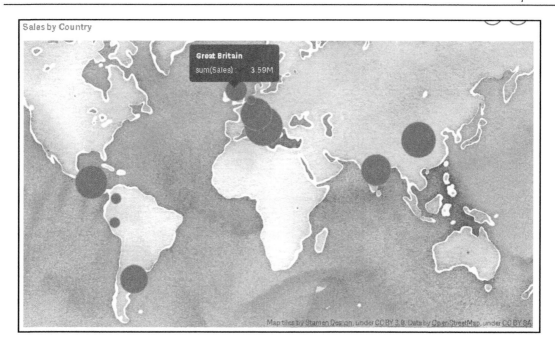

14. When we hover over any bubble, the tooltip shows the relevant country and sales.

How it works...

While loading the script for this recipe, we made use of the GeoMakePoint() function. This function creates and tags a point with its latitude and longitude information. Each country is thus linked to point data, which is plotted on the map. When we use a KML file as a source, Qlik Sense automatically detects the Geopoint field, therefore, there is no need to use a special function to define it. While changing the background for the map, we insert the required URL that connects to the file server we want to use. For copyright reasons, the attribution string should correspond to the desired URL.

There's more...

Point data can also be read from Excel files:

1. If the point data is stored in a single column called `Location`, that is, if each point is specified as an array of `x` and `y` coordinates and represented as `[x, y]`. Here, `x` is longitude and `y` is latitude, then:

   - The geospatial coordinates for latitude and longitude should be tagged with `$Geopoint` so that the `Location` field is recognized as a point data field.
   - As an example, imagine that the `Location` data is being extracted from a file called `Country.XLS` that has three columns, `Country`, `Location`, and `Sales`, where `Location` contains the point data. The script in such a case would look like the following:

   ```
   LOAD
   Country,
   Location,
   Sales
   FROM 'lib:///Country.xls' (biff, embedded labels, table
   is (Sheet1$));Tag Field Location with $Geopoint;
   ```

   - Run the script and add the point dimension to the map.

2. If the point data is stored in two columns, that is, one for latitude and the other for longitude, then:

   - The `GeoMakePoint()` function should be used to generate point-based data

3. Similarly, you can make use of KML files, which contain point data, area data, or both, in order to create maps in Qlik Sense. The following URL explains the process of generating maps in Qlik Sense using KML files: `https://community.qlik.com/docs/DOC-7354`.

4. Finally, if you use the Data Manager to load a dataset, the data profiling automatically identifies columns with geolocation data, such as `Country`, `City`, `State` (for limited countries), just by reading the data being loaded. Depending on the level of detail of the geo data, Qlik Sense will give you the option to plot data as points or areas on the map.

Reference lines in a Sales versus Target gauge chart

Recently, while delivering a proof of concept, I was asked by a customer if we could create a "Stephen Few Bullet chart" in Sense. This is not possible out of the box, for the simple reason that a bullet chart involves overlaying a bar chart on top of a gauge chart, and overlaying objects in Sense is not allowed. So, I thought of delivering the same result using just the gauge chart and making use of reference lines.

Getting ready

Load the following script in the Qlik Sense **Data load editor**; it gives information about the Sales and Target values for four countries:

```
LOAD * INLINE [
Country, Sales, Target
USA, 10000, 8500
UK, 7000, 9500
Germany, 5000, 4500
Japan, 6000, 6000
];
```

How to do it...

1. Drag a **Gauge** chart object onto the sheet from the Assets panel on the left.
2. Click on **Add measure** and type in the following expression. Label it as Sales vs Target:

   ```
   Sum(Target)
   ```

3. Under **Add-ons**, click on the **Reference lines** and add a **Reference line expression** with the following definition:

   ```
   =Sum (Sales).
   ```

4. Label the **Reference line expression** as Sales. Change the color of the reference line to red by clicking on the color dropdown.

5. Under **Appearance,** click on **Presentation** and set the **Max range Limit** as follows:

    ```
    =Sum(Target)*1.2
    ```

6. Select the representation as **Bar** and orientation as **Horizontal.**
7. Check the **Use segments** box.
8. Next, click on the **Add limit** button and add the following limit as the first segment:

    ```
    =Sum (Target)*0.30
    ```

9. Click on the segment area to change the default color to Gray.
10. Again, click on the **Add limit** button to create a second segment with the following limit:

    ```
    =Sum (Target)*0.60
    ```

11. Click on the segment area to change the default color to Red.
12. Finally, click on the **Add limit** button to create a third segment with the following limit:

    ```
    =Sum (Target)
    ```

13. Click on the segment area to change the default color to Yellow.
14. Set the color of the last segment as Green. Check the **Gradient** box for the last segment.
15. Click on 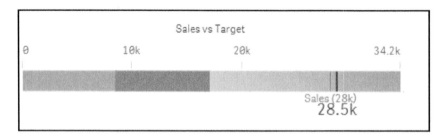 when finished.
16. The resulting chart will look similar to the following screenshot:

How it works...

The color segments signify how the sales of a particular country are performing, compared with the target values. The red reference line indicates the sales value. The color red does not signify anything else and is used only to highlight sales, so you can use any other color of your choice. The sales can be more than the set target, so the **Max range limit** is set to 1.2 times the target value. Due to this setting, the target value is represented by the black line at the end of the bar. Sure, sales can surpass targets by more than 20 percent, so the **Max range figure** can be altered to, say, 1.5 times the target value. One look at the graph and we can easily make out whether we are in the red zone or are doing better than expected.

There's more...

A similar concept is explored in the Capventis Redmond Pie-Gauge chart designed by Stephen Redmond. The gauge in this object is more of a modified bullet chart. If the sales are more than the target, then good performance is shown as a shaded sector to the right of the vertical, and if performance is below par, it is shown as a shaded sector to the left of the vertical, as shown in the following diagram:

The Capventis Redmond Pie-Gauge can be downloaded from GitHub at `https://github.com/stred/Qlik-Sense-Redmond-Pie-Gauge`.

See also

- *Creating treemaps*

Effectively using the KPI object in Qlik Sense®

A visualization should provide the user with a clear and effective presentation of the data. Numbers have an impact and they contain a message. Key performance indicators demonstrate the importance of numbers in business and also communicate the health of the business to the audience.

Getting ready

We will make use of the application from the preceding recipe. The application has the following script loaded; it gives information on the Sales and Target values for four countries:

```
LOAD * INLINE [
Country, Sales, Target
USA, 10000, 8500
UK, 7000, 9500
Germany, 5000, 4500
Japan, 6000, 6000
];
```

How to do it...

1. Go to the **App overview** and create a new sheet.
2. Name the sheet KPI and open it.
3. Go to Edit mode by clicking on ✎ **Edit** .
4. Drag the #1 KPI object from the assets panel onto the sheet.
5. Next, add the following measure:

   ```
   (Sum(Sales)-Sum(Target))/Sum(Target)
   ```

6. Name the label Sales vs Target.
7. Once we add the measure, we can see a host of properties, such as number format, color, and so on, for the measure directly beneath the **Expression** editor box.

8. For the measure, change the **Number formatting** to **Number** and select the percentage format (**12.3%**) from the available formats under the dropdown.

9. Next, add the limits to define colors. Switch on **Conditional colors**.

10. Click on **Add limit** and set the limit under the function to **0**.

11. Click on the first segment of the color bar and set the color as red with the symbol. Click on the second segment of the color bar and set the color as green with the  symbol.

12. The KPI object appears as follows:

13. Under **Appearance,** click on **General**, switch on **Show titles**, and add the title `Sales vs Target`.

14. Add the subtitle as follows:

```
IF(getselectedcount(Country)>0,Country,' ')
```

15. Next, go to the **Presentation** dropdown and uncheck **Show title**.

16. Add the **Filter pane** object from the assets panel on the sheet and select the dimension as **Country**. Select different countries to see how your organization is faring with respect to each country:

17. Next, we will link our KPI object to a sheet that shows detailed reports.

18. Create a new sheet called `Reports`.

19. Create a **Table** report on the reports sheet with **Country** as the dimension and the following measures:
    - Sum(Sales): Label it Sales.
    - Sum(Target): Label it Target.
    - (Sum(Sales)-Sum(Target))/Sum(Target): Label it Sales vs Target. For the measure, change the **Number formatting** to **Number** and select the percentage format (**12.3%**) from the available formats under the dropdown.
20. Move back to the KPI sheet and enter Edit mode by clicking on ✎ Edit .
21. Select the **KPI** object. This will activate the Properties panel on the right.
22. Under **Appearance**, go to **Presentation** and switch on **Link to sheet**. Under **Select a sheet**, select the **Reports** sheet and click on ✎ Done .
23. When we click on the **KPI** object in the user interface, it directs us to the reports sheet where you can analyze all the sales and target figures for each country:

How it works...

The KPI object is an important visualization object on any dashboard. The color segments we defined in the properties determine whether the country is doing better than its set target value or not. If the sales are below the target values, then the KPI figure is shown in red, or else in green. Linking the KPI to the **Reports** sheet helps the user to dig deeper into the data and see the more granular figures.

There's more...

The KPI object can also be represented using two measures. We can show a comparison between key figures in a single KPI object. For example, the absolute sales and target values can be shown adjacent to each other as separate figures. If the sales are greater than the target, then the value is represented in green, or else in red. This can be achieved by following these steps:

1. Create a new KPI object by following the steps given in the previous recipe. Label the object `Sales vs Target-1`.
2. Add the following measures:
   - `Sum(Sales)`: Label it `Sales`
   - `Sum(Target`
   - `)`: Label it `Target`
3. For `Sales`, switch on the **Conditional colors**.
4. Click on **Add limit**.
5. Set the limit under the function as:

   `=Sum(Target)`

6. Set the first color as red with the ▼ symbol and the second as green with the ▲ symbol.
7. For `Target`, set the font color as **Blue.**
8. The resultant object will be similar to the following:

See also

- *Creating text and images*

Creating treemaps

Treemaps (previously called block charts in QlikView) are a good way to show how different parts combine to form a whole. To add more depth to the visualization, you can easily highlight areas of importance by adding color coding.

Getting ready

For this recipe, we will make use of inline data loading, which provides product sales information. Load the following code into the data load editor:

```
LOAD * INLINE [
Product Line, Product Group, Product Sub Group, Year, Sales,
Cost
Drink, Beverages, Juice, 2015, 12000, 6000
Drink, Beverages, Juice, 2014, 16000, 7000
Drink, Beverages, Soda, 2015, 42000, 26000
Drink, Beverages, Soda, 2014, 68000, 57000
Drink, Beverages, Water, 2015, 18000, 8000
Drink, Beverages, Water, 2014, 10000, 6000
Drink, Dairy, Milk, 2015, 25000, 22000
Drink, Dairy, Milk, 2014, 22000, 20000
Food, Dairy, Cheese, 2015, 22000, 8000
Food, Dairy, Cheese, 2014, 31000, 30000
Food, Produce, Nuts, 2015, 50000, 30000
Food, Produce, Nuts, 2014, 46000, 26000
Food, Produce, Tofu, 2015, 26000, 21000
Food, Produce, Tofu, 2014, 15000, 7000
Food, Snacks, Chips, 2015, 31000, 6000
Food, Snacks, Chips, 2014, 15000, 9000
Food, Snacks, Dips, 2015, 10000, 6000
Food, Snacks, Dips, 2014, 6000, 3000
];
```

How to do it...

1. Drag a **Treemap** object onto the content page.
2. Add **Product line** as a dimension.
3. Add **Product Group** as a dimension.

4. Add **Product Sub Group** as a dimension.

5. Add `Sum(Sales)` as a measure and label it `Sales`.

6. From the Properties panel on the right-hand side of the screen, under **Appearance** | **Colors and legend**, toggle the **Colors** option from **Auto** to **Custom**.

7. In the drop-down window, select **By expression** and enter the following expression:

```
If(Sum({<Year={2014}>}Sales)>Sum({<Year={2015}>}Sales),
Red(),Green())
```

8. Click on **Done**.

9. The finished result should resemble the following screenshot:

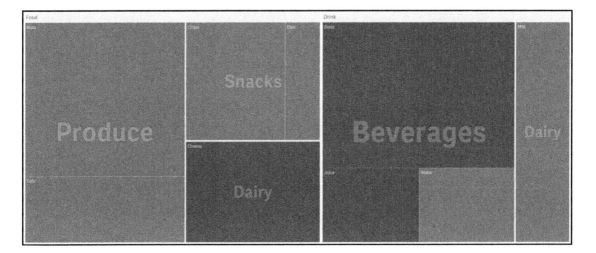

How it works...

The **Treemap** object groups the data based on the order of the dimensions you added. By adding the color coding expression, we can quickly see the products that are doing better this month compared to the previous month.

There's more...

The red and green indicators used in the preceding image can be useful for spotting products that are not performing in line with similar products. To get more value from these types of indicators, we can change the density of the color to reflect the magnitude of change. Replace the color expression we used in step *7* of the *How to do it...* section with the following code:

```
If((Sum({<Year={2015}>}Sales)-
    Sum({<Year={2014}>}Sales))/Sum({<Year={2015}>}Sales)>0,
  ColorMix1((Sum({<Year={2015}>}Sales)-
    Sum({<Year={2014}>}Sales))/Sum({<Year={2015}>}Sales),
    white(),RGB(50,255,50)),
if((Sum({<Year={2015}>}Sales)-
    Sum({<Year={2014}>}Sales))/Sum({<Year={2015}>}Sales)<0,
  ColorMix1(fabs((Sum({<Year={2015}>}Sales)-
    Sum({<Year={2014}>}Sales))/Sum({<Year={2015}>}Sales)),
    white(),RGB(255,50,50))))
```

The chart should now resemble the following screenshot:

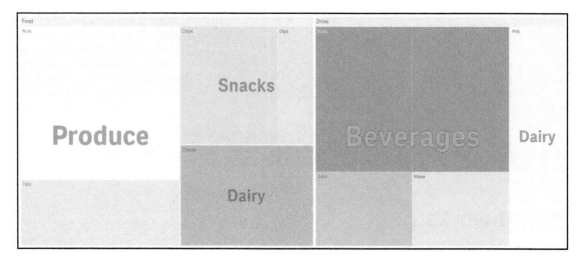

Based on the values returned by the expression, the `ColorMix1` function automatically assigns a range of colors. In the preceding example, we set up two color ranges: the first `If` statement goes from white to green for the positive numbers and the second goes from white to red for the negative numbers. The `ColourMix1` function only works with positive numbers, so we use the `Fabs` function to convert the negatives into positives once they are identified by the second `if` statement.

Creating dimensionless bar charts in Qlik Sense®

A bar chart is usually defined by one or two dimensions and a measure. However, we need to have dimensionless bar charts when designing KPIs on dashboards, and also in certain other scenarios. By default, Qlik Sense will not allow this. However, there is a workaround, which is discussed in the following sections.

Getting ready

We will make use of the same application that we developed for the KPI recipe. The application has got the following script loaded, which gives information on the Sales and Target values for four countries. In addition, we will add a new column called Dummy. Make sure to save and load the script once the Dummy field is added:

```
LOAD * , 1 as Dummy INLINE [
Country, Sales, Target
USA, 10000, 8500
UK, 7000, 9500
Germany, 5000, 4500
Japan, 6000, 6000
];
```

We want to display the overall sales for the company and change the color of the bar, based on the threshold value.

How to do it...

1. Go to **App overview** and create a new sheet.
2. Name the sheet Dimensionless Bar Chart and open it.
3. Go to Edit sheet mode by clicking on [✎ Edit].
4. From the assets panel, drag the ▫▪ Bar chart object onto the sheet.
5. Go to the **Master items** ⌀ in the assets panel and create a dimension with the name Dummy, as shown here:

   ```
   =Valuelist('Dummy')
   ```

6. In the chart under **Dimensions**, use the just-created **Dummy** master dimension as the dimension.

7. Add the measure as **Sum(Sales)** and label it `Sales`.

8. Under **Appearance**, click on **Presentation**, make the chart **Horizontal**, and switch on the **Value labels**.

9. Under **Appearance**, click on **General** and add `Company Sales` as the chart title under the **General** properties.

10. Under **Appearance**, click on **Colors and legend**. Switch off auto colors and select **By expression** from the dropdown menu.

11. Add the following color code expression:

```
If(Sum(Sales)>Sum(Target),RGB(0,255,0),RGB(255,0,0))
```

12. Make sure that **The expression is a color code** is checked.

13. Go to **Labels and title**, click on the **Title only** option under ▼ Y-axis: Dummy , and select **None**.

14. Under ▼ X-axis: Sales , switch off the **Auto** range and select **Min/max** under **Custom**. Set the min value to **0** and the max value to **30000**.

15. The final chart looks like the following:

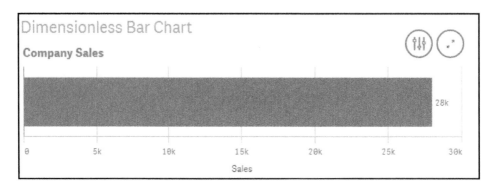

16. Create a **Filter pane** object with **Country** as the dimension. Now, select different countries and view the results.

How it works...

Qlik Sense doesn't allow dimensionless bar charts. So, we need to create a **Dummy** dimension that has only a single field value. When we select **None** under the **Labels and title** option, it hides this field value from the axis, thus serving our purpose. The color code used for the bars will turn the bar red if the sales for a country are less than or equal to the target values:

There's more...

We can use the **Dummy** dimension directly from our source data, instead of creating a master dimension in the frontend. Another approach is to use a calculated dimension, =1, and name it Dummy. Both of these approaches will yield the same result. To make the chart more informative, one can add reference lines for the target.

See also

- *Adding reference lines to trendline charts*

Adding reference lines to trendline charts

It is impossible to overstate the importance of adding context to analysis. Take the example of having the headline number **Average Call Time** displayed on a dashboard. While this might clearly be an important metric for a call center, on its own it portrays very little.

As shown in the *Dimensionless bar chart* recipe, we use reference lines to add the context required to make the number meaningful. Sticking to the example of **Average Call Time**, we may also want to also see a previous point-in-time position, the national or a competitor's average, the internal target, and so on. This recipe extends the use of reference lines further.

Getting ready

For this recipe, we will make use of inline data loading, which gives us the call bounce rates for different periods. Add the following code into the data load editor and reload the Qlik Sense application:

```
WebStats:
LOAD * INLINE [
    Period, BounceRate
    1, 0.26
    2, 0.25
    3, 0.24
    4, 0.24
    5, 0.27
    6, 0.28
    7, 0.21
    8, 0.34
    9, 0.24
    10, 0.25
];
```

How to do it...

1. Add a **Line chart** object to the contents page.
2. Add **Period** as a dimension.
3. Add **AVG(BounceRate)** as a measure.
4. From the Properties panel, under **Add-ons**, click on the **Reference lines** button and then on **Add reference line.**
5. Set the **Label** as Upper Threshold and set the **Reference line expression** to the following:

    ```
    =Avg(BounceRate)+Stdev(Total Aggr( Avg(BounceRate),Period))
    ```

6. Set the color to Red.

7. Click **Add reference line** again, this time setting the label to `Lower Threshold` and the expression to the following:

```
=Avg(BounceRate)-Stdev(Total Aggr( Avg(BounceRate),Period))
```

8. Set the color to Yellow.

9. Click **Add reference line** for the third time and set the label to `Average` and the expression to the following:

```
=Avg(BounceRate)
```

10. Set the color to Green.

11. The final visualization should resemble the following screenshot:

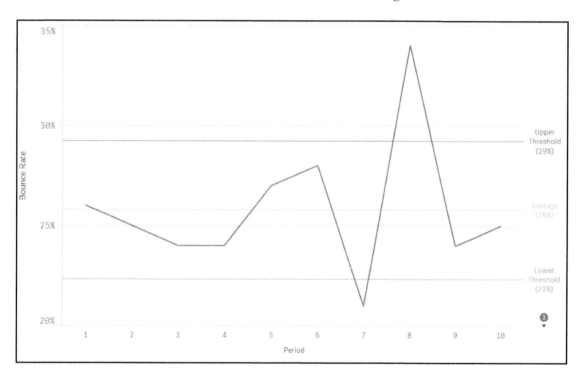

How it works...

The preceding chart is often referred to as a **Statistical Process Control** (**SPC**) chart. The upper and lower threshold reference lines set the boundaries of its normal operation. Data points that fall outside of these reference lines differ from the norm and are highlighted as such. The upper and lower limits are simply the average, plus or minus the standard deviation. We use the Aggr function to pre-calculate the average over the period dimension and then apply the Stdev function to this number.

Definition

Standard deviation (represented by the sigma symbol, σ) shows how much variation or *dispersion* exists from the average (mean) or expected value. A low standard deviation indicates that the data points tend to be very close to the mean; high standard deviation indicates that the data points are spread out over a large range of values (http://en.wikipedia.org/wiki/Standard_deviation).

Creating text and images

Images in Qlik Sense for Desktop are stored in the following location by default: C:\Users\<*your own user folder*>\Documents\Qlik\Sense\Content\Default\. Once images have been added to the folder, they are automatically made available in Qlik Sense.

Getting ready

For this recipe, we will make use of inline data loading, which gives us sales information. Load the following code into your Qlik Sense application:

```
SalesData:
LOAD * INLINE [
    ID, Sales, Quantity, Cost
    1, 15000, 50, 11000
    2, 30000, 100, 25000
];
```

How to do it...

To add images, follow these steps:

1. Place your desired image file in the `C:\Users\<\*your own user folder*>\My Documents\Qlik\Sense\Content\Default\` folder.
2. Add the **Text & image** object from the assets panel to the content area.
3. With the **Text & image** object selected, click on **Click to add text and measures**.
4. The design bar will appear; click on the Insert an image button on the far right, as shown in the following screenshot:

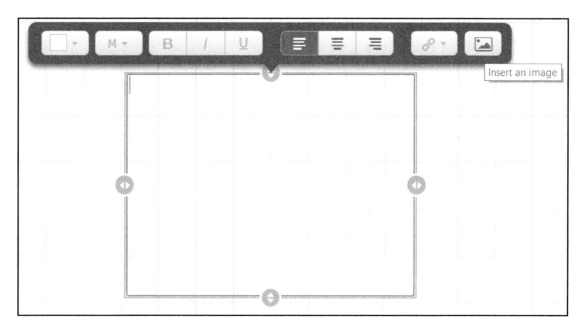

5. Select and insert the desired image from the **default** folder.

6. You can edit the sizing options of the image without clicking on the image button in the design bar, as shown in the preceding step. To do this, go to the properties of the **Text & image** object and set the same image as a background; using this method now gives you access to size options, as shown in the following screenshot:

Adding text, perform the following steps:

1. Add another **Text & image** object from the Assets panel to the content area.
2. If you double-click on the object in the content page, you can immediately start typing the text. You will see some basic formatting options above the object, as seen in the following screenshot:

3. Type the following into the `Sales` = textbox.

4. Next, from the properties pane under **Data**, add the following measure and label it `Sales`:

    ```
    SUM(Sales)
    ```

5. From the **Number formatting** drop-down menu, select **Number**, and from the next drop-down menu below the first, select the top option with no decimal places (for example, 1,000).

6. You can repeat the process using more text objects and different expressions if you like. Multiple measures can be added to the same object, or they can be separated out, as shown in the following examples:

7. An example of textboxes and images is the following:

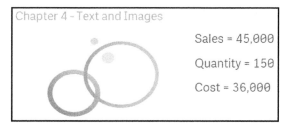

How it works...

Adding text or images to a dashboard can be key to helping users learn more about what they are looking at, not just the company branding. In the preceding example, we have added a metric into the textbox. Normally, we suggest using the KPI object in these instances. However, textboxes are essential if you wish to add a narrative beyond a single number. If all you are trying to do is show one number, using a textbox does give the benefit of horizontal labeling, for example, the "date of the last reload."

Applying limitations to charts

While outliers can reveal all kinds of useful intelligence, such as issues in data capture or associated process patterns, they can cause problems when you are building data visualizations. The most common issue is to do with scale, and we will show you how to solve this in this recipe.

Getting ready

For this recipe, we will make use of inline data loading, which gives us the information on the number of calls made for each month. Add the following code into the data load editor and reload the Qlik Sense application:

```
Data:
LOAD * INLINE [
    Month, Date, Calls
    Jan, 27/01/15, 25
    Jan, 28/01/15, 27
    Jan, 29/01/15, 25
    Jan, 30/01/15, 600
    Jan, 31/01/15, 22
    Feb, 01/02/15, 20
    Feb, 02/02/15, 19
    Feb, 03/02/15, 21
    Feb, 04/02/15, 1
    Feb, 05/02/15, 600
];
```

How to do it...

1. Add a **Bar chart** object onto the content page.
2. Add **Month** as a dimension.
3. Add **Avg(Calls)** as a measure. Label it `Average Calls`.
4. Click on **Done**. Notice that the values in both months are just below **150**:

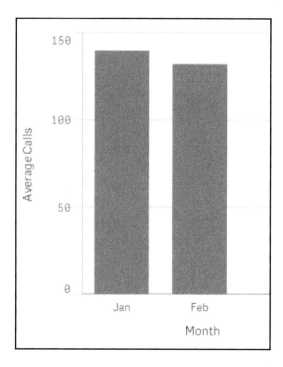

5. Next, go back into Edit mode and replace the measure with the following code:

```
Avg(If (Calls > Aggr(NODISTINCT Fractile(Calls, 0.1),
Month) and Calls < Aggr(NODISTINCT Fractile(Calls, 0.9),
Month),Calls))
```

6. Click on **Done**.

7. The chart should now resemble the following image. It not only has both bars significantly reduced, down to below 30, but there is also a much bigger gap between January's and February's average call volumes:

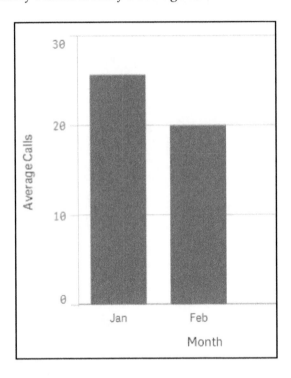

How it works...

If we look at the source data we loaded at the beginning of the recipe, it is clear that there are some outliers present. To exclude these and get a real picture of the normal, average amount of calls, we remove the top and bottom 10 percent of the value. This is done using the `fractile` function. The `fractile` function calculates the cut-off point for 10 and 90 percent, based on our data. The `Aggr` function is needed because `fractile` is an aggregation function nested inside another aggregation.

There's more...

Another method of handling outliers is not to exclude them from the expression, but hide them from what is visualized. For example, if a data point far exceeds the norm, you can set the axis limit to the second largest value; this focuses the visualization on the points that are closely related. You can do this by going to the object properties:

1. Under **Appearance**, click on **Y-axis**.
2. Switch off **Auto Range** and set the **Max value** by using an expression such as the following:

```
=Max(aggr(avg(Calls),Date),2)
```

Here, we simply work out what the second largest number is and set that as the axis limit. This way, we can produce an all-inclusive line graph by date, albeit one data point will be off the screen.

Adding thumbnails to a clear environment

It is easy to skip over minor features of a BI platform. Unlike Qlikview, which has a large amount of options for chart customizations, Qlik Sense features are more universal. The majority of components will be relevant to you and, as such, should be given due consideration. Here, our aim is to simplify the environment by adding thumbnails and metadata descriptions at a high level to the application and the sheets within.

Getting ready

Open the Qlik Sense Desktop hub and either open up an existing application or create a new one.

How to do it...

1. Find an image you want to use as the thumbnail for your application. Copy the image into the following folder: `C:\Users\*your own user folder*\Documents\ Qlik\Sense\Content\Default\`

2. From the **App overview** screen, click on the edit button in the top-right corner.

3. Give your application a **Title** and **Description**.

4. Adjacent to the **Title** and **Description** window is the area for the application thumbnail. Click the Change thumbnail image  .

5. Select the image that you added to the Qlik folder in step 1 and then click **Insert**.

6. Finally, click the Stop editing tick button in the top-right corner:

7. Depending on the image you have chosen, the color of the background will also change, as shown in the preceding image.

8. You can repeat the process for sheets by clicking on the button next to each sheet description.

9. You can see a great example of how this should be implemented in the default helpdesk management application that is available with each fresh install of Qlik Sense Desktop. Take special note of the sheet descriptions, which include questions you can answer:

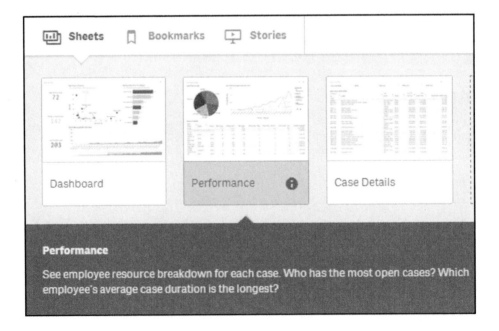

How it works...

I have seen many unorganized BI environments before, and it really has a negative impact on the user experience. When you first go into the Qlik Sense hub, which of these do you prefer to be presented with the following screenshot:

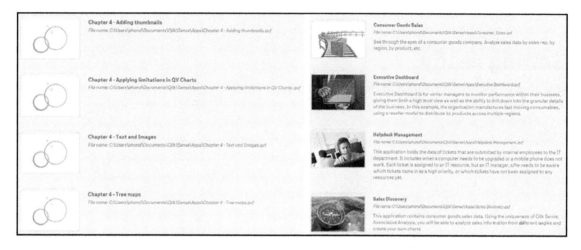

On the left: default image and text; on the right: with thumbnails and descriptions

The left-hand image looks more pleasing and professional to the eye. User experience is an important factor in the adoption of a tool. If the first screen you see looks rushed or is confusing, it will start the user off on a bad footing. The thumbnails and descriptions also apply to sheets within an application. By default, small thumbnails are displayed as an image, showing objects by type and placement. These can be replaced with something clearer and more meaningful to the audience. This is hardly storyboarding, but you should know what each page is trying to achieve. Actually, asking questions about each screen can help you get a feel for the shape of the application and the flow of analysis. Are you asking these questions:

- Who are the users of this screen?
- What is the page showing?
- What questions will the page answer?
- What actions will that enable?

While not universal, asking questions such as these regularly will help keep your focus on the audience.

Navigating many data points in a scatter chart

The following recipe showcases an interesting concept in the use of scatter charts in Qlik Sense. This feature is available from version 2.0+ of Qlik Sense.

Getting ready

Load the following code into your Qlik Sense application:

```
Transactions:
Load
  Round(1000*Rand()*Rand()*Rand()) as Sales,
  Round(10*Rand()*Rand()*Rand()) as Quantity,
  RecNo() as TransID
Autogenerate 1000000
  While rand()<0.5 or IterNo()=1;
```

How to do it...

1. Create a new sheet and drag a **Scatter plot** chart object onto the content page.
2. Add **TransID** as a dimension.
3. Add **Sum(Sales)** as the first measure. Label it `Sales`.
4. Add **Sum(Quantity)** as the second measure. Label it `Quantity`.
5. Click on **Done**.
6. Name the chart `Sales vs Quantity`.
7. You will notice that you cannot select data inside the chart as you can with every other Qlik Sense visualization. To navigate the data, you have to scroll in and out using the mouse wheel. The object will look like the following screenshot try scrolling in:

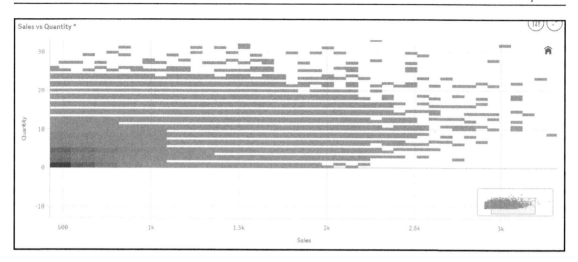

8. As you zoom further into the chart, the number of data points being displayed reduces. You will eventually see the details of each data point displayed in each block. The higher-density blocks are also color-coded, as shown in the following screenshot:

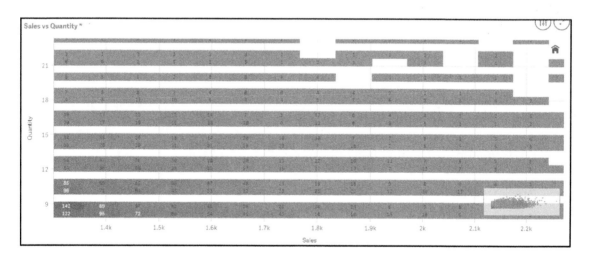

9. Eventually, you can zoom in enough and reduce the number of data points to a point where they are identifiable individually. At this point, the graphic will revert its display to a more standard scatter chart look. Those with enough space around them actually have their value displayed, as shown in the following screenshot:

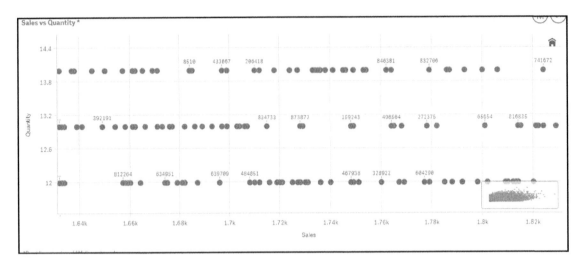

How it works...

This is a very intelligent addition by Qlik to the normal scatter chart display. This chart plots over a million data points effortlessly. Doing this the traditional way is very process-intensive. When you want to extract data volumes of this size, you normally tend to look at the pattern and not at the individual numbers. This archives both by displaying the individual points at the point they would make sense, and not before.

There's more...

While the color coding is fixed at a high level, you can apply color coding expressions as normal. This only gets applied when you zoom in far enough to see the individual data points.

Using alternative dimensions and measures

Alternative dimensions and measures can be made available in charts, and the user might select them to be used in the current visualization. These alternative dimensions and measures can be changed.

Getting ready

For this recipe, we will reuse the same data loading as for the *Creating treemaps* recipe.

How to do it...

1. Drag a **Bar chart** object onto the content area.
2. Add **Product line** as a dimension.
3. Add **Product Group** using the **Add alternative** button in the alternative dimensions section.
4. Add **Product Sub Group** using the **Add alternative** button in the alternative dimensions section.
5. Add `Sum(Sales)` as a measure and label it `Sales`.
6. Add `Avg(Sales)` using the **Add alternative** button in the alternative measures section and label it `Sales Average`.
7. Click on **Done**.
8. The finished result should resemble the following screenshot:

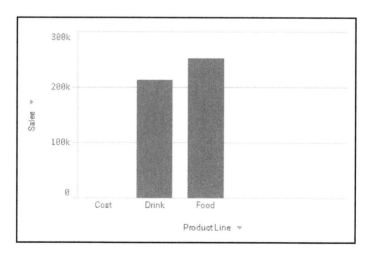

9. Click on the **Product Line** label in the dimensions axis. A pop-up menu will show the current dimension selected with a tick and the alternate dimensions.

10. Select the **ProductGroup** dimension.

11. Now, you should see the following chart:

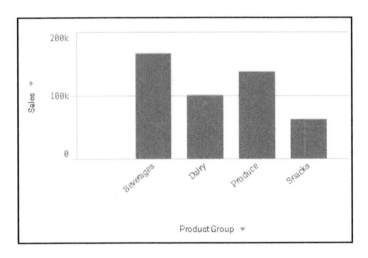

12. Now, click on the **Sales** label in the measure axis. A pop-up menu will show the current measure selected with a tick and the alternative measures.

13. Select the **Sales Average** measure.

14. Now, you should see the following chart:

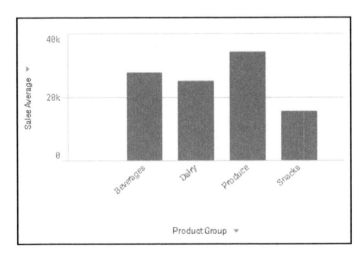

How it works...

Most chart objects provide a way to select an alternate dimension or a measure that is not in use in the visualization. Only **Bar chart**, **Line chart**, **Combo chart**, **Pie chart**, and **Scatter plot chart** show the alternative selection on the axis label.

There's more...

You can use the visual exploration menu to change the alternative dimensions or measures for a chart, and other chart properties as well. I will show you how it works in the next recipe.

Using the visual exploration menu

You can use the visual exploration menu to change some properties without editing the sheet. For example, you can change dimension order, change to an alternative dimension or measure, sort data, change coloring by dimension or measure, and change how labels are displayed.

Getting ready

For this recipe, we will reuse the charts used in the *Creating treemaps* recipe and the bar chart from the *Using alternative dimensions and measures* recipe.

How to do it...

1. If you are in edit mode, click on **Done**.
2. Hover your mouse over the **Treemap** object.
3. Click the **Sliders** button at the top-right of the visualization, or right-click on the visualization and select **Open Exploration menu**.

4. Open the **Presentation** section and set on in the **Value labels** property.
5. The result should resemble the following screenshot:

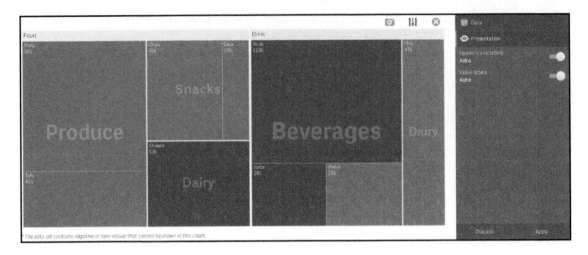

6. The value labels are shown on each block.
7. Click on **Close full screen** to close the menu and go back to visualization mode.
8. Now, go to the sheet with the bar chart created in the last recipe.
9. Open the visual exploration menu for the bar chart.
10. Open the **Sorting** section.
11. Select the measure on the second line and drag it over to the first line to change the sorting criteria to by measure.
12. Click the arrow on the left of the measure to open the sorting property and select **Descending**.

13. The result should resemble the following screenshot:

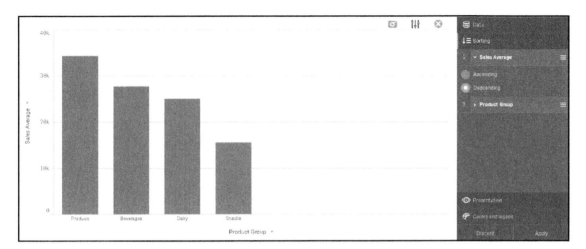

14. Click on **Close full screen** to close the menu and go back to visualization mode.

How it works...

When you change the properties and click on the **Close full screen** button, you accept the changes in the chart automatically.

There's more...

You can go back to the visual exploration menu and click on **Discard** to get the original properties back. If you are editing your app on Qlik Sense Desktop or it's an unpublished app in the Qlik Sense Server, the **Apply** button will be available as well. If you click on **Apply**, all changes are effectively part of the original object. To discard the changes, you need to enter edit mode and click on the undo button.

5
Useful Functions

In this chapter, we will focus on some interesting and useful functions available in Qlik Sense:

- Using an extended interval match to handle slowly changing dimensions
- Using the `Previous()` function to identify the latest record for a dimensional value
- Using the `NetworkDays()` function to calculate the working days in a calendar month
- Using the `Concat()` function to display a string of field values as a dimension
- Using the `MinString()` function to calculate the age of the oldest case in a queue
- Using the `RangeSum()` function to plot cumulative figures in trendline charts
- Using the `Fractile()` function to generate quartiles
- Using the `FirstSortedValue()` function to identify the median in a quartile range
- Using the `Declare` and `Derive` functions to generate `Calendar` fields
- Setting up a moving annual total figure
- Using the `For Each` loop to extract files from a folder
- Using the `Peek()` function to create a currency exchange rate calendar
- Using the `Peek()` function to create a trial balance sheet
- Using the `subfield()` function to split field into multiple records
- Using the `dual()` function to set the sort order of dimensions

Introduction

In this chapter, we will shift our focus to the functions available in Qlik Sense. In certain situations, the functions can be used in the script or they can be used in frontend expressions to get solutions for complex requirements. All the functions discussed in this chapter will find their way into most of the Qlik Sense implementations.

Using an extended interval match to handle slowly changing dimensions

Sometimes, while developing the data model for a Business Intelligence application, you encounter dimensional values that tend to change over time. Such dimensions are known as *slowly changing dimensions*. For example, an employee joins a company at a Junior Executive level and stays in the same position for one year. After one year, the designation changes to Senior Executive and then changes to Project Manager after three years. The position field, in this case, will be treated as a *Slowly Changing Dimension*. Such Slowly Changing Dimensions can be represented in Qlik Sense, provided the historical data is stored at the source with a proper "Position Start Date" and "Position End Date." In order to match the discrete date values to the date intervals, we will make use of the `intervalmatch` function. At the same time, we will match the values of the primary key. This will help us to build an optimized data model and properly link the transactions to the Slowly Changing Dimensions.

Getting ready

The following recipe assumes a hypothetical situation wherein an HR department is trying to track the employee journey within an organization that is tracking the various positions the employee has held within his or her tenure with the company, and the related compensation against each position. For this purpose, we will create the following `Inline` tables within Qlik Sense:

- **2 dimension tables**: `Employee` and `Position`
- **1 date intervals table to track changes in position for the employee**: `Employment`
- **1 fact table**: `EmpSalary`

The steps to do so are as follows:

1. Create a new Qlik Sense application.
2. Load the following script in Qlik Sense:

```
// ============= Load the Employee table =============
Employee:
LOAD * INLINE [
    EmployeeID,EmployeeName
    11,Susan Sayce
    22,Adam Holliaoak
    33,Rod Marsh
    44,Alex Gerard
    55,Pete Cox
];
// ============= Load the Position table =============
Position:
LOAD * INLINE [
PositionID,Position
1,HR Analyst
2,HR Director
3,HR Executive
];

// ==== Load the Employee table with the Date Intervals ====
EmployeeInt:
LOAD *,
    Autonumber(EmployeeID & '-' & PositionFrom & '-' &
PositionTo)
    as DatePositionKey;
LOAD DATE(Date#( PositionFrom,'DD/MM/YYYY')) as PositionFrom,
DATE(Date#( PositionTo,'DD/MM/YYYY')) as PositionTo,
PositionID,
    EmployeeID
  INLINE [
    PositionFrom, PositionTo,PositionID,EmployeeID
    01/09/2009, 31/10/2010,2,11
    01/08/2008, 31/08/2009,1,11
    10/08/2008, 15/03/2010,1,22
    03/03/2008, 08/12/2008,2,33
    15/02/2008, 15/03/2010,3,44
    01/06/2008, 08/12/2008,3,55
];

// ============= Load the Employee Salary table =============
EmployeeSalary:
LOAD EmpID ,DATE(Date#( DateInToPosition,'DD/MM/YYYY')) as
    DateInToPosition, EmployeeSal INLINE [
```

```
        EmpID,DateInToPosition,EmployeeSal
        11,01/09/2009,90000
        11,01/08/2008,50000
        22,10/08/2008,45000
        33,03/03/2008,100000
        44,15/02/2008,60000
        55,01/06/2008,55000
    ];
```

How to do it...

1. Open the **Data model viewer**. The data model is shown in the following screenshot. We can see that the `EmployeeSalary` table is not linked to the data model. If we try to link the table through the `EmpID` field, then the employees who have changed their positions would reflect the same salaries for each position, which is not correct.

2. Open the **App overview** and create a new sheet. Drag a **Table** object onto the content area.

3. Add the following dimensions to the table: `EmployeeID`, `EmployeeName`, `Position`, `PositionFrom`, and `PositionTo`.

4. Under **Sorting**, promote `EmployeeName` to the top. Promote `PositionFrom` to the second position and set the sort order as numeric and **Ascending**:

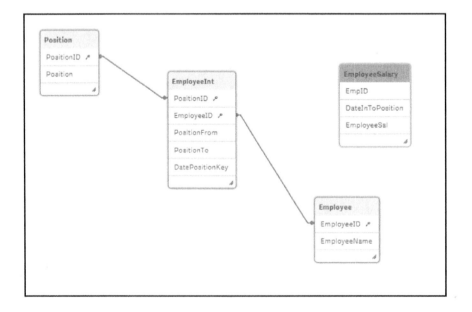

5. In the preceding script, `Susan Sayce` has changed her position from `HR Analyst` to `HR Director`. There is a `DateInToPosition` value associated with each position, which comes from the `EmployeeSalary` table.

6. We will make use of the `IntervalMatch` function, which will match the `DateInToPosition` to the date interval of `PositionFrom` and `PositionTo`.

7. Load the following script on a separate section:

```
// === Link Table using the IntervalMatch prefix ===
LinkTable:
IntervalMatch (DateInToPosition,EmpID)
Load distinct PositionFrom, PositionTo, EmployeeID AS EmpID
    Resident EmployeeInt;

Left Join (EmployeeSalary)
Load
EmpID,
DateInToPosition,
Autonumber(EmpID & '-' & PositionFrom & '-' & PositionTo)
    AS DatePositionKey
Resident LinkTable;

// ============ Cleanup ============
Drop Table LinkTable;
Drop Field EmpID;
```

8. On the final load, the data model should look like this:

Extended interval match

EmployeeID	EmployeeName	Position	PositionFrom	PositionTo
11	Susan Sayce	HR Analyst	01/08/2008	31/08/2009
11	Susan Sayce	HR Director	01/09/2009	31/10/2010
22	Adam Holliaoak	HR Analyst	10/08/2008	15/03/2010
33	Rod Marsh	HR Director	03/03/2008	08/12/2008
44	Alex Gerard	HR Executive	15/02/2008	15/03/2010
55	Pete Cox	HR Executive	01/06/2008	08/12/2008

9. Open the **App overview** via the navigation dropdown in the top-left corner. Go back to the sheet created in Step 2.

10. In the **Table** object, add the following measure and label it `Salary`:

    `Sum(EmployeeSal)`

11. Make sure that the sorting order remains the same as mentioned in Step 4, that is, to promote `EmployeeName` to the top. Promote `PositionFrom` to the second position and set the sort order as numeric and Ascending.

12. The resultant table would look like this:

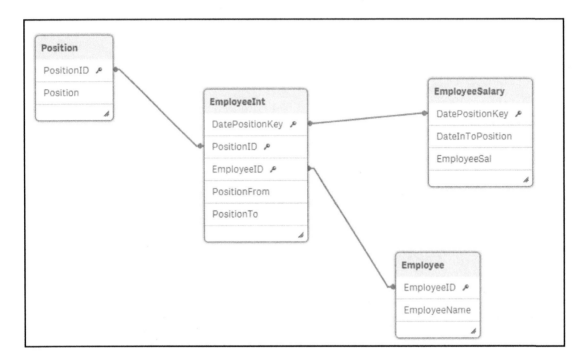

13. Select a particular employee to see all the associated positions, start dates, end dates, and salaries.

How it works...

The dimension tables are loaded first. A composite key comprising `EmployeeID`, `PositionFrom`, and `PositionTo` is created in the `EmployeeInt` table. The fact table, `EmployeeSalary`, is loaded with the `EmployeeID` value represented as `EmpId`. Under `LinkTable`, an interval is assigned to each combination of `EmpID` and `DateInToPosition` using the `intervalmatch` function. Finally, a key is created in `LinkTable` with the same combination of `EmployeeID`, `PositionFrom`, and `PositionTo`. The `LinkTable` is joined back to the `EmployeeSalary` table. The problem of slowly changing dimensions can be solved using the extended `intervalmatch` syntax explained in the preceding steps. The employee, positions, and salaries will all be properly linked.

There's more...

In the preceding example, we have joined `LinkTable` to the `EmployeeSalary` table. However, you should bear in mind that this can only be done if there is a *Many-One* relationship between the `Employee` and `Position`. If this doesn't hold true, that is, if an employee knowingly or unknowingly has more than one position for the same start and end dates in the source data, then the join between the link and the `EmployeeSalary` table will result in an increase in the number of records. In such a situation, the left join should be avoided. Instead, `LinkTable` must simply be linked through the `DatePositionKey` composite key to the `EmployeeInt` table. Another composite key comprising `DateInToPosition` and `EmpID` must be created, which should link back to the same key in `EmployeeSalary`. The resident load for the `Link` table would be as follows:

```
Link:
Load
Autonumber(EmpID & '-' & DateInToPosition)AS DateInToPositionKey,
Autonumber(EmpID & '-' & PositionFrom & '-' & PositionTo)
AS DatePositionKey
Resident LinkTable;
```

The resident load for the `Employee` table would be as follows:

```
EmployeeSalary_1:
Load
*,
Autonumber(EmpID & '-' & DateInToPosition)AS DateInToPositionKey
Resident
EmployeeSalary;
DROP TABLE EmployeeSalary;
```

On loading the script, the resulting data model would be as follows:

Extended interval match					
EmployeeID 🔍	EmployeeName 🔍	Position 🔍	PositionFrom 🔍	PositionTo 🔍	Salary
Totals					**400000**
11	Susan Sayce	HR Analyst	01/08/2008	31/08/2009	50000
11	Susan Sayce	HR Director	01/09/2009	31/10/2010	90000
22	Adam Holliaoak	HR Analyst	10/08/2008	15/03/2010	45000
33	Rod Marsh	HR Director	03/03/2008	08/12/2008	100000
44	Alex Gerard	HR Executive	15/02/2008	15/03/2010	60000
55	Pete Cox	HR Executive	01/06/2008	08/12/2008	55000

See also

- *Using the Previous() function to identify the latest record read for a dimensional value*

Using the Previous() function to identify the latest record read for a dimensional value

In a line-level table, there are multiple records stored for a single dimensional value. For example, an `Order Line` table will have multiple lines for the same `OrderID`. Business requirements may warrant us to only consider the first or the latest line for each order. This can be done using the `Previous()` function available in Qlik Sense.

Getting ready

For the sake of continuity, we will make use of the same script and application as in the previous recipe. We will determine the most recent position of any employee during their tenure within the organization.

How to do it...

1. Open the **Data load editor**. Change the name of the `EmployeeInt` table in the script to `EmployeeIntTemp`.

2. Insert the following lines of code after the `EmployeeIntTemp` table `LOAD` command. If you are copying and pasting the code in the **Data load editor**, make sure that the single quotes are copied in a proper format:

```
EmployeeInt:
LOAD *,
if([EmployeeID]= previous([EmployeeID]),'No','Yes') AS
    LatestRecordFlag
RESIDENT EmployeeIntTemp
ORDER BY [EmployeeID] ASC, PositionFrom DESC;

DROP TABLE EmployeeIntTemp;
```

3. The code will look like the following:

```
EmployeeIntTemp:
LOAD *,
     Autonumber(EmployeeID & '-' & PositionFrom & '-' &
PositionTo)
     as DatePositionKey;
LOAD DATE(Date#( PositionFrom,'DD/MM/YYYY')) as PositionFrom,
DATE(Date#( PositionTo,'DD/MM/YYYY')) as PositionTo,
PositionID,
   EmployeeID
 INLINE [
    PositionFrom, PositionTo,PositionID,EmployeeID
    01/09/2009, 31/10/2010,2,11
    01/08/2008, 31/08/2009,1,11
    10/08/2008, 15/03/2010,1,22
    03/03/2008, 08/12/2008,2,33
    15/02/2008, 15/03/2010,3,44
    01/06/2008, 08/12/2008,3,55
];

EmployeeInt:
LOAD *,
if([EmployeeID]= previous([EmployeeID]),'No','Yes') AS
    LatestRecordFlag
RESIDENT EmployeeIntTemp
ORDER BY [EmployeeID] ASC, PositionFrom DESC;

DROP TABLE EmployeeIntTemp;
```

```
// ============ Load the Employee Salary table ============
EmployeeSalary:
LOAD EmpID ,DATE(Date#( DateInToPosition,'DD/MM/YYYY')) as
     DateInToPosition, EmployeeSal INLINE [
     EmpID,DateInToPosition,EmployeeSal
     11,01/09/2009,90000
     11,01/08/2008,50000
     22,10/08/2008,45000
     33,03/03/2008,100000
     44,15/02/2008,60000
     55,01/06/2008,55000
  ];
```

4. Save and load the script.
5. Add the field `LatestRecordFlag` to the **Table** object we created in the previous recipe.
6. Under **Sorting**, make sure that `PositionFrom` is promoted to the top. Switch off the **Auto sorting** feature for `PositionFrom`. No sorting options should be selected, as this will then show the `PositionFrom` date in the load order.
7. The table should look like this:

EmployeeID	EmployeeName	Position	PositionFrom	PositionTo	Salary	LatestRecordFlag
Totals					**400000**	
11	Susan Sayce	HR Director	01/09/2009	31/10/2010	90000	Yes
11	Susan Sayce	HR Analyst	01/08/2008	31/08/2009	50000	No
22	Adam Holliaoak	HR Analyst	10/08/2008	15/03/2010	45000	Yes
33	Rod Marsh	HR Director	03/03/2008	08/12/2008	100000	Yes
44	Alex Gerard	HR Executive	15/02/2008	15/03/2010	60000	Yes
55	Pete Cox	HR Executive	01/06/2008	08/12/2008	55000	Yes

Extended interval match

8. Select employee **Susan Sayce**. We can see that there are two positions associated with Susan. If we select the **LatestRecordFlag** value as **Yes**, it will only show the latest position for Susan: **HR Director**.

How it works...

The `LatestRecordFlag` can be used in calculations to determine the most recent position of any employee. In our script, we create the `LatestRecordFlag` using the `Previous()` function. The `Previous()` function basically parses the `EmployeeID` column. If the current record that is being read has the same `EmployeeID` value as the previous record, then it is flagged as `No`, or else `Yes`. The *ordering* of the fields plays an important role here. Because I wanted to determine the latest position for the employee, the `PositionFrom` field is arranged in descending order.

There's more...

We can also make use of the `Peek()` function in the preceding script. In our example, both `Peek()` and `Previous()` would yield the same result. However, `Peek()` is more effective when the user is targeting a field that has not previously loaded in the table, or if the user wants to target a specific row. The `Previous()` function is more effective when the user wants to compare the current value with the previous value for the field in the input table.

See also

- *Using the Peek() function to create a trial balance sheet*

Using the NetworkDays() function to calculate the working days in a calendar month

One of the KPIs that companies often concentrate on is the average sales in a month. The average sales are calculated by dividing the total sales by the number of working days in a month. Every month has a different number of working days. While calculating the number of working days for the current month, we only need to consider the days passed in the month and not the total days of the month in order to calculate the actual working days. In order to arrive at the exact number of working days in a month, we need to exclude all the Fridays and Saturdays as well as the public and bank holidays from our calculations. The `Networkdays()` function helps us to achieve this.

Getting ready

For this exercise, we first need to prepare a list of all public holidays, either in Excel or inline in the Qlik Sense script.

How to do it...

1. Copy and paste the following part of the script in the **Data load editor**. This is a list of public holidays for 2014 and 2015:

```
HolidayTmp:
LOAD DATE(Date#( Date,'DD/MM/YYYY')) as Date INLINE [
Date
01/01/2015
03/04/2015
06/04/2015
04/05/2015
25/05/2015
31/08/2015
25/12/2015
28/12/2015
01/01/2014
18/04/2014
21/04/2014
05/05/2014
26/05/2014
25/08/2014
25/12/2014
26/12/2014
];
```

2. Next, we will store the list of public holidays in a variable inside the script:

```
ConcatTmp:
LOAD concat(chr(39) & Date & chr(39),',') AS HolidayDates
RESIDENT HolidayTmp;
LET vPublicHolidays = FieldValue('HolidayDates',1);

LET vCurMonth=month(today());
```

3. Copy and paste the following fact table. Insert the last of the `PostingDates` in your table as today's date and put a sales figure against it. This is to demonstrate the use of `today()` in the `WorkingDays` calculation:

```
SalesTmp:
LOAD DATE(Date#( PostingDate,'DD/MM/YYYY')) as PostingDate,
    Sales INLINE [
PostingDate, Sales
05/08/2014, 5000
04/09/2014,522
24/10/2014,400
15/11/2014,5000
24/12/2014, 822
29/12/2014, 633
02/01/2015, 1000
02/02/2015, 2000
25/03/2015,2200
25/04/2015,266
09/05/2015, 3000
18/05/2015, 4000
15/06/2015,5000
22/07/2015,456
08/09/2015,4200
26/10/2015,1875
];
```

4. Next, calculate the number of working days:

```
Sales:
LOAD *,
Month(PostingDate) as Month,
MonthName(PostingDate) AS MonthYear,
IF(Year(PostingDate)=Year(TODAY()) AND
Month(PostingDate)=MONTH(TODAY()),
    NETWORKDAYS(MONTHSTART(today()),(Today()),
    '$(vPublicHolidays)'), NETWORKDAYS(MONTHSTART(PostingDate),
    MonthEnd(PostingDate),
'$(vPublicHolidays)')) AS WorkingDays RESIDENT
SalesTmp;
DROP table SalesTmp;
    DROP table HolidayTmp;
```

5. Load the script.

6. On the Qlik Sense sheet, create a **Table** object and name it `Average Monthly Sales`.

7. Add **MonthYear** and **WorkingDays** as dimensions.

8. Add the following measure and label it as `Avg Sales`:

```
Sum(Sales)/WorkingDays
```

9. Set the number formatting for **Avg Sales** to **Money**.
10. Under **Sorting**, make sure that the `MonthYear` field is promoted to the top.
11. Go to **Appearance** | **Presentation** and switch off **Totals**.
12. The final table object should look like this:

Average Monthly Sales

MonthYear	WorkingDays	Avg Sales
Aug 2014	20	£250.00
Sep 2014	22	£23.73
Oct 2014	23	£22.22
Nov 2014	20	£250.00
Dec 2014	21	£69.29
Jan 2015	21	£47.62
Feb 2015	20	£100.00
Mar 2015	22	£100.00
Apr 2015	20	£13.30
May 2015	19	£368.42
Jun 2015	22	£227.27
Jul 2015	23	£19.83
Sep 2015	22	£190.91
Oct 2015	18	£104.17

How it works...

The `Concat` function stores the aggregated string concatenation of all the holiday dates. These holiday dates are stored in a variable, `vPublicHolidays`, which is further used in the `Networkdays()` function. The `Networkdays()` function has three parameters. The first two parameters define the range of dates to consider. If the `PostingDate` date lies in the current month, the range of dates is defined by the first day of the month and today. From this range, we exclude the non-working days, Saturdays, Sundays, and public holidays. If the posting date is in a month prior to the current month, the first and the last day of said month determine the range of the days for calculating the working days.

See also

- *Using the Concat() function to display a string of field values as a dimension*

Using the Concat() function to display a string of field values as a dimension

A line-level table is normally the most granular data in a data model. For example, consider an `Order Line` table. The orders for each customer are stored one row per product line, and we have corresponding costs for each product on each line. When we generate a table report for such data, we will have a separate line for each product, which, in itself, is not wrong. Recently, however, a customer asked me to initiate an export for the Table report in such a way that all the products for a particular order are contained in a single cell, and the sales column should show the aggregated figure for all the products under `OrderID`. To tackle this requirement, I created a calculated dimension using the `Concat` function. The process is explained in the following recipe.

Getting ready

1. Create a new Qlik Sense application.
2. Add the following `INLINE` table that contains the `Order Line` table details:

```
Orders:
LOAD * INLINE [
    Customer,OrderID,Product,Cost
    1,201,Chain,20
    1,201,Seat,40
    1,201,Mudguard,50
    2,202,Gloves,15
    2,202,Basket,60
    3,203,Helmet,70
    ];
```

3. Load the data and save the file. Open **App overview** by clicking on the Navigation dropdown in the top-left corner.

How to do it...

1. Create a new sheet.
2. Drag the **Table** object from the left-hand side Assets panel on to the sheet. Name it `Sales by Order`.
3. Add **OrderID** and **Customer** as dimensions.
4. Add the following as a third, calculated dimension, and label it `Products`:

   ```
   =AGGR(Concat(DISTINCT Product,','),OrderID)
   ```

5. Add the following expression as the measure. Label it `Total Sales`:

   ```
   Sum(Cost)
   ```

6. Click on **Save**, and click on [✎ **Done**].
7. The resulting table on the screen will look like this:

Sales by Orders			
OrderID 🔍	Customer 🔍	Products 🔍	Total Sales
Totals			**255**
201	1	Chain,Mudguard,Seat	110
202	2	Basket,Gloves	75
203	3	Helmet	70

8. As you can see, all the products for a particular `OrderID` value are stringed together in a single cell, and the sales figures are the aggregated figures for each OrderID value.

How it works...

The `Concat()` function gives us the aggregated string concatenation of all the product values separated by the , delimiter. The `Concat()` function is an aggregation function, and hence needs to be used with `AGGR` in order to be used as a dimension. For the sake of our dimension, the products are grouped by the `OrderID`. The same functionality could have been achieved by defining products within a calculation in a measure, as follows:

```
Concat(DISTINCT Product,',')
```

But, by doing so, we won't be able to select the products for a particular `OrderID` value inside the table. When we use the calculated dimension, we get the advantage of selecting all the products for the `OrderID` value in a single go by selecting a cell in the products column.

There's more…

The `Concat()` function can also be used in the script along with the `Group By` clause.

See also

- *Using the* `Fractile()` *function to generate quartiles*

Using the Minstring() function to calculate the age of the oldest case in a queue

Support centers for any organization log several customer cases during the day. These cases are sometimes tagged with a specific status such as contact, and review. Each case goes through different statuses in the workflow until it reaches *closed* or *sign off* in the queue. The following example calculates the number of cases in each status of the workflow, and then makes use of the `Minstring()` function to calculate the number of days passed since the oldest case logged for a particular status.

Getting ready

Load the following script, which gives information on the cases logged at a debt collection agency:

```
LET vToday=num(today());
Case:
LOAD  CaseID ,DATE(Date#( DateLogged,'DD/MM/YYYY')) as DateLogged,
Status INLINE [
CaseID,DateLogged,Status
101,01/01/2002,Advice
101,25/04/2002,Contact
101,21/06/2003,Creditors Meeting
101,24/06/2003,Draft Allocation
```

```
101,30/06/2003,Sign off
102,18/10/2009,Contact
102,28/10/2009,Advice
102,11/02/2010,Creditors Meeting
102,20/03/2010,Draft Allocation
102,30/06/2010,Review
103,11/02/2013,New Business
103,19/06/2013,Draft Allocation
104,30/06/2010,New Business
105,30/06/2010,Contact
105,11/02/2013,New Business
106,19/06/2013,Drafting
106,30/06/2010,Advice
];
```

How to do it...

1. Drag the **Table** object from the left-hand side Assets panel. Name it `Oldest case in Queue (in days)`.
2. Add **Status** as the dimension.
3. Next, add the following expression as the first measure, and label it `Case Volume`:

    ```
    Count(CaseID)
    ```

4. Add the following expression as the second measure, and label it `Oldest item in Queue (in Days)`:

    ```
    Num($(vToday)-(MinString({$<DateLogged=>}
        [DateLogged])),'#,##0')
    ```

5. Under **Sorting**, promote **Status** to the top.
6. Under **Appearance**, click on **Presentation** and uncheck **Totals**.
7. Click on [✎ Done] when finished.
8. The resulting table should look like the following screenshot. The figures you get for the **Oldest case in Queue (in days)** table may be different, as the calculation is based on today's date, which will be different in your case:

Oldest case in Queue (in days)'

Status	Case Volume	Oldest Item in Queue in Days
Advice	3	4,951
Contact	3	4,837
Creditors Meeting	2	4,415
Draft Allocation	3	4,412
Drafting	1	764
New Business	3	1,849
Review	1	1,849
Sign off	1	4,406

How it works...

Today's date is stored in a number format in the `vToday()` variable. The `MinString()` function finds the oldest value in the `DateLogged` field from the total number of cases for each status. Next, we take the difference between `Today()` and the minimum date for each status to get the number of days for the oldest case.

There's more...

By making use of the `Peek()` and `Previous()` functions and using the correct sort order during load, we can determine the case volume for each change of status, for example, *count of cases* that went from *advice* to *contact, contact* to *creditors meeting*, and so on.

See also

- *Using the RangeSum() function to plot cumulative figures in trendline charts*

Using the RangeSum() function to plot cumulative figures in trendline charts

The charts in Qlik Sense don't provide the user with the inbuilt functionality to calculate the cumulative totals, as is the case with QlikView. In order to achieve the cumulative totals in a trendline chart, we make use of the `RangeSum()` function.

Getting ready

Load the following script that gives information on monthly sales figures for two years:

```
Sales:
LOAD
Month(Date#(Month,'MMM')) as Month,
Year,
Sales
INLINE [
Month,Year,Sales
Jan,2014,1000
Feb,2014,1520
Mar,2014,1600
Apr,2014,3000
May,2014,2500
Jun,2014,4500
Jul,2014,6000
Aug,2014,6500
Sep,2014,7800
Oct,2014,6800
Nov,2014,3000
Dec,2014,2500
Jan,2015,750
Feb,2015,1200
Mar,2015,800
Apr,2015,600
May,2015,2100
Jun,2015,3500
Jul,2015,4700
];
```

How to do it...

1. Click on **App overview** under the Navigation dropdown and create a new sheet.
2. Drag across the Line chart object from the Assets panel on the sheet, and name it `Cumulative Sales`.
3. Add **Year** and **Month** as the dimensions.
4. Next, add the following measure, and label it `Cumulative Sales`:

   ```
   RANGESUM(ABOVE(TOTAL Sum(Sales),0, ROWNO(TOTAL)))
   ```

5. Go to **Appearance | Presentation**. Tick on **Show data points**.
6. Save the application and click on .
7. The final trendline chart should look like the following:

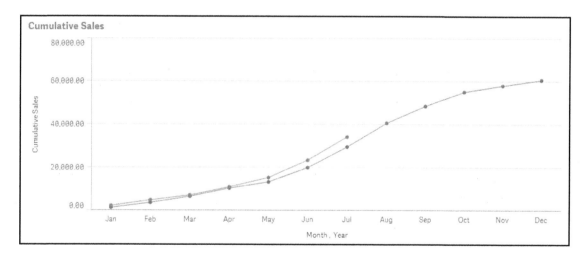

How it works...

There are three arguments defined in the syntax used for the `Above()` function:

- `Expression = Sum(Sales)`
- `Offset = '0'`

  Since this is zero, the function evaluates the expression on the current row.

- `Count = RowNo(Total)`

> The third argument tells the `Above()` function to evaluate the expression over a range of values. In this case, because we are specifying a total inside the `Rowno()` function, the result would be the number of the row the user is currently on.

The `Above()` function will return a range of values. Hence, we will use the `RangeSum()` function to sum up all the values.

See also

- *Using the FirstSortedValue() function to identify the median in a quartile range*

Using the Fractile() function to generate quartiles

Qlik Sense provides a host of statistical functions that can be put to effective use based on requirements in user reports. At a recent implementation, one of the requirements that popped out was to divide the data values into four quartiles. Quartiles are equivalent to percentiles that divide the data into four groups. The first quartile is determined by every value that is equal to and less than the twenty-fifth percentile. The second quartile is determined by every value that is between the twenty-fifth and the fiftieth percentile. The third quartile is determined by every value that is between the fiftieth and the seventy-fifth percentile. The fourth quartile will be all the data values above and beyond the value of the seventy-fifth percentile. In order to generate quartiles in Qlik Sense, we make use of the `Fractile()` function. The following recipe explains the process.

Getting ready

For the sake of this recipe, we create a hypothetical situation and make use of an inline data load that gives case-level information for an insurance company. Load the following script in Qlik Sense:

```
Case:
LOAD * INLINE [
CaseID,Value,Status
101,1500,Active
```

```
102,1800,Active
103,800,Closed
104,2590,Closed
105,3500,Closed
106,1200,Active
107,5600,Active
108,8000,Closed
109,5960,Closed
110,5000,Active
111,4000,Active
112,2500,Active
];
```

How to do it...

1. Click on **App overview** under the Navigation dropdown and create a new sheet.
2. Enter the Edit mode by clicking on ✎ Edit .
3. Drag the **Table** object on to the sheet.
4. Add the following calculated dimension, and label it Quartile:

```
=If (Value <= Fractile (TOTAL Value, 0.25), 'Quartile 1',
    If (Value <= Fractile (TOTAL Value, 0.50), 'Quartile 2',
    If (Value <= Fractile (TOTAL Value, 0.75),'Quartile 3',
    'Quartile 4')))
```

5. Add the second dimension, CaseID.
6. Add the following measure, and label it Value:

```
Sum(Value)
```

7. Under **Sorting,** promote Value to the top and sort it as numeric **Descending**.

8. The resultant table would be as follows:

Quartiles	CaseID	Value
Totals		**42450**
Quartile 4	108	8000
Quartile 4	109	5960
Quartile 4	107	5600
Quartile 3	110	5000
Quartile 3	111	4000
Quartile 3	105	3500
Quartile 2	104	2590
Quartile 2	112	2500
Quartile 2	102	1800
Quartile 1	101	1500
Quartile 1	106	1200
Quartile 1	103	800

9. As seen in the preceding screenshot, each CaseID value is now grouped under the Quartile.

How it works...

The Fractile() function finds the value corresponding to the stated quartile in the range of the data values given by the expression. For example, a Fractile (TOTAL Value, 0.25) works in the following way. A value corresponding to the twenty-fifth percentile is calculated. The total qualifier disregards the chart dimensions. In our calculated dimension, every CaseID having the value below the twenty-fifth percentile mark is tagged as *Quartile 1*, between twenty-fifth and fiftieth as *Quartile 2*, and so on.

There's more...

We can make use of a distinct qualifier inside the Fractile() function. In such a case, only the unique values of the Value field are evaluated.

See also

- *Using the FirstSortedValue() function to identify the median in a quartile range*

Using the FirstSortedValue() function to identify the median in a quartile range

Our next task is to find a claim corresponding to the median value in each quartile. A median is nothing but a value corresponding to the fiftieth percentile. We can achieve this using the `FirstSortedvalue()` and `median()` functions.

Getting ready

Continue with the same application as in the preceding recipe.

How to do it...

1. Go to the Edit mode by clicking on ✎ **Edit** .
2. Select the table we created just now in the preceding recipe.
3. Edit the **CaseID** dimension, and put in the following calculation:

```
=if(Match(CaseID,
'$(=FirstSortedValue(distinct{<Value={"<=$(=Median({<Value=
{'>=$(=fractile(Value, 0))<=$(=Fractile(Value, 0.25))'}>}
Value))"}>} CaseID, -Value))',
'$(=FirstSortedValue(distinct{<Value={"<=$(=Median({<Value=
{'>$(=fractile(Value, 0.25))<=$(=fractile(Value,
0.5))'}>} Value))"}>} CaseID, -Value))',
'$(=FirstSortedValue(distinct{<Value={"<=$(=Median({<Value=
{'>$(=fractile(Value, 0.5))<=$(=fractile(Value,
0.75))'}>} Value))"}>} CaseID, -Value))',
'$(=FirstSortedValue(distinct{<Value={"<=$(=Median({<Value=
{'>$(=fractile(Value, 0.75))<=$(=fractile(Value, 1))'}>}
Value))"}>} CaseID, -Value))' ), CaseID, Null() )
```

4. Uncheck **Show Null Values** for **CaseID**.

5. The resultant table appear as follows:

Quartiles 🔍	CaseID 🔍	Value
Totals		**13660**
Quartile 4	109	5960
Quartile 3	111	4000
Quartile 2	112	2500
Quartile 1	106	1200

6. As you can see, every quartile is now showing only the claim corresponding to the median value in each quartile.

How it works...

The calculated dimension for `CaseID` gives us the claims corresponding to the median values in each quartile. As you can see, a `Match()` function is being used to match the `CaseID` with each of the four expressions within. Let's decipher the first expression inside the `Match()` function:

```
'$(=FirstSortedValue(distinct
{<Value={"<=$(=Median({<Value={'>=$(=fractile(Value,
    0))<=$(=fractile(Value, 0.25))'}>} Value))"}>} CaseID, -Value))'
```

The details of the expressions are as follows:

- The innermost set gives us the range of values that are between the 0th quartile value and the twenty-fifth quartile value
- The `Median()` function then gives us the value that lies at the median of this range
- The `FirstSortedvalue()` returns the value of the output field (`CaseID`) based on the sorted values of the value field

In situations where the number of claims in any quartile is an even number, there will be two claims that will correspond to the median values. In such a scenario, we want to select only the claim that is higher in the sorting order. Hence, we use a `-Value` as the sort weight.

There's more...

Similar to medians, we can derive the quartiles within quartiles using the `Fractile()` function.

See also

- *Using the Fractile() function to generate quartiles*

Using the Declare and Derive functions to generate Calendar fields

Defining a master calendar in Qlik Sense is a common requirement, and can be done using the `Time` and `Date` functions. With Sense, Qlik has introduced the `Declare` and `Derive` functions, which make it easier to create the `Calendar` definition. This is still not commonly used, as most Qlik Sense developers stick to their old calendar scripts, and there is nothing wrong with that. However, these functions are worth exploring.

Getting ready

Load the following part of the script, which gives information on organization sales, into the Qlik Sense application:

```
OrgSales:
LOAD Product, OrderNo ,DATE(Date#( InvoiceDate,'DD/MM/YYYY')) as
    InvoiceDate,
Sales INLINE [
InvoiceDate,Product,OrderNo,Sales
1/1/2013,Chains,101,5500
8/2/2014,Seats,101,4800
3/3/2014,Brake Oil,102,6500
9/5/2015,Helmets,104,4500
];
```

How to do it...

Using the `INLINE` table specified in the preceding code, we will generate a master calendar. We will generate the fields and `Group` definition using the `Declare` function:

1. In the **Data load editor**, type in the following script:

```
Calendar:
Declare Field Definition Tagged '$date'
Parameters
    first_month_of_year=1
 Fields
       Year($1)  as Year Tagged '$year',
       Month($1) as Month Tagged '$month',
       Date($1) as Date Tagged '$date',
       Week($1,first_month_of_year) as Week Tagged '$week'

       Groups
       Year,Month,Date type collection as YearMonthDate;
```

2. Once the `Calendar` definition is created, it needs to be linked back to the date field using the `Derive` function. Insert the following statement in the script and reload the application:

```
Derive Fields from Fields InvoiceDate using Calendar;
```

3. On a new sheet, click on **Edit sheet** and then on the **Fields** tab on the Assets panel to the left. At the bottom of the panel, you will see there is a new tab for the time and date functions. Once you expand this, you should be able to see all the fields we created under the `Declare` statement.

How it works...

The `Declare` function is used to create the `Calendar` definition and tag it to `$date`. The `Calendar` definition is then used to derive related dimensions such as **Year**, **Month**, **Week**, and so on. The `first_month_of_year` parameter indicates what the first month of the year should be. It contains comma-separated values, but it is optional and can be skipped if needed. Next, we define the fields we want to generate in the `Calendar` table. `$1` represents the data field from which the date field will be generated, which is `InvoiceDate` in our case. When the field definition is used, a comma-separated list of fields is generated. The `Derive` function is used in order to generate the derived fields such as **Year**, **Month**, and so on from the `InvoiceDate` field. The groups are defined at the end of the script that creates a drilldown group for **Year**, **Month**, and **Date**.

There's more...

The `Derive` function can be used to link back the `Calendar` to multiple dates separated by a comma, for example, "derive fields from the fields `InvoiceDate`, `ShippingDate` using `Calendar`". Similar to the resident load, a `Calendar` table can be loaded again in the script. We can change the parameter value of the first month of the year to 3. The earlier value of the parameter is overridden by doing this. This is achieved with the following commands:

```
MyCalendar:
DECLARE FIELD DEFINITION USING Calendar WITH
   first_month_of_year=3;
DERIVE FIELDS FROM FIELDS InvoiceDate USING MyCalendar;
```

See also

- *Using the Peek() function to create a currency exchange rate calendar*

Setting up a moving annual total figure

A **moving annual total (MAT)** is the total value of a variable, such as sales figures for a product, over the course of the previous 12 months. This is a rolling yearly sum, so it changes at the end of each month with data from the new month added to the total and data from the first month of the period taken away. You can read more about MAT at `http://www.pmlive.com/intelligence/healthcare_glossary_211509/Terms/m/moving_an nual_total_mat`.

Getting ready

We are going to make use of variables in this recipe. We will define three variables in the script: `vMonthFormat`, `vRolling12Months`, and `vMaxMonth`. Load the following script into your Qlik Sense application:

```
LET vMonthFormat = 'MMM-YYYY';
LET v12MonthsBack = 'Date(AddMonths(max([MonthYear]), -
   12),$(vMonthFormat))';
LET vMaxMonth='Date(max([MonthYear]),$(vMonthFormat))';


Sales:
LOAD
```

```
Date(Date#(MonthYear, 'MMMYYYY'), 'MMM-YYYY') as MonthYear,
Month(Date#(MonthYear, 'MMMYYYY')) as Month,
Year(Date#(MonthYear, 'MMMYYYY')) as Year,
Sales INLINE [

MonthYear, Sales
Jan2014, 1000
Feb2014, 1520
Mar2014, 1600
Apr2014, 3000
May2014, 2500
Jun2014, 4500
Jul2014, 6000
Aug2014, 6500
Sep2014, 7800
Oct2014, 6800
Nov2014, 3000
Dec2014, 2500
Jan2015, 750
Feb2015, 1200
Mar2015, 800
Apr2015, 600
May2015, 2100
Jun2015, 3500
Jul2015, 4700
Aug2015, 2100
Sep2015, 3500
Oct2015, 4700
];

FOR vMonth = 0 to 11
MATMonthYear:
LOAD
[MonthYear],
Date(AddMonths([MonthYear], $(vMonth)),'$(vMonthFormat)') as [MAT
    MonthYear]
RESIDENT Sales
WHERE AddMonths([MonthYear], $(vMonth)) < today()
;
next
```

How to do it...

1. Once the data is loaded, open the **App overview** window and create a new sheet.
2. Enter the Edit mode by clicking on ✎ **Edit** .

Quartiles Q	CaseID Q	Value
Totals		**13660**
Quartile 4	109	5960
Quartile 3	111	4000
Quartile 2	112	2500
Quartile 1	106	1200

3. Drag across the 〰 **Line chart** object from the Assets panel on the sheet.
4. Name it `Moving Annual Total`.
5. Add `[MAT MonthYear]` as the dimension.
6. Next, add the following measure and label it `MAT Sales`:

```
SUM({<[MAT
    MonthYear]={">=$(vRolling12Months)<=
    $(vMaxMonth)"}>}Sales)
```

7. Save the application and click on ✎ **Done** .
8. Under **Appearance**, select the chart style as ⊿ .
9. Check the **Show Data** points.
10. Switch on the **Value Labels** options to show values on each data point.
11. Under **X-Axis:MAT MonthYear**, switch off **Continuous** and disable **Use Continuous scale**.

12. The final trendline chart should look as follows:

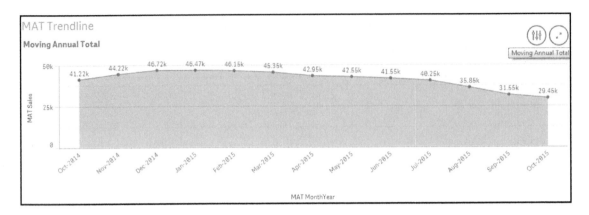

How it works...

The MAT curve helps in smoothing out the spikes that occur in a single month by making use of the annual totals. This is achieved by calculating the rolling 12 months accumulated sales data for each data point. We create a **MAT MonthYear** field. You will notice that when we select any month and year value in this field, it associates the field value with the current `MonthYear`, and the 11 `MonthYears` prior to the current, in the `MonthYear` field. In the **MAT Sales** expression, we make sure that the rolling 12 months are always shown in the chart. This is achieved by restricting the **MAT MonthYear** values shown in the chart between the `vRolling12Months` and the `vMaxMonth` variables. Selecting any **MAT MonthYear** will result in the trendline chart populating the MAT figures for the selected month and 11 months prior to that.

There's more...

There is a similar concept known as cumulative sums, which we discussed in the *Using the Rangesum() function to plot cumulative figures in trendline charts* recipe. However, there is a glaring difference between the two. While cumulative takes into consideration all the previous months and years to the current, an MAT will always consider the previous 12 months. In a way, it is a rolling 12-month sum at any given point in time.

See also

- *Using the Rangesum() function to plot cumulative figures in trendline charts*

Using the For Each loop to extract files from a folder

Picture a scenario where the month end sales data in an organization is stored in a folder on the network from where it needs to be picked up for reporting purposes. Control statements such as *For Each next* can be used in Qlik Sense as an approach toward script iteration. The following recipe deals with extracting files in Qlik Sense from a folder, processing them to create QVD files, and then transferring the source files to another folder. In the process, we will also deal with the incremental update of the QVD.

Getting ready

This recipe requires the legacy mode to be activated. The steps are as follows:

1. To activate the Legacy mode, open the `Settings.ini` file under `C:\Users\<username>\Documents\Qlik\Sense`.

2. Change the value of the `StandardReload` parameter from 1 to 0.

3. For this recipe, we make use of four Excel files: `January.xlsx`, `February.xlsx`, `March.xlsx`, and `April.xlsx`. These files are provided with the chapter and can be downloaded from the Packt Publishing website.

4. Save the file `January.xlsx` under `C:\QlikSense`. If you are not able to write to this location, then you may change the storage location for the file. Note that in this case, you will have to make relevant changes to the file location paths for the load script discussed in the *How to do it...* section for this recipe.

5. Create another folder named `Processed` inside the `QlikSense` folder we created in Step 1. The path for the folder would be `C:\QlikSense\Processed`.

6. Create a third folder named `QVD` inside the QlikSense folder created in Step 1. The path for the folder would be `C:\QlikSense\QVD`.

How to do it...

1. Create a new Qlik Sense application.
2. Open the **Data load editor**.

3. Load the following script:

```
For each File in filelist ('C:\QlikSense\*.xlsx')

ProdSales:
LOAD
 left(FileBaseName(),18) AS ProdSalesFileName,
filename() as FileName,
 [Product],
[Sales]
FROM [$(File)]
(ooxml, embedded labels, table is Sheet1)
WHERE Sales >250000;

Execute cmd.exe /C move "$(File)" "C:\QlikSense\Processed";

next File
SET rowCount = 0;
LET rowCount = NoOfRows('ProdSales');

IF rowCount > 0 AND
    Alt(FileSize('C:\QlikSense\QVD\ProdSales.QVD'),0) > 0 THEN

    Concatenate(ProdSales)
    LOAD * FROM C:\\QlikSense\QVD\ProdSales.QVD (qvd);
    STORE ProdSales INTO C:\QlikSense\QVD\ProdSales.QVD;

ELSE

    STORE ProdSales INTO C:\QlikSense\QVD\ProdSales.QVD;

END IF

DROP TABLE ProdSales;

LOAD * FROM C:\QlikSense\QVD\ProdSales.QVD (qvd);
```

4. Now, add the remaining three Excel files, that is, `February.xlsx`, `March.xlsx`, and `April.xlsx`, to the source location; in the case of this recipe, it is `c:\QlikSense`.

5. Load the script again. You will notice that all the files have been processed and moved to the processed folder. At the same time, the new data is appended to the `ProdSales.QVD` file.

6. In order to test the data loaded into the QVD, go to **App overview** and create a new sheet.

7. Drag a **Table** object on to the sheet.

8. Add **ProdSalesFileName** as the first dimension and label it `Month`.

9. Add **Product** as the second dimension.

10. Add the following expression and label it as `Sales`:

    ```
    Sum(Sales)
    ```

11. The resultant table would look like the following, with each month showing records only with sales > 250,000:

Month	Product	Sales
Totals		6882967
April	2589	589686
April	4545	526352
April	7852	323256
February	2563	658968
February	2589	489868
February	7852	451185
January	4545	658936
January	7852	458788
January	2563	456698
January	4568	452658
January	7856	452563

How it works...

The `for each next` loop iterates through each file in the `Source` folder and processes it to pick up records with sales greater than 250,000. Once processed, the files are transferred to the processed folder using the command prompt. The `if` condition checks for the row count of the processed file. If it is greater than zero, then the file is concatenated to the existing `ProdSales.QVD` file. The `LOAD` statement inside the `if` condition has a `WHERE` not exists clause, which makes sure to append only new files to the QVD.

Using the Peek() function to create a currency exchange rate calendar

Organizations dealing in multiple currencies may use a web service to extract the exchange rates. They may even store the currency exchange rates in Excel files, or sometimes in a database table. The exchange rates for any currency may be stored only for each RateStartDate, that, is for the day when the rate changes its value. However, for our reporting purposes, we need exchange rates for each day and not just for the day when the rate changes. For this purpose, it is beneficial to create an exchange rate calendar.

Getting ready

Create a new Qlik Sense application and load the following script into your Qlik Sense application:

```
ExchangeRatetemp:
LOAD FromCurrency,ExchangeRate,
DATE(Date#(RateStartDate,'DD/MM/YYYY')) as RateStartDate INLINE [
FromCurrency, ExchangeRate, RateStartDate
EUR,0.687,01/08/2012
EUR,0.757,02/09/2012
EUR,0.74,08/09/2013
EUR,1.10,24/10/2014
SGD,0.52,01/08/2012
SGD,0.68,27/02/2014
SGD,0.88,28/03/2015
USD,0.75,14/12/2013
USD,0.77,16/01/2014
USD,0.85,26/06/2015
];
```

How to do it...

We will now generate the end dates for each currency exchange rate:

1. Load the following script to generate the RateEndDate for each exchange rate:

```
ExchangeRate:
LOAD
FromCurrency,
ExchangeRate,
Date (RateStartDate) AS RateStartDate,
```

```
If (FromCurrency=Peek (FromCurrency), Date (Peek
    (RateStartDate)-1), Today ()) AS RateEndDate
RESIDENT
ExchangeRatetemp
ORDER BY FromCurrency, RateStartDate DESC;

DROP TABLE ExchangeRatetemp;
```

2. Go to the **App overview** window and open a new sheet.

3. Enter the Edit mode by clicking on 🖉 **Edit**.

4. Drag the **Table** object on to the screen and add all the four dimensions to it. Promote **RateStartDate** to the top of the sorting order and set the sort order as numeric **Ascending**.

5. The result would be as follows:

FromCurrency	ExchangeRate	RateStartDate	RateEndDate
EUR	0.687	01/08/2012	01/09/2012
EUR	0.757	02/09/2012	07/09/2013
EUR	0.74	08/09/2013	23/10/2014
EUR	1.10	24/10/2014	27/07/2015
SGD	0.52	01/08/2012	26/02/2014
SGD	0.68	27/02/2014	27/03/2015
SGD	0.88	28/03/2015	27/07/2015
USD	0.75	14/12/2013	15/01/2014
USD	0.77	16/01/2014	25/06/2015
USD	0.85	26/06/2015	27/07/2015

6. As we can see, every record for a currency now has a rate end date.

7. We will now use the `RateStartDate` and `RateEndDate` fields as our base dates for the exchange rate calendar.

8. Now, copy and paste the following script after the `DROP TABLE ExchangeRatetemp` statement:

```
//--------------------------------------------------
// Generate calendar dates
//--------------------------------------------------

LET ExStartDate = Num(Peek ('RateStartDate', -1,
    ExchangeRate));
```

```
LET ExEndDate = Num(Peek('RateEndDate', 0, ExchangeRate));

ExchangeRateCalendar:
LOAD
Date($(ExStartDate) + RecNo() - 1) AS ExchangeRateDate
AUTOGENERATE
($(ExEndDate) - $( ExStartDate) + 1);

//--------------------------------------------------
// INTERVAL MATCH JOIN the month records to the calendar
 // table
//--------------------------------------------------

LEFT JOIN (ExchangeRateCalendar)
INTERVALMATCH (ExchangeRateDate)
LOAD
RateStartDate,
RateEndDate
RESIDENT
ExchangeRate;

LEFT JOIN (ExchangeRateCalendar)
LOAD * RESIDENT ExchangeRate;

DROP TABLE ExchangeRate;

ExchangeRate:
LOAD
FromCurrency,
ExchangeRateDate,
ExchangeRate
RESIDENT
ExchangeRateCalendar;

DROP TABLE ExchangeRateCalendar;
```

9. Again, create a **Table** object on the sheet and get all the dimensions from the ExchangeRate **table**.

10. We will have exchange rates for each of the missing dates as well, as shown in the following screenshot:

FromCurrency	ExchangeRate	ExchangeRateDate
EUR	0.74	14/12/2013
EUR	0.74	15/12/2013
EUR	0.74	16/12/2013
EUR	0.74	17/12/2013
EUR	0.74	18/12/2013
EUR	0.74	19/12/2013
EUR	0.74	20/12/2013
EUR	0.74	21/12/2013
EUR	0.74	22/12/2013
EUR	0.74	23/12/2013
EUR	0.74	24/12/2013
EUR	0.74	25/12/2013
EUR	0.74	26/12/2013
EUR	0.74	27/12/2013

How it works...

The main purpose of creating this exchange rate calendar is to tag the exchange rates for every missing date in the range. The initial data only comes with the rate start dates. So, we create a rate end date for each exchange rate using the `Peek()` function. The `Peek()` function checks for the last read record for `FromCurrency` and, if it matches, it generates a rate end date of `current RateStartDate -1`. If `FromCurrency` doesn't match, then the rate end date is set to today's date. Using these start and end dates, the calendar is generated.

There's more...

The exchange rate calendar generated in the preceding recipe can be set for a daily update and stored in a QVD file that can then be used in any Qlik Sense application involving monetary analysis.

See also

- *Using the Peek() function to create a trial balance sheet*

Using the Peek() function to create a trial balance sheet

A trial balance sheet captures the activity across different accounts of a company with regard to the opening and closing balances. The following recipe focuses on the creation of a trial balance sheet in Qlik Sense.

Getting ready

The recipe will make use of the `Trial Balance.xlsx` file, which can be downloaded from the Packt Publishing website. Store the file on your system at the following location: `C:/QlikSense`.

How to do it...

1. Create a folder connection to the `Trial Balance.xlsx` file. Name it `QlikSenseCookBook _TB`.
2. Load the data from the `TrialBalance.xlsx` file in the Qlik Sense file. We need to make use of the cross-table functionality to load the data in a proper format:

```
Let  vMaxMonth=Max(Month);

TrialBalancetemp:
CrossTable(Month, Amount, 4)
LOAD [Company Number],
  [Account Number],
  [Year],
    Forwarded,
  [January],
  [February],
  [March],
  [April],
  [May],
  [June],
```

```
[July],
[August],
[September],
[October],
[November],
[December]
FROM [lib://QlikSenseCookBook_TB/Trial Balance.xlsx]
(ooxml, embedded labels, table is Sheet1);
```

3. Next, we will generate the `Month` and the `MonthYear` field in a resident load. Copy and paste the following script:

```
TrialBalancetemp1:
NoConcatenate LOAD
[Company Number],
[Account Number],
 Forwarded,
Year,
Month(Date#(Month,'MMM')) as Month,
Date(MakeDate(Year, Month(Date#(Month,'MMM'))), 'MMM YYYY')
    as MonthYear,
Amount
Resident TrialBalancetemp;
DROP Table TrialBalancetemp;
```

4. The final step is to create the `Opening Balance` and `Closing Balance` fields using the `Peek()` function. Copy and paste the following script in the editor:

```
TrialBalance:
NoConcatenate LOAD
CompanyAccountKey,
[Company Number],
[Account Number],
MonthYear,
Year,
Month,
Amount,
if(Rowno() = 1 OR CompanyAccountKey <>
 Peek(CompanyAccountKey), Forwarded, Peek(Closing)) as
 Opening,
    if(Rowno() = 1 OR CompanyAccountKey <>
      Peek(CompanyAccountKey), Forwarded + Amount,
      Peek(Closing) + Amount) as Closing
;
NoConcatenate LOAD
[Company Number] & '_' & [Account Number] as
 CompanyAccountKey,
[Company Number],
```

```
       [Account Number],
       Year,
       Month,
       MonthYear,
       Forwarded,
       Amount
       Resident TrialBalancetemp1
       Order By [Company Number], [Account Number], MonthYear;
       DROP Table TrialBalancetemp1;
```

5. Load the data and save the file. Open **App overview** by clicking on the Navigation dropdown ⊘ ▾ in the top-left corner:

6. Add the **Table** object to the sheet.

7. Add MonthYear, Company Number, and Account Number as dimensions.

8. Next, we will add the expressions for measures. We specify a range of months in the set analysis expression. When we define the range, it is enclosed within double quotes (" "). If you try to copy this expression and paste it in the Qlik Sense expression editor, sometimes, the double quotes are not copied in the correct format. If the format for the quotes is incorrect, the vMaxMonth variable is highlighted in purple. In this case, the user must make sure that a proper format of double quotes is in place.

9. Add the first expression to the table, and label it Opening:

    ```
    Sum({<Month={"<=$(vMaxMonth)"}>} Opening)
    ```

10. Add the second expression to the table, and label it Amount:

    ```
    Sum({<Month={"<=$(vMaxMonth)"}>} Amount)
    ```

11. Add the third expression to the table, and label it Closing:

    ```
    Sum({<Month={"<=$(vMaxMonth)"}>} Closing)
    ```

12. Under **Sorting**, promote **Account Number** to the top and set the sort order as numerically ascending.

13. Promote **Company Number** to the second position in sorting, and set the sort order as numerically ascending.

14. The final table report will look like this:

MonthYear	Company Number	Account Number	Opening	Amount	Closing
Totals			**151000**	**9000**	**160000**
Jan 2015	1	1001	10000	1000	11000
Feb 2015	1	1001	11000	1000	12000
Mar 2015	1	1001	12000	1000	13000
Apr 2015	1	1001	13000	-1000	12000
May 2015	1	1001	12000	1000	13000
Jun 2015	1	1001	13000	1000	14000
Jul 2015	1	1001	14000	1000	15000
Aug 2015	1	1001	15000	1000	16000
Sep 2015	1	1001	16000	1000	17000
Oct 2015	1	1001	17000	1000	18000
Nov 2015	1	1001	18000	1000	19000

TrialBalance

How it works...

The script uses a rowno() function and a Peek() function to calculate the **Opening** and **Closing** balances. The rowno() function determines the position of the current row. If we are at the first row, then the **Forwarded Amount** is taken as the opening balance. If the company and account have changed, then we use the Peek() function to determine the previous closing balance, which is taken as the opening balance. Similarly, if we are at the first row, then the **Forwarded Amount** + **Amount** added for the particular month is taken as the closing balance. If the company and account have changed, then we use the Peek() function to determine the previous closing balance and add this value to the amount to get the final closing balance.

See also

- *Using the Peek() function to create a currency exchange rate calendar*

Using the subfield() function to split field into multiple records

Sometimes, we have nested data stored in a field, instead of several lines to save space in a database. This is manageable for storage and record-by-record retrieval. However, for analysis, we need to split data into multiple records. For this purpose, we use the `subfield()` function.

Getting ready

Create a new Qlik Sense application and load the following script into your Qlik Sense application:

```
LOAD * INLINE [
OrderID, CustomerID, LineItems
200, 1, Gloves;100|Helmet;75
201, 2, Raincoat;50|Gloves;70|Seat;90
202, 3, Seat;80
203, 4, Mudguard;90
];
```

How to do it...

We will need to split the data stored in `LineItems` into several records and, after that, split data into multiple columns.

1. Load the following script to generate the records for each order item, and separate the product name and sale value data into two new columns. You can add this on top of the initial LOAD as a preceding LOAD:

```
Orders:
LOAD
    OrderID,
    CustomerID,
    subfield(LineItems,';',1) as ProductName,
    subfield(LineItems,';',2) as Sale;
LOAD
    OrderID,
    CustomerID,
    subfield(LineItems,'|') as LineItems;
LOAD * INLINE [
OrderID, CustomerID, LineItems
```

```
200, 1, Gloves;100|Helmet;75
201, 2, Raincoat;50|Gloves;70|Seat;90
202, 3, Seat;80
203, 4, Mudguard;90
];
```

2. Go to the **App overview** window and open a new sheet.

3. Enter the Edit mode by clicking on [✏ **Edit**].

4. Drag the **Table** object on to the screen, and add `OrderID`, `CustomerID`, and `ProductName` as dimensions to it. Add `Sale` as a measure.

5. Promote `OrderID`, `ProductName` to the first and second column of the sorting order.

6. The result would be as follows:

Sales by OrderID and Product ⊗

CustomerID	OrderID	ProductName	Sum(Sale)
Totals			**555**
1	200	Gloves	100
1	200	Helmet	75
2	201	Gloves	70
2	201	Raincoat	50
2	201	Seat	90
3	202	Seat	80
4	203	Mudguard	90

7. As we can see, for every order there is a record for each product, and the product data is split into the `ProductName` and `Sale` columns.

How it works...

The items for each order are stored in the `LineItems` field. Each item record is separated by "|" (pipe), and columns on each record are separated by ";" (semicolon). When using `subfield(LineItems, '|')` with two parameters, it creates multiple records using the second parameter as the record separator. When using `subfield(LineItems, ';', 1)` with three parameters, it uses the second parameter as a column separator and the third parameter as the column index; 1 for the first column, 2 for the second column, and so on.

There's more...

Using the preceding LOAD, you can reuse data generated by the bottom load and apply a new data transformation without the need for creating a temporary table.

See also

- *Using a For each loop to load data from multiple files*

Using the dual() function to set the sort order of dimensions

The following recipe shows you a way to overcome a problem with the sort order when creating a range dimension. You create a calculated dimension to the group set of values as custom ranges and describe it as with labels such as "above 10", "< 30", "< 60", and "up to 100". If you sort it alphabetically, then it will not show in the same order. We can assign a numeric value to each label using the dual() function. Using this approach, you can simply set the sort order of the dimension as numerical and it will sort correctly.

Getting ready

For this recipe, we will generate sales data in the script, as defined in the following script. Load the following script into the **Data load editor**:

```
load round(rand()*100) as Value
AutoGenerate(100);
```

How to do it...

1. Go to the **App overview** window and open a new sheet.
2. Enter the Edit mode by clicking on ⬚ **Edit** .
3. Create a **Table** chart.
4. Add a new dimension, and click on the **fx** button to create it as an expression.

5. Insert the following expression:

```
=if(Value < 10, dual('less than 10',1),
if(Value < 30, dual('<30',2),
if(Value < 60, dual('<60',3),
dual('above 60',4))))
```

6. Type `Range` as a label for the dimension.
7. Add `Count(Value)` as a measure.
8. The result would be as follows:

Range Q	Count(Value)
Totals	**100**
less than 10	6
<30	22
<60	27
above 60	45

9. Change the sorting order of `Range` dimensions from automatic to **Custom**, and set sort to numerically.
10. The result would be as follows:

Range Q	Count(Value)
Totals	**100**
above 60	45
<60	27
<30	22
less than 10	6

11. As we can see, the sort order is correct now.

How it works...

The dual() function creates an internal index for each label. When you set the sort order numerically, Qlik Sense uses the index for sorting.

There's more...

If you need to create buckets of values with the same size, you can use the class() function.

See also

- The *Distribution* recipe in Chapter 2, *Visualizations*

6

Set Analysis

In this chapter, we will focus on the concept of Set Analysis and its use in Qlik Sense. We will cover the following topics:

- Cracking the syntax for Set Analysis
- Using flags in Set Analysis
- Using the = sign with variables in Set Analysis
- Point in Time using Set Analysis
- Using comparison sets in Set Analysis
- Using embedded functions in Set Analysis
- Creating a multi-measure expression in Set Analysis
- Using search strings inside a set modifier
- Capturing a list of field values using a `Concat()` function in Set Analysis
- Using the element functions `P()` and `E()` in Set Analysis
- Using the intersection between sets for Basket Analysis
- Using alternate states

Introduction

I will say it outright that Set Analysis is one of the most important technical features of Qlik solutions. It allows you to do things dynamically that just wouldn't be possible with the default selections you have made. Set analysis can be termed as **Selection Analysis**. The user tells Qlik Sense what set of records needs to be picked for calculation, which is similar to making a selection from a **Filter pane** or active objects. The only difference is that you define the selection inside the calculation, so that the expression can still look at the records you specified inside the Set Analysis expression even if you clear all the default selections.

Cracking the syntax for Set Analysis

Set Analysis is a very powerful concept in Qlik Sense. In very simple terms, each set contains a *group* of selected dimensional values. The sets allow users to create independent selections, other than the one being used in the active Qlik Sense objects. The aggregations inside the set are compared with current selections to get the desired results.

 Any set that has been created in Qlik Sense only alters the context of the expression that uses it. Unless they are referencing label names inside the same visualization, all expressions using the set syntax are independent of each other. As such, basic expressions not using Set Analysis will react to normal selections made inside the Qlik Sense document.

A Set Analysis expression consists of three main parts:

1. Set identifiers, for example, $, 1, and 1-$
2. Set operators
3. Set modifiers (optional)

A set expression is defined inside curly brackets { }. Set identifiers are separated from modifiers by angular (<>) brackets.

Set identifiers define the relationship between the set expression and the field values or the expression that is being evaluated (Qlik, help).

The set modifier is made up of one or several field names, each followed by a selection that should be made in the field (Qlik, help).

For example, to compare sales from the current year against last year's sales for three countries, we can write the following Set Analysis expression:

```
Sum({$<Year={2014,2015},Country={USA, 'UNITED KINGDOM', GERMANY}>}Sales)
```

When using set modifiers, you need to specify sets of elements. They can be enclosed by single quotes or not. The following is an explanation regarding single quote usage:

- For numerical elements, you don't need to use single quotes
- For string elements with a single word, single quotes are optional
- String elements with two or more words, such as 'United Kingdom,' need to be enclosed it by single quotes
- Date and time elements need to be enclosed by single quotes as well

You can also create a set of elements with a search expression using the same syntax used in a **Filter pane** in your dashboard interface. In this case, it's mandatory to enclose the set using double quotes.

You will learn more about these rules in the following recipes.

Getting ready

Load the following script, which gives information on the Sales values for four customers:

```
Sales:
LOAD * INLINE [
Customer,Month,Volume,Sales
ABC,Jan,100,7500
DEF,Feb,200,8500
GHI,Mar,400,12000
JKL,Apr,100,4500
];
```

The following section will explain the basics of set expressions. The aim is to retrieve customers with volumes greater than or equal to 200.

How to do it...

1. Drag the **Table** object across on to the sheet from the Assets panel. Name it Set Analysis.
2. Add **Customer** as a dimension.
3. Add **Sum(Sales)** as the measure and label it as Sales.
4. In order to define the set, open the **Expression editor** window by clicking on the *fx* button.
5. Start constructing the set expression by first inserting the curly brackets, { }, just before the word Sales.
6. Inside the curly brackets, insert the set identifier, $.
7. Finally, we will define the set modifier. As mentioned earlier, the modifiers are separated from the identifier using angular brackets, < >. Insert < > after the $ sign. Type in Volume = {} inside the angular brackets.

8. Inside the angular brackets after, `Volume`, type in `">=200"`. Note the double quotes.
9. The final Set Analysis expression will look similar to the following:

    ```
    Sum({$<Volume ={">=200"}>} Sales)
    ```

10. Click on Stop editing sheet icon when finished.
11. The table should look similar to the following:

Set Analysis		
Customer	🔍	Sales
Totals		**20500**
DEF		8500
GHI		12000

How it works...

The set identifier, `$`, represents the records for the current selection.

The set modifier retrieves the records for customers `DEF` and `GHI` who have volumes of `200` and `400` respectively. It is mandatory to use double quotes when specifying a range of values in the set modifier. Hence, in our case, the value `">=200"` is in double quotes.

There's more...

A set modifier can consist of multiple field names with selections made on them. We can also exclude selections in a particular field by specifying the field name followed by a = sign. For example, if we want to exclude the month selection, then our expression will become:

```
Sum({$<Month=,Volume ={">=200"}>} Sales)
```

See also

- *Creating a multi-measure expression in Set Analysis*

Using flags in Set Analysis

Set Analysis expressions tend to become overly complex when there are too many comparison sets and conditions put in place. In order to reduce the complexity, you can make use of the flags created in the script in the Set Analysis expression. The flags can be set up to be simple binary values, 0 and 1. The use of flags optimizes the performance of frontend calculations. The following recipe explores this possibility by creating flags in the script to identify *On-time* and *Late* shipments.

Getting ready

For the purpose of this recipe, we will be using an inline data load that contains shipment details for each customer. Load the following script in the Qlik Sense **Data load editor**:

```
SalesTemp:
LOAD DATE(Date#(DeliveryDate,'DD/MM/YYYY')) AS DeliveryDate,
DATE(Date#(ShipmentDate,'DD/MM/YYYY')) AS ShipmentDate,
Invoiceno.,Customer,Month,Sales INLINE [
Invoiceno.,Customer,Month,DeliveryDate,ShipmentDate,Sales
101,ABC,Jan,01/01/2015,29/12/2014,10000
102,ABC,Feb,02/02/2015,25/01/2015,10000
103,ABC,Mar,03/03/2015,02/03/2015,12000
104,ABC,Apr,04/04/2015,24/01/2015,10000
105,DEF,Feb,03/02/2015,03/02/2015,25000
106,DEF,Mar,25/03/2015,21/03/2015,25000
107,DEF,Apr,18/04/2015,14/04/2015,25000
108,GHI,Jan,24/01/2015,18/01/2015,8500
109,GHI,Mar,14/03/2015,09/03/2015,7000
110,GHI,Jun,06/08/2015,07/06/2015,5000
];


Sales:
LOAD * ,
IF(num(DeliveryDate)-num(ShipmentDate)>=0 AND
Num(DeliveryDate)-num(ShipmentDate)<5 ,1,
IF(num(DeliveryDate)-num(ShipmentDate)>=5 AND
Num(DeliveryDate)-num(ShipmentDate)<25 ,2,3)) AS
    OntimeLateFlag
RESIDENT SalesTemp;
DROP TABLE SalesTemp;
```

How to do it...

1. Drag the **Table** object across on to the sheet from the left-hand side Assets panel. Name it `Invoiced Sales`.

2. Add the following dimensions:
   - `Invoiceno.`
   - `DeliveryDate`
   - `ShipmentDate`

3. Add the following expression under **Data** and label it `Sales`:

   `Sum({$<OntimeLateFlag={1}>}Sales)`

4. Under **Sorting,** promote `Sales` to the top.

5. Click on **Save** and Done.

6. The resulting table on the screen should look similar to the following:

Invoiced Sales			
Invoiceno. 🔍	DeliveryDate 🔍	ShipmentDate 🔍	Sales
Totals			97000
105	2/3/2015	2/3/2015	25000
106	3/25/2015	3/21/2015	25000
107	4/18/2015	4/14/2015	25000
103	3/3/2015	3/2/2015	12000
101	1/1/2015	12/29/2014	10000

7. Note that only the invoices with a delivery time of fewer than five days are shown in the preceding table.

How it works...

The calculation to identify the *On-time* and *Late* shipments is executed in the script and performed only once. Every `OnTime` shipment is flagged as 1, a slight delay as 2, and late as 3. Use of these flags in the frontend objects will filter the data in the table accordingly.

There's more...

In order to give a more meaningful representation to the flags in the frontend, we may use the Dual() function. A Dual() function combines a number and a string into a single record. The number representation of the record can be used to sort, and also for calculation purposes, while the string value can be used for display purposes.

In order to do this:

1. Rename the Sales table to SalesTemp1.
2. Add the following Resident load:

```
Sales:
LOAD *,
IF(OntimeLateFlag =1, Dual('OnTime',1),
IF(OntimeLateFlag =2, Dual('SlightDelay',2),
    Dual('Late',3))) As Flag
RESIDENT SalesTemp1;
DROP Table SalesTemp1;
```

3. Save and reload the application.
4. In the frontend, drag the **Filter pane** object across and add the **OntimeLateFlag** and **Flag** dimension to it.
5. Note that every **OntimeLateFlag** value is now associated with the text:

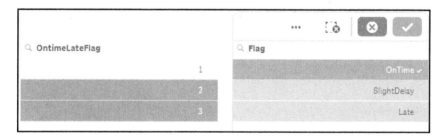

Using flags with a string format in Set Analysis expressions may not always be the most efficient way of optimizing the performance of Qlik Sense objects. With a big dataset, using a flag with a string representation in the expression does not offer a massive advantage from a performance standpoint is concerned. However, if we have the binary flags 0 and 1, then multiplying these flags by the measures results in faster performance in the user interface.

Hence, we conclude the following:

- To make selections in the application, use the `String` representation of flags in the **Filter pane** objects
- To calculate a condition inside a Set Analysis expression, use a numeric representation of flags

See also

- *Using embedded functions in Set Analysis*

Using the = sign with variables in Set Analysis

We can make use of variables and calculations in set modifiers. The following recipe explains the syntax for using variables for comparison in sets and how to effectively use the = sign in the dollar sign expansions.

Getting ready

For the purpose of this recipe, we will be using an inline data load that contains shipment details for each customer. Load the following script in the Qlik Sense **Data load editor**. Make sure that the last record in this script has the `Month` set to the current month and the `DeliveryDate` set to today's date:

```
Let vToday=Today ();

Sales:
LOAD DATE(Date#(DeliveryDate,'DD/MM/YYYY')) AS DeliveryDate,
DATE(Date#(ShipmentDate,'DD/MM/YYYY')) AS ShipmentDate,
Customer,Month,Volume,Sales,Supplier
INLINE [
Customer,Month,DeliveryDate,ShipmentDate,Volume,Sales,Supplier
ABC,Jan,01/01/2015,29/12/2014,100,10000,DEF
ABC,Feb,02/02/2015,25/01/2015,100,10000,DEF
ABC,Mar,03/03/2015,02/03/2015,400,12000,DEF
ABC,Apr,04/04/2015,24/01/2015,100,10000,GHI
DEF,Feb,03/02/2015,03/02/2015,200,25000,GHI
DEF,Mar,25/03/2015,21/03/2015,300,25000,GHI
```

```
DEF,Apr,18/04/2015,14/04/2015,200,25000,ABC
GHI,Jan,24/01/2015,18/01/2015,200,8500,ABC
GHI,Mar,14/03/2015,09/03/2015,200,7000,ABC
GHI,Jun,06/08/2015,07/06/2015,200,5000,ABC
];
```

How to do it...

1. Drag the **Table** object across on to the sheet from the Assets panel.
2. Add **Customer** as a dimension.
3. Now add the following calculation as the measure and label it `Sales`:

   ```
   Sum({$<DeliveryDate={'$(vToday)'}>}Sales)
   ```

4. Click on **Save** and then click on the **Stop editing** sheet.
5. The resultant table is similar to the following screenshot, with only one record for the customer **GHI**:

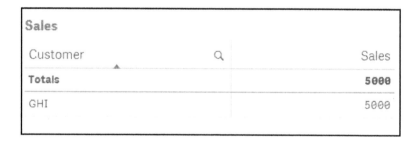

6. Next, update the `Sales` calculation as shown:

   ```
   Sum({$<DeliveryDate={'$(TODAY())'}>}Sales)
   ```

7. When you save this calculation, Qlik Sense won't be able to interpret the result and we will get the following output:

8. Tweak the sales calculation by adding a = sign in front of `TODAY()`:

```
Sum({$<DeliveryDate={'$(=TODAY())'}>}Sales)
```

9. The result will be as seen earlier, with one record for the customer **GHI**.

How it works...

We have defined the `vToday` variable in the script. This variable stores the values for today's date. When we use this variable inside the set modifier, we just use a simple $ sign expansion.

The `vToday` variable is calculated before the script is executed. However, Qlik Sense fails to interpret the result when we use the `TODAY()` function inside the set modifier instead of `vToday`, the reason being that the $ sign expansion needs to perform a calculation in the form of `TODAY()` and without the preceding = sign, the date for today won't be calculated.

Hence, we proceed to `TODAY()` with the = sign. Once the = sign is in place, the sales with today's delivery date are calculated.

If we are not using any calculations inside the set modifier, then the variable can be defined with or without the = sign.

See also

* *Point in Time using Set Analysis*

Point in Time using Set Analysis

"How is this month looking compared to the last?" This is one of the most common questions asked in BI solutions. In this recipe, we will build two charts and both will compare one year to another. The first chart expression will limit the range of data and make use of the `Year` dimension. The second chart will not use the `Year` dimension but will build the year comparison directly into the expression itself.

Getting ready

For the purpose of this recipe, we will make use of an inline data load that gives yearly sales information for different fruits. Load the following data into the Qlik Sense **Data load editor**:

```
Data:
LOAD * INLINE [
    Fruit, Year, Sales
    Apple, 2013, 63
    Apple, 2014, 4
    Cherry, 2014, 1150
    Cherry, 2013, 1180
    Fig, 2013, 467
    Fig, 2013, 374
    Fig, 2014, 162
    Fig, 2014, 267
    Fig, 2014, 586
    Orange, 2013, 10
    Orange, 2013, 50
    Orange, 2013, 62
    Orange, 2013, 131
    Orange, 2013, 145
    Orange, 2014, 93
    Orange, 2014, 102
    Pear, 2013, 27
    Pear, 2013, 157
    Pear, 2013, 384
    Pear, 2014, 489
    Pear, 2014, 782
    Plum, 2013, 148
    Plum, 2014, 36
    Plum, 2014, 412
    Plum, 2012, 700
];
```

How to do it...

1. Drag a **Line chart** object from the Assets panel onto the content area. Title it `Changes in Rank`.
2. Add **Year** as a dimension and **Fruit** as a dimension.
3. Add the following expression and label it `Sales`:

```
sum({<Year={">=$(=MAX(Year)-1)<=$(=MAX(Year))"}>}Sales)
```

4. Under **Appearance** | **Colors and legend**, switch on **Show legend** and click on the **Stop editing** sheet.

5. Next, drag a **Bar chart** onto the content area and title it `Deviation`.

6. Add **Fruit** as a dimension.

7. Add a measure with the following expression and label it as `Sales Change, current year vs previous`:

$$
\begin{aligned}
&\text{sum(\{<Year=\{\$(=MAX(Year))\}>\}Sales)-} \\
&\quad\text{sum(\{<Year=\{\$(=MAX(Year)-1)\}>\}Sales)}
\end{aligned}
$$

8. Select **Horizontal** under **Appearance** | **Presentation**.

9. Under **Sorting**, drag the measure to the top to occupy the first position.

10. Under **Appearance** | **Colors and legend**, toggle the Colors button to uncheck **Auto** colors and switch on Custom colors. Select **By dimension** and check the **Persistent** colors button.

11. Your graphs will look similar to the following screenshot:

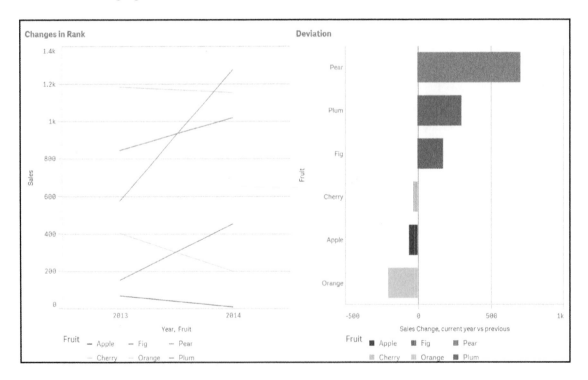

How it works...

The first Set Analysis expression makes use of a search string, hence defining the set of records we want to calculate across. The pseudo-code will read like this:

```
Sum where the Year = {"Search for records that fulfill a
    particular requirement "}
```

Using the double quotes denotes that we will be doing a search starting with < or >. Only values that fulfill the numeric requirement will be matched.

In our example, we define the numeric requirement of the search string dynamically using the following code:

```
={">=$(=MAX(Year)-1)<=$(=MAX(Year))
```

This code evaluates the max year and the year previous to that. If we changed the -1 in the preceding code to -2, the calculation would cover three years and not just two; this is the benefit of using search strings in Set Analysis. For the second chart, we have not used a search string but specified literals. We have kept the dynamic part of the expression as:

```
{$(=MAX(Year))}
```

Now, the max year available will be picked up automatically as opposed to saying `Year={2015}` and updating the expression next year.

Using comparison sets in Set Analysis

The following chart is a stacked bar chart, a standard way of comparing separate entities. Each value that you select is displayed as a segment in each bar by year:

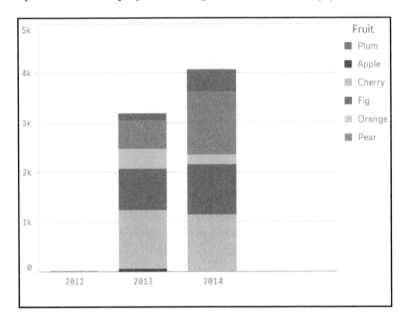

Using a comparative analysis allows you to group the separate selections dynamically so that you can compare them against one another. In the preceding example, we can group together **Plum** and **Apple** versus **Fig** and **Orange**.

Getting ready

For the purpose of this recipe, we will make use of an inline data load that gives yearly sales information for different fruits. Load the following script in the Qlik Sense **Data load editor**:

```
Data:
LOAD * INLINE [
    Fruit, Year, Sales
    Apple, 2013, 63
    Apple, 2014, 4
    Cherry, 2014, 1150
    Cherry, 2013, 1180
    Fig, 2013, 467
```

```
    Fig, 2013, 374
    Fig, 2014, 162
    Orange, 2013, 131
    Orange, 2013, 145
    Orange, 2014, 102
    Pear, 2014, 489
    Pear, 2014, 782
    Plum, 2013, 148
    Plum, 2014, 412
];

DataIslandFruit:
LOAD * INLINE [
FruitAlt
Apple
Cherry
Fig
Orange
Pear
Plum
];
```

How to do it...

1. Drag a **Bar chart** onto the content area and call it `Comparison Analysis`.
2. Add **Year** as a dimension.
3. Add the following expression and label it `Group 1 Sales`:

   ```
   Sum(Sales)
   ```

4. Add the following expression and label it `Group 2 Sales`:

   ```
   Sum({<Fruit={$(=GetFieldSelections(FruitAlt))}>}Sales)
   ```

5. Under **Appearance | Colors and legend,** switch on the **Show legend** option.
6. Create a **Filter pane** object and add the first dimension as `Fruit`. Label the dimension as `Group1`.
7. Add `FruitAlt` as the second dimension to the **Filter pane** and label the dimension as `Group2`.
8. The final chart should resemble one of the following screenshots if you have already made the selections to test the comparative analysis.

The following is an example where no selections are made:

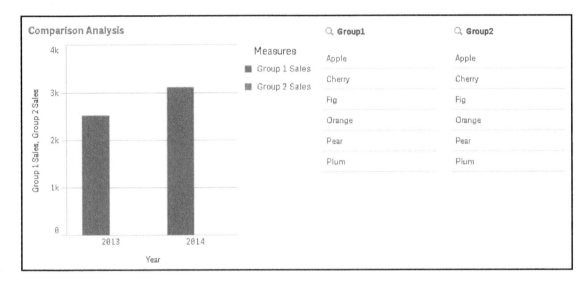

The following is an example where selections are made:

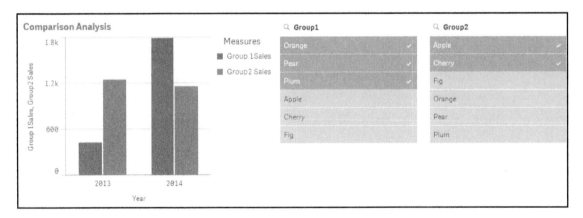

How it works...

The second table we loaded is what's known as a data island; this table is not connected to the rest of the data model in any way. However, we can use its content in our Set Analysis expression to compare different groups in the same field.

The first expression is completely standard. The second expression gives the total sales, where the `Fruit` field (part of the complete dataset) matches the values selected in the `FruitAlt` field (part of the disconnected data island). This method allows us to select groups of data for aggregation in our graph, something that we couldn't ordinarily do, by effectively breaking the association (green, white, and gray) using Set Analysis.

Using embedded functions in Set Analysis

As you have seen in the previous recipes, we have used functions, such as `Max()` and `GetFieldSelections()` inside our Set Analysis. Embedding functions inside a Set Analysis expression, specifically in the rules area that defines the set of records we want to calculate across, is known as Dollar-sign expansion.

A set of records in the simplest literal form is defined as `Year= {2015}`.

The expression needs to know the year you want to use and dollar sign expansion allows us to generate the text dynamically. Understanding how to use dollar sign expansion in your Set Analysis expressions enriches the amount of analysis you can perform. Sometimes, just using the function alone or specifying literals in Set Analysis is either too time-consuming or adds unnecessary maintenance to the application.

Getting ready

For the purpose of this recipe, we make use of product sales data as defined in the following script. Load the following data into the Qlik Sense **Data load editor**:

```
Transactions:
Load
 date(today()-IterNo()) AS Date,
 Pick(Ceil(3*Rand()),'Standard','Premium','Discount') AS
   ProductType,
 floor(date(today()-IterNo())) AS DateNum,
 Round(1000*Rand()*Rand()*Rand()) AS Sales
Autogenerate 1000
 While Rand()<=0.9 or IterNo()=1;
```

How to do it...

1. Create a new sheet and double-click on the **Table** object to add it to the main content area.
2. Add `ProductType` as a dimension.
3. Add the following expression as the first measure and label it `Total Sales`:

   `sum(Sales)`

4. Add the following expression as the second measure and label it `WTD`:

   `sum({<DateNum={">=$(=Today()-7)"}>}Sales)`

5. Add the following expression as the third measure and label it `Previous WTD`:

   `sum({<DateNum={">=$(=Today()-14)<$(=Today()-7)"}>}Sales)`

6. Add the following expression as the fourth measure and label it `Weekly Variance`:

   `(COLUMN(2)-COLUMN(3))/COLUMN(2)`

7. For the expression in Step 6, change the **Number formatting** to **Number** and then select the percentage format from the dropdown list.
8. You should have a table that looks similar to the following screenshot. The screenshots may not be similar to the following screenshot as we are using the `Rand()` function to generate the initial set of data in the script:

ProductType	Total Sales	WTD	Previous WTD	Weekly Variance
Totals	**£1,213,426**	**£640,889**	**£295,293**	**53.9%**
Premium	£410,761	£218,494	£97,393	55.4%
Standard	£407,902	£209,730	£103,621	50.6%
Discount	£394,763	£212,665	£94,279	55.7%

How it works...

When calculating something such as the week-to-date sales, the set of records you identify in your Set Analysis expression will change every day. When you use functions such as `Today()` inside a Set Analysis expression, the literal text values that the expression uses change automatically. Ultimately, using dollar sign expansion is just a replacement for the text strings that you could use.

If the date today is `06/08/2015`, then the user sees the set condition as:

```
DateNum={">=$(=Today()-7)"}
```

While Qlik Sense sees the set condition as:

```
DateNum={">=31/07/2015"}
```

This is because the function inside the dollar sign is evaluated first and it simply expands into the text/field values that we want to calculate across.

There's more...

The fourth expression is written as `(COLUMN(2)-COLUMN(3))/COLUMN(2)`. Here, we pick up the column numbers instead of the actual field names for our calculation.

We can also write the expression in the following manner:

```
([WTD]-[Previous WTD])/[WTD]
```

We will get a bad field name `([WTD]-[Previous WTD])/[WTD]` at the bottom of the **Expression editor** window. But don't worry, as Qlik Sense will still interpret the results correctly. This chink may be ironed out in future releases of Qlik Sense.

The expression does not make use of the fields that we have loaded into the application's data model. It instead uses the expression labels we have already created for the previous calculations. This is always a best practice option if you need to use the same calculation in the same table more than once. It make things simpler; you only have to change something once and, best of all, it is optimized and the calculation is already cached in RAM.

Creating a multi-measure expression in Set Analysis

Sometimes, you may have groups of expressions you want to view that either don't need to be viewed at once, or you don't have the room to display them all. In these cases, you do not have to go and create another sheet; you can add a control to let users select what is calculated.

The output of this recipe is similar to the preceding recipe, only with slightly different expressions to add depth of analysis to the same object.

Getting ready

For the purpose of this recipe, we make use of product sales and margin data, as defined in the following script. Load the following data into the Qlik Sense **Data load editor**:

```
Transactions:
Load
Date(today()-IterNo()) AS Date,
Pick(Ceil(3*Rand()),'Standard','Premium','Discount') AS
    ProductType,
Floor(date(today()-IterNo())) AS DateNum,
 Round(1000*Rand()*Rand()*Rand()) AS Sales,
 Round(10*Rand()*Rand()*Rand()) AS Quantity,
 Round(Rand()*Rand(),0.00001) AS Margin
Autogenerate 10000
While Rand()<=0.9 or IterNo()=1;

Measures:
LOAD * INLINE [
    Measures
    Sales
    Quantity
    Margin
];
```

How to do it...

1. Create a **Filter pane** object and add `Measures` as the dimension.
2. Next, drag the **Table** object across on to the main content area.
3. Add `ProductType` as a dimension.
4. Add the following expression as the first measure and label it `Total Sales`:

   ```
   sum($(=GetFieldSelections(Measures)))
   ```

5. Add the following expression as the second measure and label it `WTD`:

   ```
   sum({<DateNum={">=$(=Today()-
       7)"}>}$(=GetFieldSelections(Measures)))
   ```

6. Add the following expression as the third measure and label it `Previous WTD`:

   ```
   sum({<DateNum={">=$(=Today()-14)<$(=Today()-7)"}>}
       $(=GetFieldSelections(Measures)))
   ```

7. Add the following expression as the fourth measure and label it `Weekly Variance`:

   ```
   (COLUMN(2)-COLUMN(3))/COLUMN(2)
   ```

8. For the expression in Step 7, change the **Number formatting** to **Number** and then select the percentage format from the drop-down list.
9. If you come out of Edit sheet mode and select one value from the **Filter pane** object, you will see the calculation changing.
10. You should have a table that looks similar to the following screenshot. The figures may not be exactly similar to the following screenshot since we are using the `Rand()` function to generate the initial set of data in the script:

Select one option below to view the figures

Chart Options	ProductType	Total	WTD	Previous WTD	Weekly Variance
Sales ✓	Totals	£12,739,229	6,609,537	£3,243,454	50.9%
Margin	Discount	£4,278,988	2,218,842	£1,088,209	51.0%
Quantity	Premium	£4,237,879	2,203,479	£1,080,869	50.9%
	Standard	£4,222,362	2,187,216	£1,074,376	50.9%

How it works...

Here, we capture the field values that we want to calculate using a data island. When we use a data island, we simply pick an option from the **Measures** box without filtering the data in any way. But this approach allows us to control what calculations are being returned.

The `GetFieldSelections (Measures)` function simply returns `Sales`, `Margin`, or `Quantity`, depending on what you have selected. As such, writing the expression `Sum (GetFieldSelections (Measures))` means we can have any of the three options displayed just by selecting the value from the **Filter pane**.

As mentioned in the previous recipe, we can write the `Weekly Variance` expression, using the expression labels defined previously, in the table as follows:

```
([WTD]-[Previous WTD])/[WTD]
```

We will get a warning for **Bad field** at the bottom of the **Expression editor** window. Ignore it, as this chink may be ironed out in future releases of Qlik Sense.

Using search strings inside a set modifier

A set modifier contains one or several field names that make up the set expression. We can define a *range of values* within the selection made in the set modifier. The following recipe makes use of search strings to calculate sales within a specified date range.

Getting ready

For the purpose of this recipe, we will be using an inline data load that contains shipment details for each customer. Load the following script in the Qlik Sense **Data load editor**:

```
Sales:
LOAD DATE(Date#(DeliveryDate,'DD/MM/YYYY')) AS DeliveryDate,
DATE(Date#(ShipmentDate,'DD/MM/YYYY')) AS ShipmentDate,
Customer,Month,Volume,Sales,Supplier INLINE [
Customer,Month,DeliveryDate,ShipmentDate,Volume,Sales,Supplier
ABC,Jan,01/01/2015,29/12/2014,100,10000,DEF
ABC,Feb,02/02/2015,25/01/2015,100,10000,DEF
ABC,Mar,03/03/2015,02/03/2015,400,12000,DEF
ABC,Apr,04/04/2015,24/01/2015,100,10000,GHI
DEF,Feb,03/02/2015,03/02/2015,200,25000,GHI
DEF,Mar,25/03/2015,21/03/2015,300,25000,GHI
```

```
DEF,Apr,18/04/2015,14/04/2015,200,25000,ABC
GHI,Jan,24/01/2015,18/01/2015,200,8500,ABC
GHI,Mar,14/03/2015,09/03/2015,200,7000,ABC
GHI,Jun,11/06/2015,07/06/2015,200,5000,ABC
];
```

How to do it...

1. Drag the **Table** object across on to the sheet from the Assets panel.
2. Add `Customer` as a dimension.
3. Add the following expression, which calculates the sales for delivery dates ranging between `14/01/2015` and `14/04/2015`. Label it `Sales`:

    `Sum({< DeliveryDate = {">=14/01/2015<=14/04/2015"} >} Sales)`

4. Click on **Save** and the click on the **Stop editing** sheet.
5. The resultant table will be as follows. Note that we get a subset of the `Sales` value based on the date range specified in the set modifier:

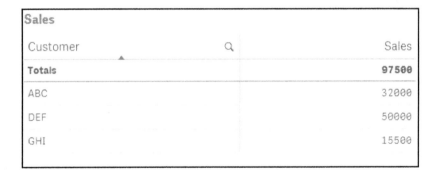

Sales	
Customer 🔍	Sales
Totals	**97500**
ABC	32000
DEF	50000
GHI	15500

6. Drag across the **Filter pane** object on to the sheet and add the **DeliveryDate** as a dimension.
7. Select any random delivery dates. Observe that the **Sales** figure for each customer remains unchanged.

How it works...

In the set modifier, we specify two dates enclosed within double quotes ("). The first date is the start date of the range and it is preceded by a >= sign, while the second date is the end date of the range and is preceded by a <= sign. We can use dates as literals in a search string without quotes when the field has the same date format.

There's more...

The preceding recipe considers two static dates for the date range. We can also make the date range dynamic by tweaking our Set Analysis expression in the following way:

```
Sum({<DeliveryDate =
    {">=$(=min(ShipmentDate))<=$(=max(ShipmentDate))"} >} Sales )
```

Here, we are comparing the delivery date to the shipment date and calculating sales for the delivery dates lying between the range of shipment dates.

For example:

1. Add `ShipmentDate` as a new dimension to the **Filter pane** object.
2. Select the shipment dates from `18/01/2015` to `25/01/2015`.
3. The resultant table shows the sales value only for the delivery date, as `24/01/2015`:

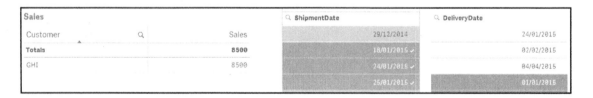

See also

- *Using the = sign with variables in Set Analysis*

Capturing a list of field values using a Cconcat() function in Set Analysis

While we have used the search strings in previous recipes to do a numeric search, we can also perform text searches by using the wildcard character, *. Occasionally, however, you might want to compare the values in one field to the values stored in another. We can also achieve this using Set Analysis and the `Concat()` function.

Getting ready

For the purpose of this recipe, we make use of product sales data as defined in the following script. Load the following script in the Qlik Sense **Data load editor**:

```
Transactions:
Load *,
    If(Len(TmpSubCategory)=0,Null(),TmpSubCategory) AS
     SubCategory;
Load * INLINE [
    ProductType, Category, TmpSubCategory, Sales
    Premium,A4,A4,300
    Standard,A4,A4,100
    Premium,A5,A5,500
    Standard,A5,A5,200
    Premium,A6,A6,1000
    Standard,A6,A6,600
    Premium,A1,,700
    Standard,A1,,300
    Premium,A2,,300
    Premium,A3,,200
    Standard,A3,,60
];
```

How to do it...

1. Drag a **Table** object onto the content area and label it `Product Sales`.
2. Add `ProductType` as a dimension.
3. Add the following expression as the first measure and label it `Total Sales`:

   ```
   Sum(Sales)
   ```

4. Add the following expression as the second measure and label it `Sub Category Sales`:

```
Sum ({<Category = {$(=concat (distinct [SubCategory],
    ','))} >} Sales)
```

5. You should have a table that looks similar to the following screenshot:

Product Sales

ProductType ⌕	Total Sales	Sub category Sales
Totals	**4260**	**2700**
Premium	3000	1800
Standard	1260	900

How it works...

The `concat()` function wraps around a field name; when expressed, it lists every field value separated by a delimiter. As such, the `concat (Distinct Subcategory,',')` function returns A4, A5, and A6, which are all the values in the subcategory field with no selections made.

Using the `concat()` function means you can avoid having to write out long lists of text strings in your Set Analysis expression. It is even better if these lists come from a source system where they are automatically updated with data.

Using the element functions P() and E() in Set Analysis

So far, we have seen how sets can be used to manipulate the result of an expression. To take the concept a bit further, we will now see how to use the `P()` and `E()` functions inside a Set Analysis expression. In the previous Set Analysis expressions, all field values were explicitly defined in the sets or variables or, in certain cases, through defined searches. The `P()` and `E()` functions make use of nested set definitions.

A P() function returns a set of all possible values, while an E() function returns a set of all excluded values.

Getting ready

For the purpose of this recipe, we make use of customer sales data as defined in the following inline data load. Load the following script in the Qlik Sense **Data load editor**:

```
P_E:
LOAD * INLINE [
Customer,Month,Volume,Sales,Supplier
ABC,Jan,100,10000,DEF
ABC,Feb,100,10000,DEF
ABC,Mar,400,12000,DEF
ABC,Apr,100,10000,GHI
DEF,Feb,200,25000,GHI
DEF,Mar,300,25000,GHI
DEF,Apr,200,25000,ABC
GHI,Jan,200,8500,ABC
GHI,Mar,200,7000,ABC
GHI,Jun,200,5000,ABC
];
```

How to do it...

1. On a new sheet, drag and drop the **Table** object from the Assets panel on to the left-hand side of the screen. Name the table Possible Sales.

2. Add Customer and Month as dimensions.

3. Add the following expression for Sales:

   Sum({$<Customer=P({1<Month={'Jan'}>})>}Sales)

4. Click on the **Stop editing** sheet.

5. The resultant table will look similar to the following. Note that it only shows all the records for customers ABC and GHI:

Possible Sales		
Customer 🔍	Month 🔍	Sales
Totals		**62500**
ABC	Mar	12000
ABC	Apr	10000
ABC	Feb	10000
ABC	Jan	10000
GHI	Jan	8500
GHI	Mar	7000
GHI	Jun	5000

6. Next, create another table with the same dimensions, such as **Customer** and **Month**, and name it Excluded Sales.

7. Add the Sales expression as follows:

```
Sum({$<Customer=E({1<Month={'Jan'}>})>}Sales)
```

8. The resultant table will look similar to the following screenshot. Note that we only have one customer, DEF, in the table:

Excluded Sales		
Customer 🔍	Month 🔍	Sales
Totals		**75000**
DEF	Apr	25000
DEF	Feb	25000
DEF	Mar	25000

How it works...

1. The `P()` function selects all the possible values from the set. In the first expression:

   ```
   Sum({$<Customer=P({1<Month={'Jan'}>})>}Sales)
   ```

   We select the customers who have made purchases in the month of January.

2. However, the `E()` function selects all the excluded values from the set. In the second expression:

   ```
   Sum({$<Customer=E({1<Month={'Jan'}>})>}Sales)
   ```

   We select the customers who have made purchases in all months except January.

There's more...

The concept of `P()` and `E()` can also be used with two fields for comparison inside the nested sets.

For example: if you need to find out all those customers where the suppliers had a volume of `300`, the set expression in the `Sales` measure will be defined in the following way:

```
Sum({$<Customer=p({1<Volume={300}>}Supplier)>}Sales)
```

Here, the `P()` element function returns a list of possible suppliers who had a volume of `300`. The list of suppliers is then matched to the customers to make the relevant selections.

The resultant table will look similar to the following:

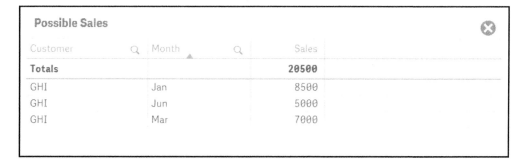

Customer	Month	Sales
Totals		20500
GHI	Jan	8500
GHI	Jun	5000
GHI	Mar	7000

An E() function in place of P() will result in all the customers whose suppliers never had a volume of 300:

Excluded Sales		
Customer	Month	Sales
Totals		**117000**
ABC	Mar	12000
ABC	Apr	10000
ABC	Feb	10000
ABC	Jan	10000
DEF	Apr	25000
DEF	Feb	25000
DEF	Mar	25000

See also

- *Using embedded functions in Set Analysis*

Using the intersection between sets for Basket Analysis

In the previous recipe, you learned how to use the P() function inside a Set Analysis expression. A P() function returns a set of all possible values.

To take the concept a bit further, we will now see how to use the P() function combined with the intersection operator * to help us locate invoices where two or more products were sold together.

Getting ready

For the purpose of this recipe, we make use of product sales data by invoice, as defined in the following inline data load. Load the following script in the Qlik Sense **Data load editor**:

```
Basket:
LOAD * INLINE [
BasketInvoiceno, BasketProduct, BasketSales
101, Apple, 10000
101, Orange, 5000
101, Lemon, 6000
102, Apple, 30000
103, Orange, 4000
103, Strawberry, 4000
104, Lemon, 4000
106, Apple, 3000
106, Orange, 2000
107, Strawberry, 4000

];
```

How to do it...

1. On a new sheet, drag and drop the **Filter pane** object from the Assets panel on the left-hand side of the screen.
2. Add `BasketProduct` as a dimension to use a filter.
3. Now, drag and drop the **Table** object from the Assets panel on the left-hand side of the screen. Name the table `Basket Sales`.
4. Add **BasketInvoiceno** and **BasketProduct** as dimensions.
5. Add the following expression for `Sales`:

   ```
   Sum( {<BasketProduct=, BasketInvoiceno=$(=concat( distinct
   'p({<BasketProduct = {'''&BasketProduct&'''} >})','*'))>}
   BasketSales)
   ```

6. Click on the **Stop editing** sheet.
7. Select **Apple** on the **Filter pane**.

8. The resultant table will look similar to the following. Note that it will only show data if you choose almost one product on `BasketProduct` filter:

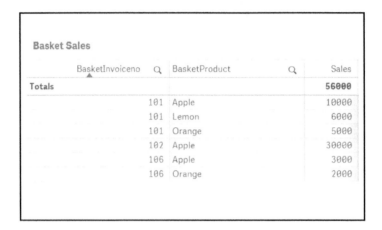

9. Now select **Orange** on the **Filter pane**.
10. The resultant table will now only show invoices where **Apple** and **Orange** exist together:

Basket Sales			
	BasketInvoiceno	BasketProduct	Sales
Totals			26.000
	101	Apple	10.000
	101	Lemon	6.000
	101	Orange	5.000
	106	Apple	3.000
	106	Orange	2.000

How it works...

1. The P() function selects all the possible values of `BasketInvoiceno` from the set. In the inner expression:

```
p({<BasketProduct = {'''&BasketProduct&'''} >})'
```

We select the `BasketInvoiceno` from customers who have sold the selected products over the last month.

2. The `concat()` function creates a combination of elements for each product selected in the `BasketProduct` field. It's enclosed by a dollar expansion sign to create a set expression dynamically according to the products selected:

```
$(=concat( distinct 'p({<BasketProduct =
{'''&BasketProduct&'''} >})','*'))
```

If we select **Apple** and **Orange**, the expression generated is as follows:

```
Sum( {<BasketProduct=, BasketInvoiceno=p({<BasketProduct =
{'Apple'} >})*p({<BasketProduct = {'Orange'} >})>} BasketSales)
```

If we select **Apple**, **Orange**, and **Lemon**, the expression generated is:

```
Sum( {<BasketProduct=, BasketInvoiceno=p({<BasketProduct =
{'Apple'} >})*p({<BasketProduct = {'Orange'}
>})*p({<BasketProduct = {Lemon'} >})>} BasketSales)
```

There's more...

The use of operator with `P()` can also be used to exclude or include values.

For example, if you need to find out all those invoices including apples, but exclude those that include lemons:

```
Sum( {<BasketProduct=, BasketInvoiceno=p({<BasketProduct = {'Apple'} >}) -
p({<BasketProduct = {'Lemon'} >})>}  BasketSales)
```

Here, the `P()` element function, preceded by "-", will exclude from the result all invoices matched with `Lemon`.

The resultant table will look similar to the following:

Basket Sales			⊗
BasketInvoiceno 🔍	BasketProduct 🔍	Sales	
Totals		**35000**	
102	Apple	30000	
106	Apple	3000	
106	Orange	2000	

See also

- *Using embedded functions in Set Analysis*

Using alternate states

The Qlik Sense associative engine allows you to work with two states of selections: {1} for all records with no selections applied, and {$} for all records with current selections applied. They are also known as identifiers.

Considering these two states, we can create set expressions that ignore all selections except those you explicitly identify in your selection.

To take the concept a bit further, we will now see how to create a dashboard with objects that only accept selections in calendar fields.

Getting ready

For the purpose of this recipe, we make use of product sales data by invoice, as defined in the following inline data load. Load the following script in the Qlik Sense **Data load editor**:

```
Transactions:
Load
 date(today()-RowNo()) AS Date,
 Pick(Ceil(4*Rand()),'Apple','Orange','Lemon','Strawberry') AS
  Product,
 Pick(Ceil(2*Rand()),'Standard','Premium') AS
  ProductType,
 Round(1000 * Rand()) * Ceil(4*Rand()) AS Sales
Autogenerate 1000;

Calendar:
Load distinct
   Date,
    Year(Date) as Year,
    Month(Date) as Month,
    MonthName(Date) as MonthYear
Resident Transactions;
```

How to do it...

1. Create a new sheet and label it `Dashboard with alternate states`.
2. Double-click on the **Filter Pane** object to add it to the main content area.
3. Add `Year`, `Month`, `MonthYear`, and `Date` as dimensions.
4. Adjust the size of the object to be just one line in the grid at the top area.
5. Double-click on the **Pie chart** object to add it to the main content area.
6. Add `Product Type` as a dimension.
7. Add the following expression as a measure and label it `Total Sales`:

   ```
   sum(Sales)
   ```

8. Double-click on the **Bar chart** object to add it to the main content area.
9. Add `Product` as a dimension.
10. Add the following expression as a measure and label it `Total Sales`:

    ```
    sum(Sales)
    ```

11. You should have a dashboard that looks similar to the following screenshot. The screenshots may not be similar to the following screenshot as we are using the Rand function to generate the initial set of data in the script:

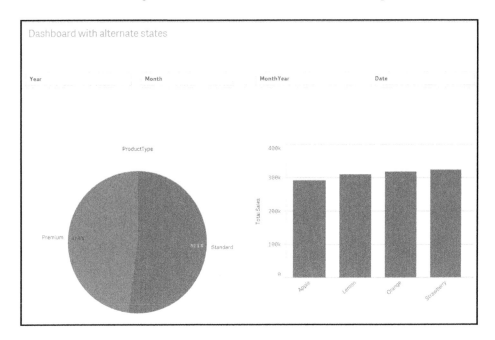

12. At this point, the expressions show the data, as usual, relating to current selections.

13. Now change the expressions on the charts to the following:

```
Sum( {1<Year= $::Year , Month = $::Month>} Sales)
```

14. After this, the objects will reflect data selections in the **Year** or **Month** Field.

How it works...

When defining a set expression, the first thing to do is define the state it will apply. In the recipe, the identifier, 1, between { and <, is used as an alternate state with all records with no selection.

The modifiers for Year and Month using $: : enable the selected values from the $ state to be passed into the 1 state, applying the selection to just these fields.

There's more...

It's possible to create a dynamic formula to create a set that modifies the selection state for all fields in the Calendar table.

We can also write the expression in the following manner:

```
Sum( {1< $(=concat( {<$Table={Calendar}>} $Field&'=$::'&$Field,',' )) >}
Sales)
```

The set expression is created dynamically with the concat() function, selecting all fields from the Calendar table using the system fields $Table and $Field.

Qlik Sense doesn't provide out-of-the-box functionality to create and manage several alternate states within an app. You can address this issue using several extensions, available at branch.qlik.com.

See also

- *Using the intersection between sets for Basket Analysis*
- *Finding extensions on Qlik Branch*

Using Extensions in Qlik Sense

7

In this chapter, we will focus on the use of some useful extensions in Qlik Sense, and discuss the following topics:

- Finding extensions on Qlik Branch
- How to import extensions (Desktop and Server)
- Using the variable extension
- Using the Reload button extension
- Using the simple KPI extension
- Using the ShowHide Container extension

Introduction

Qlik Sense has an extensive library of chart objects to display data. However, of late, there has been an increase in the demand for custom visualizations from business users, and such visualizations are used in specific circumstances. The visualization extension objects in Qlik Sense are developed using open standards, such as HTML5, CSS, and JavaScript.

There are plenty of useful extensions created by the Qlik Sense community, and most of them available for free.

The following discussed recipes include where to find extensions, how to import and use them in your Qlik Sense environment, and recommendations for the most reliable and useful extensions.

Finding extensions on Qlik Branch

Qlik Branch is a place where developers share and collaborate on open source projects.

It is the starting point for every Qlik Sense developer looking for an extension. Most of the extensions created by the community are published there.

There are thousands of projects published there, but how can you know if the extension is popular and consequently reliable?

In the following steps, I will show you how to identify popular and reliable extensions, and download them to use in your apps.

Getting ready

You just need a web browser to search the website.

How to do it...

1. Open your favorite web browser and go to `branch.qlik.com`.
2. Once the website successfully opens, select **Projects** in the menu at top of the page. The page will show a search box and below that a list of recent projects sorted by the most recent updated date.
3. Change the sort order to **Most Popular**. Now you will see the most popular extensions first.
4. Scroll down until you find the extension with the name **qsVariable**:

5. Click on the name to open the **qsVariable** project.
6. This extension is an object to set the value to a variable. It has different ways to render: button, select box, input field, and slider.
7. Scroll down the project page until you find the **Installation** section. There, you will see a download link to the zip file that contains the extension:

8. Click on the hyperlink to download the zip file.

How it works...

The website ranks the projects in consideration of visualizations and comments as criteria to define it as the most popular, so therefore, the most popular, the most reliable.

Extensions are stored in a zip file for distribution, and these files and the source code are stored at GitHub.

There's more...

Using the search box, you can type a keyword denoting a feature you are looking for.

Type `table`, for example, and you will see a list of several projects related to a table visualization.

Pay attention to the views, comments, and especially the last update attribute. Extensions with more than a year without updates denote they are not active and have a good chance to not function as expected in the most recent versions of Qlik Sense.

If you have web developer skills, you can customize the extension yourself, but first you need to learn about the APIs used to build extensions. More information on this subject can be found at `help.qlik.com` in **Qlik Sense Developers**.

See also

- Refer to the *How to import extensions* section

How to import extensions (Desktop and Server)

So, you found a cool extension in Qlik Branch and want to use it in your Qlik Sense app. How should you do this?

This recipe will show you how to do this using Qlik Sense Desktop.

Getting ready

This recipe is a continuation of the previous recipe. So, we will be using the same extension, `qsVariable`, to show how to import it to your desktop.

How to do it...

1. Open the extension folder located at `C:\Users\<username>\Documents\Qlik\Sense\Extensions\`.
2. Paste the file `variable.zip` and unzip it, creating a subfolder named `variable`.

3. After decompression has finished, check whether the files are stored inside `C:\Users\<username>\Documents\Qlik\Sense\Extensions\variable`.

4. Now, we will check whether Qlik Sense recognizes the new extension, so open Qlik Sense Desktop.

5. Open an existing app and edit an existing sheet.

6. Select **Custom objects** in the panel on the left.

7. Search for `Variable` in the object search box.

The resulting output will be as follows:

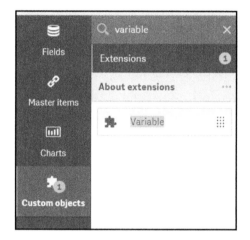

How it works...

To use an extension in Qlik Sense Desktop, first, we need to copy the extension files to the extension folder. We must pay attention to copy each extension to our folder. You can't install an extension in the same folder of an existing one.

There's more...

If you import an extension but you already have an app open, you need to press *Ctrl + F5* to refresh the screen and reload the Qlik Sense interface. With that action, it will refresh the custom objects list with the new extension.

To import an extension in Qlik Sense Enterprise Server, you need help from the Qlik Sense Administrator. Only a Qlik Sense Admin can import an extension.

You can find out more information about this at `https://help.qlik.com/ en-US/sense/February2018/Subsystems/ManagementConsole/Content/ import-extensions.htm`.

Using the Variable extension

Qlik sense has the capability to create variables that can be used in the script, and also in the user interface.

As a developer, we can use the variables editor when editing a sheet, but we can change a variable when in view mode.

There will be questions such as the following:

- How to enable the user to choose how many customers to see in a bar chart?
- How to enable end users to input data in a variable to simulate some calculation scenarios?

To answer these questions, we can use the Variable extension.

Getting ready

This recipe is a continuation of the previous recipe. So, we will be using the `Variable` extension we already downloaded.

The recipe explains how to use the extension to set values in a variable.

How to do it...

1. Open the `Automotive.qvf` app provided for `Chapter 2`, *Visualizations*, and create a new sheet.
2. Create a **Bar chart** on the sheet.
3. Add `Territory` as the dimension.
4. Add `Total Car Sales` as the measure.

5. The resulting chart will look like the following screenshot:

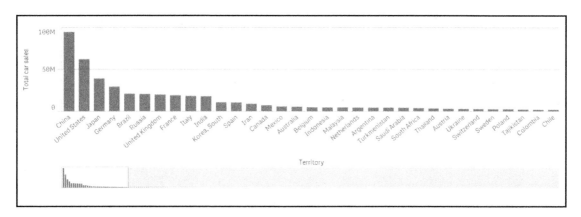

6. Adjust the `Territory` number visible at one time, changing the **Limitation** attribute in the `Territory` dimension with a fixed number of **10**:

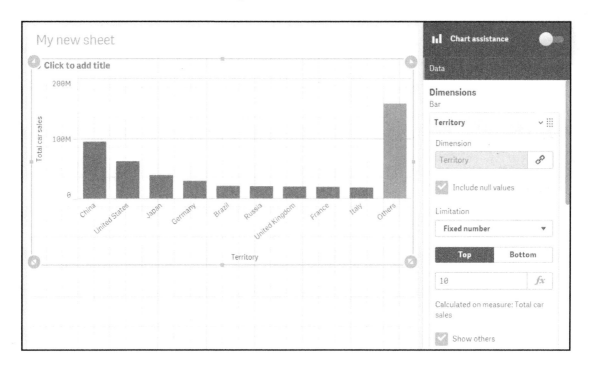

7. Keep this dynamic, so the user can choose to see 10 or 20 territories.
8. Open the variable editor, and click on Variables at the bottom of the left panel.

9. Click on **Create new** to create a new variable.
10. Set the name as `vtopn` and the definition with a default of 5.
11. Click on Save (pencil button) at the top to save the variable.
12. Click on **Close** to go back to the sheet editor.
13. Next, click in the expression editor in the **Fixed number** as **Limitation**.
14. Replace the fixed number with `$(vtopn)`.
15. Click on Apply.
16. The resulting chart will look like the following screenshot:

17. Next, we need to add the variable extension and set the correct parameters. Select **Custom objects** and search for variable extension.
18. Drag and drop the extension at the top of the sheet. The bar chart will be resized to give space to the extension automatically.

19. Now, in the property panel for **Variable** object, do the following:
    1. Set **Name** as **vtopn**.
    2. Change **Show as** to **Slider**.
    3. Set **Min** as 5 and **Max** as 20.
    4. Keep **Step** as 1.
    5. Select **Slider label**.
    6. In the **General** section, set **Title** with `Choose Top Territories`.
    7. Now, arrange the object's size in the sheet.
    8. Click on the Stop editing sheet icon to enter view mode.
20. The resulting chart will look like the following screenshot:

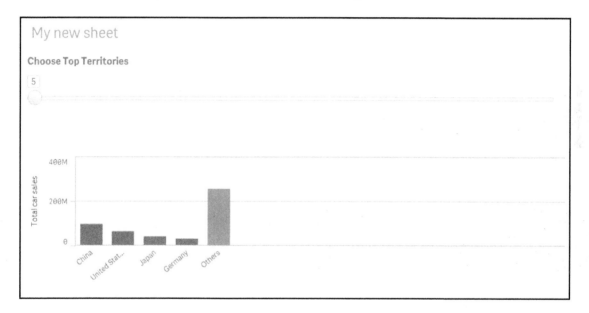

21. Drag the slider to the right to increase the number of visible territories. Drag it to the left to decrease it.

How it works...

We used a variable to store a value that limits the number of territories visible in the bar chart. The extension changes the value in the variable, and the bar graph uses this value as a new input, changing the limit of visible bars.

There's more...

The extension can be rendered as a **Button**, so that we can have several buttons and, for each of them, a specific value. This is the same for the Select option.

You can also use the variable extension as an input box, so just choose to render as **Input Field**.

Using the Reload button extension

In some use cases, we need to enable the user to reload the app by himself, but we shouldn't let the user open the **Data load editor** to do this action, or enter edit mode to push the **Reload** button under the **Fields** panel.

To solve this, we can use the **Reload** button extension.

Getting ready

To start this recipe, first you need to download the Reload button extension from Qlik Branch, by searching for the reload button in the search box:

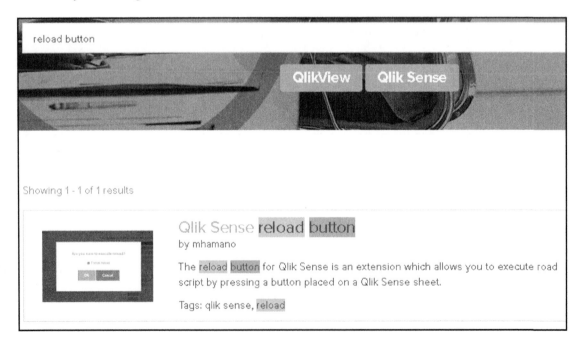

After downloading the extension, install the extension in your Qlik Sense Desktop or server, following the previous recipe about importing extensions.

The recipe explains how to use the extension to set a **Reload** button in your app.

How to do it...

1. Open an existing app you already have access to the base data you load in the app.
2. Edit an existing sheet.
3. Make some space to add the **Reload button**.
4. Search for the reload object in the **Custom objects** panel.
5. Drag and drop the **Reload button** object to the content area.
6. Add the following text as a footnote in the **Appearance** section: `Press this button to reload the data.`
7. Set the height of the object to 3 lines.
8. Click on the Done editing sheet icon.
9. The object will look like the following screenshot:

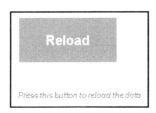

10. Click on the **Reload button**.
11. In the confirmation screen, click on OK to start the data reload process.
12. If the data load process runs with an error, it shows a **Reload Failed** warning, otherwise, it shows a **Reload Succeeded** message.
13. Click on the **Close** button in the pop-up window to go back to the app.

How it works...

The extensions trigger an API call to reload the current app.

There's more...

The extension can also trigger a partial reload process. To take full advantage of a partial reload, you need to write data **LOAD** commands with the prefix **ADD** or **REPLACE**.

When a partial reload runs, it only executes the LOAD statements with these prefixes and keeps the data for the remaining tables in the memory.

If you are developing in a server environment, look in the security constraints applied to the users with access to the app. Check with the Qlik Sense Administrator to grant the correct privileges for a user to reload an app within the extension.

Using the simple KPI extension

The Simple KPI extension is a great way to create a visualization of several KPIs, broken down by a specific dimension.

Getting ready

To start this recipe, first you need to download the Simple KPI extension from Qlik Branch, by searching for `simple kpi` in the search box:

After downloading the extension, install the extension in your Qlik Sense Desktop or server, following the previous recipe about importing extensions.

This recipe explains how to use the extension to show several examples of KPI-per-dimension data, without the need to create a separate object for each one.

How to do it...

1. Open the `Automotive.qvf` app provided for `Chapter 2`, *Visualizations*.
2. Look in the **Country car sales dashboard** sheet.
3. This sheet uses several objects, one for each of the nine top markets, to show market share as a gauge. With Simple KPI, we can a create something similar using one object:

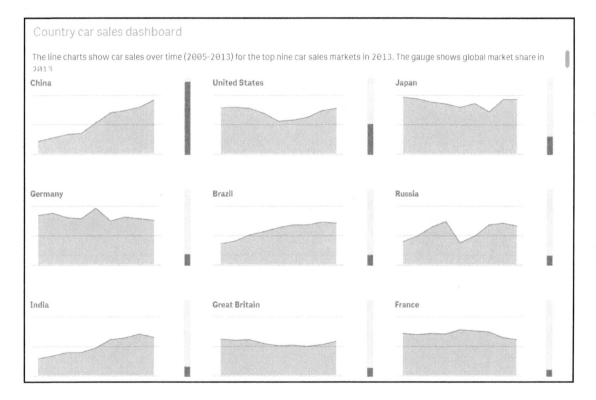

4. Duplicate the sheet and label it as `Simple KPI Dashboard`.
5. Remove all charts (**Line chart** and **Gauge**) and keep only the comment on top.
6. Drag the simple **KPI** object to the content area.
7. Add `Territory` as the dimension.

8. In the `Territory` dimension, set the limitation to **Fixed number** by **Top** as 9, and uncheck the **Show others** property.

9. Add the following expression as a measure, and label it as `MarketShare`:

```
Sum({$< [Year]={2013}>}[Car sales])/ Sum(TOTAL
{$<[Year]={2013}>}[Car sales])
```

10. Change the **Number formatting** to **Number**, and select **12.3%** as the format.
11. Open the **Appearance** section and open dimensions.
12. Change the **Show as** property to **Card.**
13. Change the **Items per row** property to **3.**
14. The resulting chart will look like the following screenshot:

15. Now, change the dimension limitation to **Top** as 12.
16. Change the **Items per row** property to **4.**

17. The resulting chart will look like the following screenshot:

How it works...

The extension accepts a single dimension that will be used to create a KPI card for each item. Using the dimension limitation, we can freely choose how many markets to show without polluting the screen with so many elements.

There's more...

You can explore several properties of the object to customize the appearance, such as **Font size**, **Font color**, **Background color**, **Label orientation**, and many more. Take a look in the sample QVF provided with the extension to see more examples of how to use this extension.

Using the ShowHide Container extension

If you already have a need to conditionally show or hide an object based on specific selections, user login, or creating a drill-down navigation using different objects for each level, this extension is a good choice.

Getting ready

To start this recipe, first you need to download the ShowHide extension from Qlik Branch, by searching for `showhide container` in the search box:

After downloading the extension, install the extension in your Qlik Sense Desktop or server, following the previous recipe about importing extensions.

The Automotive sample app has information about sales and production of cars around the world. Most of the views are separated into different sheets. This recipe explains how to use the extension to show a `Sales overview` and `Production overview`, which are in separate sheets, combined in a single sheet.

You will need to use the variable extension as well to create a button to alternate the visualization of each view.

How to do it...

1. Open the `Automotive.qvf` app provided for `Chapter 2`, *Visualizations*.
2. Go to **Sales overview**.
3. Click on the Edit sheet icon to enter edit mode.
4. Right-click on **Line chart** and select **Add to master items**.
5. Keep the name of the master item the same as the object, and click on **Add**.
6. Repeat steps 4 and 5 for the next six objects of the sheet.

7. Go to **Production overview**.
8. Right-click on **Line chart** and select **Add to master items**.
9. Keep the name of the master item the same as the object, and click on **Add**.
10. Repeat steps *4* and *5* for the next six objects of the sheet.

11. In the end, you will have 14 objects added to the visualization section on **Master items**:

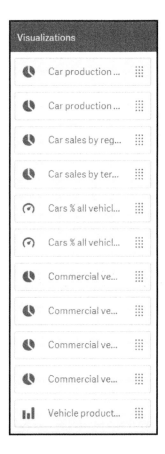

12. Create a new sheet and label it as `Sales and Production Overview`:
13. Create a new variable using the variable editor.
14. Give the **Name** as `view_selector`, and in **Definition**, write `Sales`.

15. Click on the pencil icon to save the variable definition:

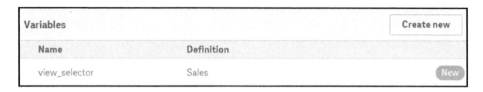

16. Click on **Close** to go back to the content area.
17. First, we need to set up an object to switch the visualization between sales and production, so add the variable extension in the top of the content area.
18. In **Variable** properties, set the name as **view_selector**.
19. Switch the **Show as** property to **Buttons**.
20. Add two new alternatives with the following parameters:
    1. **Alternative 1: Value** = Sales, **Label** = Sales
    2. **Alternative 2: Value** = Production, **Label** = Production

21. The variable object will look like the following screenshot:

22. Add the **ShowHide Container** object to the content area and align the object just under the variable object. The idea is to reproduce the same layout used on the **Sales Overview** sheet, so try to keep the following objects in the same position as in the original sheet.
23. In the property panel of the first **ShowHide Container**, set the **Master Object** as Vehicle sales by year.
24. Click on **Add Conditional Visualization**, and select **Vehicle production by year** in the **Master Object** list.
25. Set the expression for **Show Condition for Chart** to the following:

```
=if(view_selector = 'Production',1,0)
```

26. Add the second **ShowHide Container** object to the content area at the bottom left.
27. In the property panel of the first **ShowHide Container**, set the **Master Object** as **Vehicle sales by region**.

28. Click on **Add Conditional Visualization** and select **Vehicle production by region** in the **Master Object** list.

29. Set the expression for **Show Condition for Chart** to the following:

```
=if(view_selector = 'Production',1,0)
```

30. Add the third **ShowHide Container** object to the content area.

31. In the property panel of the first **ShowHide Container**, set the **Master Object** as **Car sales by territory.**

32. Click on **Add Conditional Visualization**, and select **Car production by country** in the **Master Object** list.

33. Set the expression for **Show Condition for Chart** to the following:

```
=if(view_selector = 'Production',1,0)
```

34. Add the fourth **ShowHide Container** object to the content area.

35. In the property panel of the first **ShowHide Container**, set the **Master Object** as **Commercial vehicle sales by territory.**

36. Click on **Add Conditional Visualization**, and select **Commercial vehicle production by country** in the **Master Object** list.

37. Set the expression for **Show Condition for Chart** to the following:

```
=if(view_selector = 'Production',1,0)
```

38. Add the fifth **ShowHide Container** object to the content area.

39. In the property panel of the first **ShowHide Container**, set the **Master Object** as **Car sales by region.**

40. Click on **Add Conditional Visualization** and select **Car production by region** in the **Master Object** list.

41. Set the expression for **Show Condition for Chart** to the following:

```
=if(view_selector = 'Production',1,0)
```

42. Add the sixth **ShowHide Container** object to the content area.

43. In the property panel of the first show hide container, set the **Master Object** as **Car % all vehicle sales.**

44. Click on **Add Conditional Visualization**, and select **Car % all vehicle production** in the **Master Object** list.

45. Set the expression for **Show Condition for Chart** to the following:

```
=if(view_selector = 'Production',1,0)
```

46. Add the seventh **ShowHide Container** object to the content area.

47. In the property panel of the first **ShowHide Container**, set the **Master Object** as **Commercial vehicle sales by region**.

48. Click on **Add Conditional Visualization**, and select **Commercial vehicle production by region** in the **Master Object** list.

49. Set the expression for **Show Condition for Chart** to the following:

```
=if(view_selector = 'Production',1,0)
```

50. The resulting sheet will look like the following screenshot:

51. Click on the Production button to switch all objects from the Sales to the Production view:

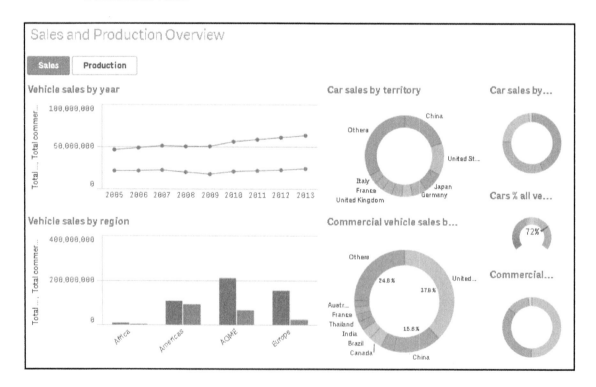

How it works...

To use this extension, first, you need to add the required objects to the master item library. The extension requires a default visualization to be shown when the conditional visualization is hidden. The condition must return 1 to show the conditional object, or 0 to hide the conditional object.

There's more...

You can add several conditional visualizations; each one will be displayed using a different show condition for the chart expression. This is very useful for creating cascading or drill-down visualizations.

8

Advanced Aggregation with AGGR

In this chapter, we will focus on understanding what the AGGR function is and how to use it. The following topics will be covered:

- Using nested aggregations
- Using Rank() with Aggr
- Combining set analysis with Aggr
- Creating an ABC analysis

Introduction

This chapter will focus on the use of the special function Aggr. In very specific cases, we need to calculate summaries over a group of dimensions.

Aggr is the only function that can enclose or be enclosed by another aggregation function.

Using nested aggregations

We know how to use several aggregation functions such as sum, max, min, and avg. When used in a measure of a chart or table, they aggregate values over the dimension stated in that chart or table.

Sometimes, you need to create a second aggregation based on the result of the first. An example could be the value and the name of the country with the most customers. This can be done using Aggr, combined with the Max() and Firstsortedvalue() functions.

Getting ready

Create a new Qlik Sense application, and load the following script that gives information on sales per country:

```
LOAD * INLINE [
Region, Country, No of Customers, Sales
Americas, Uruguay, 200, 56000
Europe, France, 900, 252000
Americas, Brazil, 1500, 330000
Europe, Croatia, 500, 160000
Americas, Mexico, 1800, 122000
Americas, Argentina, 1200, 360000
Europe, Portugal, 1100, 302500
Europe, Spain, 800, 250000
Europe, Denmark, 1500, 435000
Europe, Belgium, 700, 154000
Asia, China, 2000, 370000
Asia, Japan, 1200, 276000
];
```

How to do it...

1. Once the data is loaded, open the **App overview** window and create a new sheet.
2. Enter the Edit sheet mode on the sheet.
3. Create a **Table** object.
4. Add Country as the dimension.
5. Next, add the following measure and label it No of Customers:

   ```
   Sum([No of Customers])
   ```

6. Under **Appearance**, open **General** and, in **Title**, add the following expression:

   ```
   =Max(aggr(Sum([No of Customers]), Country))
   ```

7. Next, in **Subtitle**, add the following expression:

   ```
   =Firstsortedvalue(Country, -aggr(Sum([No of Customers]),
   Country))
   ```

The resulting table will look like this:

2000 China	
Country 🔍	Sum([No of Customers])
Totals	**13400**
Argentina	1200
Belgium	700
Brazil	1500
China	2000
Croatia	500
Denmark	1500
France	900
Japan	1200
Mexico	1800
Portugal	1100
Spain	800
Uruguay	200

How it works...

The `Aggr()` function works like the script load with the group by creating a virtual table with one measure (1ˢᵗ parameter) and one or more dimensions as 2ⁿᵈ to Nᵗʰ parameter. In this example, the aggregation dimension is `Country`.

Combining `Max()` and `Aggr()`, we found the highest value for the number of customers over the list of countries.

We used `FirstSortedValue(value, sorting_argument)` to show the corresponding country with the highest value for the number of customers. It returns the value (`Country`) that corresponds to the result of the sorting argument. In general, the sorting argument is a field, but can also be an `Aggr()` expression that was used as the sorting argument. We add a – in front of the sorting argument to start the sorting from the highest to the lowest, and not from lowest to highest, which is the default sorting criteria.

There's more...

Instead of using the expressions separated in the **Title** and **Subtitle**, you can create a single expression combining these two calculations in a **Title**:

```
='The Country of '&Firstsortedvalue(Country, -aggr(Sum([No of Customers]),
Country)) &' have the highest number of '&Max(aggr(Sum([No of Customers]),
Country))&' customers'
```

`Aggr()` is a powerful function and can be combined with other aggregation functions to create complex calculations.

See also

- *Using* `Rank()` *with* `Aggr`

Using Rank() with Aggr

The `Rank()` function is likely used to calculate the relative position of the value on the dimension of the chart, starting from 1 to *N*.

As `Rank()` requires a dimension in the object to calculate the relative position, how can we use it in a text object to show the name of the top five countries with more sales?

This recipe will show you how to use `Rank()` with `Aggr` to get this top five visualization in a dimensionless object.

Getting ready

For this recipe, we will reuse the data load for the *Using nested aggregations* recipe of this chapter.

How to do it...

1. Drag a **Text & image** object onto the content area.
2. Add the following text: Top 5 Customers, and type *Enter* to create a new line.
3. Format the text as bold.

4. Go to the property editor and open the **Data** section.

5. Add a new measure with the following expression:

```
=concat(
    aggr( if (rank(sum(Sales)) <= 5, Country), Country)   ,
    ',',
    aggr(rank(sum(Sales)),Country)
)
```

The result will look like the following screenshot:

Top 5 Customers

Mexico,Denmark,China,Argentina,Brazil

How it works...

The `Aggr` provides the Country dimension necessary according to `Rank()` to virtually create a sales ranking by country. The `If` condition is used to filter `Customers` with the rank result below or equal to 5. These are the top five countries.

We used `concat()` to concatenate the result of `Aggr` in a single row in the first parameter. The second parameter is the separator between each result, and the third parameter defines the weight to sort the concatenation. The third parameter requires a field to weight the sorting; to use an expression, it has to be inside an `Aggr()`.

To make the expression more readable, we can break each parameter of the expression into several lines.

There's more...

You can change the comma separator by the `chr(10)` funtion to show each country on a new line with the following expression:

```
=concat(
    aggr( if (rank(sum(Sales)) <= 5, Country), Country)   ,
    chr(10),
    aggr(rank(sum(Sales)),Country)
)
```

The resulting table will look like this:

Top 5 Customers
Mexico
Denmark
China
Argentina
Brazil

`Aggr()` helps us to create a calculation that depends on a dimension. You can use it on objects that are dimensionless, or even in labels and titles.

See also

- *Combining set analysis with AGGR*

Combining set analysis with Aggr

This recipe will show you how to use set analysis with aggregation functions combined with `Aggr()`.

Set analysis modifies the behavior of the filters in an aggregation expression. When using `Aggr()`, you have two aggregations, one inside `Aggr()` and the other outside `Aggr()`, as in the following example:

```
= Max( Aggr(rank(Sum(Sales)), Country))
```

Where to insert the set analysis expression? Will the result be the same?

This recipe will show how the set analysis in the inner or the outer aggregation affects the result.

Getting ready

For this recipe, we will reuse the data load for the *Using nested aggregation* recipe from ealier in this chapter.

How to do it...

1. Drag a **Table** object.
2. Add the text, `Europe Rank`, as the object title.
3. Add a dimension: `Country`.
4. Uncheck the **Include null values** property.
5. Add a new measure with the following expression, with the `Regional Rank` label:

    = Max (Aggr (rank (Sum ({<Region={'Europe'}>} Sales)), Country))

6. Add the second measure with the following expression, with the `Global Rank` label:

    = Max ({<Region={'Europe'}>} Aggr (rank (Sum(Sales)), Country))

7. Open the add-on section and uncheck **Include Zero Values**:

The result will look like the following screenshot:

Europe Rank		
Country 🔍	Region Rank	Global Rank
Totals	**6**	**11**
Denmark	1	2
Portugal	2	6
France	3	8
Spain	4	9
Croatia	5	10
Belgium	6	11

How it works...

In the first measure, the set analysis inserted in the inner aggregation filters the countries from Europe before applying the rank function, so the ranking is calculated only over the European countries.

In the second measure, the set analysis inserted in the outer aggregation filters the countries from Europe after applying the rank function, so the ranking is calculated over all countries showing the global ranking for each of them.

There's more...

If you have several aggregation expressions inside an Aggr, you can place the set analysis in the Aggr level and scope all expressions with the same set expression, as in the following expression:

```
= Max( Aggr( {<Region={'Europe'}>} Sum(Sales)/ sum ([No of Customers]),
Country))
```

With that, you simplify and make the expression more readable.

See also

- *Using nested aggregations*

Creating an ABC analysis

ABC analysis divides a set of information, such as customers, products, suppliers, or any other dimension, into three categories: "A" for those contributing to the first 80% of an indicator, such as costs or sales, "B' for those contributing to the next 10%, and "C" for the final 10 %.

This recipe will show you how to create an ABC analysis coloring a dimension with this classification, and use the classification as a dimension, so you can filter only the countries that fall under the "B" category, for example.

Getting ready

For this recipe, we will reuse the data load for the *Using nested aggregations* recipe of this chapter.

How to do it...

1. Create a new **Dimension** in the **Master items** library.
2. In the dimension editor, select the expression editor for the field.
3. Add the following expression:

```
=Aggr(
    If(Rangesum(Above(Sum(Sales)/Sum(Total
Sales),1,RowNo()))<0.8, 'A',
        If(Rangesum(Above(Sum(Sales)/Sum(Total
Sales),1,RowNo()))<0.9, 'B',
        'C')),
        (Country,(=Sum(Sales),Desc))
)
```

4. Set the label with ABCClassification.
5. Click on **Add Dimension**.
6. Click on **Done**.
7. Now, add a **Table** object to the content area.
8. Click on **Add column** and select **Dimension**, and then click on ABCClassification in the dimension list.
9. Add a second dimension and select the **Country** field.
10. Click on **Add column** and select **Measure**, and then type in the following expression. Label it as Sales:

```
=Sum (Sales)
```

11. Change the **Number formatting** of the Sales measure to **Number**.

12. The result will look like the following screenshot:

ABC Classification	Country	Sales
Totais		**3.467.500,00**
A	Argentina	360.000,00
A	Brazil	330.000,00
A	China	370.000,00
A	Denmark	435.000,00
A	France	252.000,00
A	Japan	276.000,00
A	Mexico	522.000,00
A	Portugal	302.500,00
B	Croatia	160.000,00
B	Spain	250.000,00

13. Add a **Bar chart** at the top of the content area.
14. Click on **Add dimension** and select the **Country** field.
15. Click on **Add Measure** and type in the following expression. Label it as `Sales`:

```
=Sum (Sales)
```

16. Under **Appearance**, go to **Colors and legend** and switch **Colors** to **Custom**.
17. Select **By expression** and type in the following expression:

```
=Aggr(
    If(Rangesum(Above(Sum(Sales)/Sum(Total
Sales),1,RowNo()))<0.8, green(),
     If(Rangesum(Above(Sum(Sales)/Sum(Total
Sales),1,RowNo()))<0.9, Yellow(),
      Blue())),
    (Country,(=Sum(Sales),Desc))
  )
```

18. The result will look like the following screenshot

How it works...

In the first expression created as the `ABCClassification` dimension, `AGGR()` has two parameters. The first parameter contains the conditions to categorize the countries. The second parameter of the `AGGR()` `(Country,(=Sum(Sales),Desc))` is an extended version of the simple field usage, as in the previous recipes. The structured parameter specifies the sorting criteria using the `=Sum(Sales)` expression in descending order. The equals sign in front of the expression is necessary to sort by expression.

The second `Aggr()` is a variation using colors instead of text to define the classification, and it was used to color the bar chart.

There's more...

During the development of this recipe, I found an issue in the bar chart when using the **Color** by dimension using `ABCClassification` from the **Master items**, because all the bars turned gray.

The issue was observed in previous versions, including November/2018, February/2018, and April/2018, but apparently has been fixed in the June/2018 version and Qlik Cloud.

See also

- *Using nested aggregations*

Tips and Tricks 9

In this chapter, we will focus on some useful tips and tricks, such as the following:

- Working with multiple tabs
- Using the keyboard to navigate and interact
- Working with the distinct clauses
- Managing variables in the script and layout
- Using measure names in object expressions
- Creating dynamic charts

Introduction

This chapter will focus on useful tips and tricks to keep your work more productive.

Working with multiple tabs

During the process of creating a new application, we quite often must work with the **Data load editor** to prepare the data loading process and, after reloading, go to the layout editor and check some numbers with the visualization objects, and then go back to the **Data load editor** to add another data source or fix an error in the data load process. It is a cyclical process.

This recipe will show you how to work with the **Data load editor** and the layout editor on multiple sheets at the same time using the web browser.

Getting ready

For this recipe, we will use the app created in Chapter 8, *Advanced Aggregation with AGGR*. You can also use your existing app if you have access to the data source used to load it.

How to do it...

1. Open the web browser of your preference.
2. Type in the following URL: http://localhost:4848/hub. It will show the Qlik Sense Desktop hub.
3. Open the app created in Chapter 8, *Advanced Aggregation with AGGR*.
4. Click on the **Navigation** button to open the menu.
5. Click on the **Open in new tab** icon for the **Data load editor**:

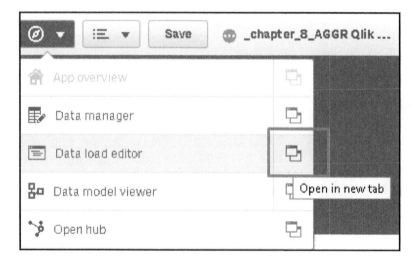

6. The **Data load editor** will be opened in a new tab.

7. Click on the title of the newly created tab, and drag it to the middle of the screen and drop it:

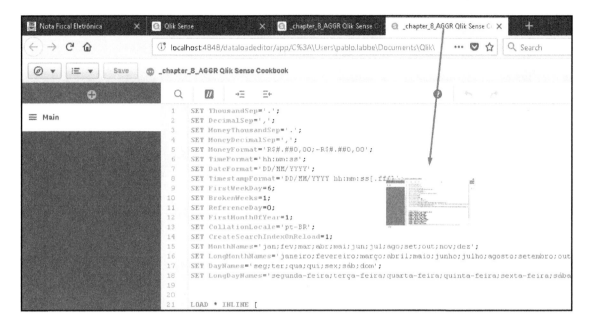

8. The tab will be detached from the main window, and a new browser window with only one tab will be created:

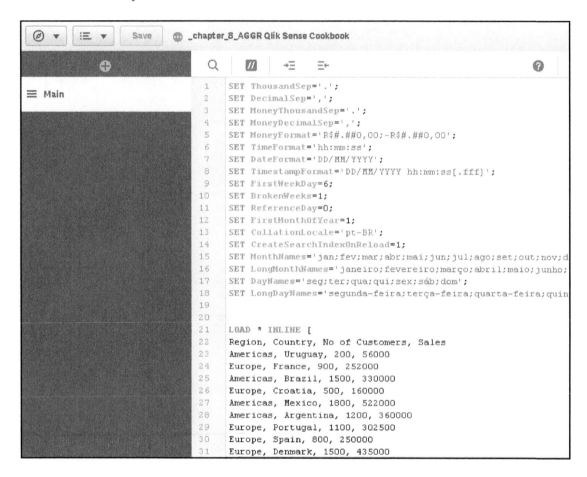

```
1   SET ThousandSep='.';
2   SET DecimalSep=',';
3   SET MoneyThousandSep='.';
4   SET MoneyDecimalSep=',';
5   SET MoneyFormat='R$#.##0,00;-R$#.##0,00';
6   SET TimeFormat='hh:mm:ss';
7   SET DateFormat='DD/MM/YYYY';
8   SET TimestampFormat='DD/MM/YYYY hh:mm:ss[.fff]';
9   SET FirstWeekDay=6;
10  SET BrokenWeeks=1;
11  SET ReferenceDay=0;
12  SET FirstMonthOfYear=1;
13  SET CollationLocale='pt-BR';
14  SET CreateSearchIndexOnReload=1;
15  SET MonthNames='jan;fev;mar;abr;mai;jun;jul;ago;set;out;nov;d
16  SET LongMonthNames='janeiro;fevereiro;março;abril;maio;junho;
17  SET DayNames='seg;ter;qua;qui;sex;sáb;dom';
18  SET LongDayNames='segunda-feira;terça-feira;quarta-feira;quin
19
20
21  LOAD * INLINE [
22  Region, Country, No of Customers, Sales
23  Americas, Uruguay, 200, 56000
24  Europe, France, 900, 252000
25  Americas, Brazil, 1500, 330000
26  Europe, Croatia, 500, 160000
27  Americas, Mexico, 1800, 522000
28  Americas, Argentina, 1200, 360000
29  Europe, Portugal, 1100, 302500
30  Europe, Spain, 800, 250000
31  Europe, Denmark, 1500, 435000
```

9. Change Mexico sales from 122000 to 522000 in the LOAD statement.

10. Reload the app, and use *ALT + TAB* to switch back to the main browser window. See how the top five ranking changed immediately after reloading finished.

11. Switch from the **Data load editor** and the **App overview** just using the keyboard, and vice versa.

How it works...

Qlik Sense Desktop can be operated via a web browser using the `http://localhost:4848/hub` URL, so we can benefit from the native browser features for tabs management to make our work more productive.

When reloading the application, you can't work on the tabs. It will show you a message of reloading in progress. After reloading is finished, the tab is released for user interaction.

There's more...

Using the browser tab management, you can work with multiple apps, and each of them on separate windows; and, on each window, you can have several tabs for each tool: Data load editor, Table visualization, and App overview/editor. You can switch between windows using *ALT + TAB*, and switch between tabs using *CTRL + TAB*.

See also

* *Using the keyboard to navigate and interact*

Using the keyboard to navigate and interact

Qlik Sense was primarily conceived to be used by touch gesture or a mouse device. The keyboard is used to type commands, expressions, text, and activate some shortcuts.

This recipe will show you how to use some useful shortcuts.

Getting ready

For this recipe, we will use the `Automotive.qvf` file, which comes as a built-in example when we install Qlik Sense Desktop.

How to do it...

1. Open the **Sales overview** sheet.
2. Type *CTRL + E* to enter Edit sheet mode.
3. Click on the **Line chart** object to select it.
4. Type *CTRL + C* and *CTRL + V* to duplicate it.
5. Type *CTRL + Z* to undo the operation.
6. Change the size of the objects, and note that the **Save** button becomes active.
7. Type *CTRL + S* to save the app with these changes.
8. Type *CTRL + E* to enter sheet view.
9. Type *CTRL + -* to zoom out of the window.
10. Type *CTRL + +* to zoom in the window.
11. Type *CTRL + O* to reset zoom in the window.
12. Click on **Brazil** in the **Car Sales by Territory** donut chart.
13. Type *Enter* to confirm the selection.
14. Click on the **Territory** field in the selection bar.
15. In the search box, type in *B** and *Enter,* and all countries starting with *B* will be selected.
16. Type *Esc* to cancel the selection.

How it works...

Qlik Sense provides shortcuts to allow primary users with disabilities to operate the software with the keyboard.

There's more...

You can play with shortcuts in the load editor as well. Here are some useful shortcuts:

- *Ctrl + Shift + Enter/Return*: Reloads the app
- *CTRL + S*: Saves the script code
- *CTRL + H*: Open
- *ALT + F9*: Show/hide the section panel on the left
- *ALT + F10*: Show/hide the Data connections panel on the right
- *ALT + F11*: Switch on/off the visualization of the command editor in fullscreen

You can find many other shortcuts at `help.qlik.com` by searching for "keyboard shortcuts" by way of keywords.

Working with the distinct clause

When building a Qlik Sense app, you often have to deal with some data issues such as duplicated records or values in a field. The duplication can be created by design, just like the customer ID in a sales transaction table, or could be an error if we find two exactly identical records created in a table.

This recipe will show you how to use the distinct clause to work with duplicated data in the **Data load editor** as well as in the object expressions.

Getting ready

For this recipe, we will make use of an inline data load that gives us sample data to demonstrate how the distinct clause works:

1. Create a new Qlik Sense file, and name it `Distinct Clause`.
2. Add the following `Inline` table that contains the location information for countries:

```
SalesData:
LOAD * INLINE [
    Product Line, Product Group, Product Sub Group, Year,
Sales, Cost
    Drink, Beverages, Juice, 2015, 12000, 6000
    Drink, Beverages, Juice, 2015, 12000, 6000
    Drink, Beverages, Juice, 2014, 16000, 7000
    Drink, Beverages, Juice, 2014, 16000, 7000
    Drink, Beverages, Soda, 2015, 42000, 26000
    Drink, Beverages, Soda, 2014, 68000, 57000
    Drink, Beverages, Water, 2015, 18000, 8000
    Drink, Beverages, Water, 2014, 10000, 6000
    Drink, Dairy, Milk, 2015, 25000, 22000
    Drink, Dairy, Milk, 2014, 22000, 20000
    Food, Dairy, Cheese, 2015, 22000, 8000
    Food, Dairy, Cheese, 2014, 31000, 30000
    Food, Produce, Nuts, 2015, 50000, 30000
    Food, Produce, Nuts, 2014, 46000, 26000
    Food, Produce, Tofu, 2015, 26000, 21000
    Food, Produce, Tofu, 2014, 15000, 7000
```

```
            Food, Snacks, Chips, 2015, 31000, 6000
            Food, Snacks, Chips, 2014, 15000, 9000
            Food, Snacks, Dips, 2015, 10000, 6000
            Food, Snacks, Dips, 2014, 6000, 3000
       ];

       ProductLine:
       LOAD DISTINCT
         [Product Line],
         [Product Group]
       RESIDENT SalesData;

       Drop field [Product Line] from SalesData; How to do it...
```

3. Drag across the **Table** object on to the sheet from the Assets panel. Name it `Distinct Table`.

4. Add `Product Line` as the **Dimension**.

5. Add `Product Group` as **Dimension**.

6. Add `Product Sub Group` as **Dimension**.

7. Add `Year` as **Dimension**.

8. Add **Sum(Sales)** as the measure and label it as `Sales`.

9. The result will look like the following screenshot:

Product Line	Product Group	Product Sub Group	Year	Sales
Totals				**493000**
Drink	Beverages	Juice	2014	32000
Drink	Beverages	Juice	2015	24000
Drink	Beverages	Soda	2014	68000
Drink	Beverages	Soda	2015	42000
Drink	Beverages	Water	2014	10000
Drink	Beverages	Water	2015	18000

10. The tables show the summary of all records but look at the first two lines. They are summing the duplicated rows that exist in the inline table in the first four lines:

```
        Drink, Beverages, Juice, 2015, 12000, 6000
        Drink, Beverages, Juice, 2015, 12000, 6000
        Drink, Beverages, Juice, 2014, 16000, 7000
        Drink, Beverages, Juice, 2014, 16000, 7000
```

11. To solve this issue, add a `DISTINCT` clause to the `LOAD` statement. The following is a sample snippet:

```
LOAD DISTINCT * INLINE [...
```

12. Reload the data, and the following screenshot will be displayed:

Product Line	Q	Product Group	Q	Product Sub Group	Q	Year	Q	Sales
Totals								465000
Drink		Beverages		Juice			2014	16000
Drink		Beverages		Juice			2015	12000
Drink		Beverages		Soda			2014	68000
Drink		Beverages		Soda			2015	42000
Drink		Beverages		Water			2014	10000
Drink		Beverages		Water			2015	18000

13. Add a new **Table** object on to the sheet. Name it `Distinct Count`.
14. Add `Product Line` as the **Dimension**.
15. Add **Count([Product Sub Group])** as the **Measure**.
16. Add **Count(Distinct [Product Sub Group])** as the **Measure**.
17. After reloading, the data should be OK now, as in the following screenshot:

Product Line	Q	Count([Product Sub Group])	Count(distinct [Product Sub Group])
Totals		18	9
Drink		10	5
Food		12	6

You can see that using the `DISTINCT` clause will show a different result than if we do not use the distinct clause. The correct number of product subgroups associated with each product line is 9, and not 18. 18 is the total number of rows in the `SalesData` table after loading in the memory.

18. Open the **Data model viewer**. There is a new table with the name **ProductLine**.

19. Select the table and open the **Preview** section. The following result shows the content of the table with only five rows created using the DISTINCT clause:

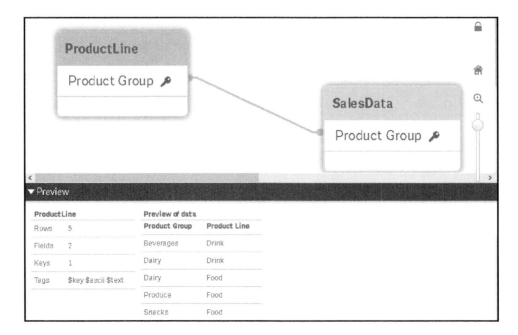

How it works...

When using the DISTINCT clause in the LOAD inline statement, the duplicated records are disregarded, keeping only the first one loaded. This is valid not only with inline tables, but also when loading records from flat files, residents, and SQLs.

When using the distinct clause in an aggregation expression, duplicated values in the **Product Sub Group** field are disregarded.

There's more...

You can create a list of Product Sub Group instances, adding the following expression as a measure:

```
concat(distinct [Product Sub Group],',')
```

Label it as Product Sub Group.

The resulting table will look like the following screenshot:

Product Line	Count([Product Sub Group])	Count(distinct [Product Sub Group])	Product Sub Group
Totals	18	9	Cheese,Chips,Dips,Juice,Milk,Nuts,Soda,Tofu,Water
Drink	10	5	Cheese,Juice,Milk,Soda,Water
Food	12	6	Cheese,Chips,Dips,Milk,Nuts,Tofu

Managing variables in the script and layout

Qlik Sense provides the option to define variables in the script and in the user interface.

The variable editor interface enlists the existing variables created in the script, and provides the user with the option to create new variables as well.

Getting ready

For the purpose of this recipe, we will make use of an inline data load that gives the sales information for four countries:

1. Create a new Qlik Sense application, and call it `QS_Variables`.
2. Load the following script in the application:

```
Sales:
LOAD * INLINE [
Country, Sales,COS
USA, 1000,500
UK, 2000,1000
France, 3000,2500
Germany, 4000,4700
];

Let vTemporary = 'Sum(Sales)';
Let vRedColor=RGB (255, 0, 0);
Let fSales= vTemporary;
Let vTemporary = null();
```

How to do it...

1. Open the QS_Variables application.
2. Create a new sheet called Sales, and go to the Edit sheet mode for the sheet.
3. While in Edit sheet mode, notice that we have a new icon, , in the lower-left corner. Click on the icon to open the **Variables** interface window.
4. The **Variables** interface window lists all the variables that we have defined in the script:

5. At the same time, it gives us the option to create new variables outside the script directly in the interface using the **Create new** button in the top-right corner.

6. Click on the **Create new** button and define a new variable, as shown here:

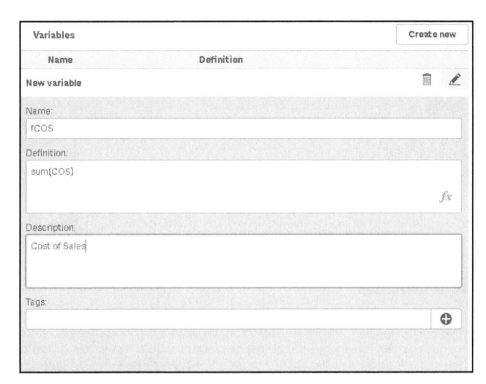

7. Click on the **Save** button and close the variable interface. Re-open to see the list of variables.
8. While still in Edit mode, drag a **Table** object on to the sheet.
9. Use **Country** as a dimension.
10. Create a measure with the following expression, and label it as Sales:

```
= $(fSales)
```

11. Create a second measure with the following expression, and label it as Cost of Sales:

```
=$(fCOS)
```

12. Define the **Background color expression** for `Cost of Sales`, as follows:

```
=if($(fCOS) > $(fSales),vRedColor, White())
```

The resulting table would look like this:

Sales			
Country ▲ 🔍		Sales	Cost of Sales
Totals		**10000**	**8700**
France		3000	2500
Germany		4000	4700
UK		2000	1000
USA		1000	500

How it works...

The variables can be put to effective use in the application to define expressions, as well as to store certain field values. If numeric values are stored in the variables, then we don't need to use the $ sign expansion while calling the variables. It is, however, a good practice to always use the $ sign, as it is needed in case of expression syntax, text, or literals.

The **Background color expression** references the variables containing the expressions we need. Referencing an existing expression as a variable instead of repeating the same code can also benefit overall chart performance. This is because the expression output can be reused from the cache memory where needed.

Note the prefix v and f before the variable names. It's best practice to differentiate the variables according to purpose, so variables starting with v store values, and variables starting with f store expression formulas.

Note, also, the variable named `vTemporary`; it receives a value as text and, at the end, a `null()` value is loaded into the variable. With that, the variables not saved in the app are not listed in the variable expression. It's good practice to set a null value to a script-only variable and not pollute the variable editor.

The variables that are defined in the script are denoted by a 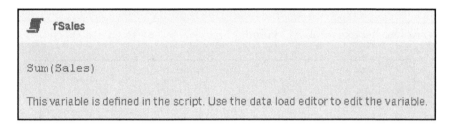 symbol in the variable interface, and can be edited only through the **Data load editor**, as shown in the following screenshot:

```
    fSales

Sum(Sales)

This variable is defined in the script. Use the data load editor to edit the variable.
```

There's more...

The variables can also be defined in external files, such as a text file, and then loaded into the application through the **Data load editor**.

In order to try this, complete the following steps:

1. Download the `Variables.xlsx` file from the Packt Publishing website and set up a library connection to the file location called `QlikSenseCookBook_SourceFiles` (to resemble the `FROM...` code used in the following code).

2. Copy and load the following code:

```
VariableDefinitions:
LOAD
    Variable,
    Expression
FROM [lib:// QlikSenseCookBook_SourceFiles/Variables.xlsx]
(ooxml, embedded labels, table is Variables);

Let vNumberOfRows = NoOfRows('VariableDefinitions');
For vI = 0 to (vNumberOfRows - 1)
Let vVariable_Name = Peek('Variable',vI,'Expression');
Let [$(vVariable_Name)] =
    Peek('Expression',vI,'Expression');
Next;
let vI = null();
Let vNumberOfRows = null();
let vVariable_Name = null();
```

If you now go back to the `Variable` list from the Edit sheet window, you will see a variable has been created for each row in the Excel file attached. The code below the FROM statement simply loops through each row of the Excel file, creating a new variable each time. The values in column *A* become the variable names, and the corresponding values in column *B* are used as the variable definitions.

This is the complete list of variables loaded:

Name	Definition
fCOS	sum(COS)
fMargin	($(fSales)-$(fCOS))
fMargin %	num($(fMargin)/ $(fSales),'0,00 %')
fSales	sum(Sales)
vRedColor	RGB(255,0,0)

Using measure names in object expressions

Qlik Sense provides the **Master items** to create dimensions and measures to be reused in the **Visualization** objects.

Each measure has a fixed label and, in some cases, we can use the measure name instead of the base expression to create new measures or for coloring a chart by expression.

Getting ready

For the purpose of this recipe, we will make use of the `QS_Variables` app created in the previous recipe. Ensure that you have already loaded the variables from the variables spreadsheet.

How to do it...

1. Open the `QS_Variables` application.
2. Open the `Sales` sheet and enter the Edit sheet mode for the sheet.
3. On the **Master items** section, go to **Measures**.
4. Add a new measure with the `$(fMargin %)` expression, and type in `Margin %` as a label.
5. Add the **Margin %** measure to the existing table.
6. Go to the Data section and expand the properties of the newly added measure.
7. Type in the following expression in **Background color expression**:

   ```
   if([Margin %]<0,vRedColor)
   ```

8. Add a new measure with expression `[Sales]-[Cost of Sales]`, and type in `Margin` as a label in the existing table object.
9. The resulting table will look like the following screenshot:

Sales				
Country 🔍	Sales	Cost of Sales	Margin %	Margin
Totals	**10000**	**8700**	**13,00 %**	**1300**
France	3000	2500	16,67 %	500
Germany	4000	4700	-17,50 %	-700
UK	2000	1000	50,00 %	1000
USA	1000	500	50,00 %	500

How it works...

When creating a new measure in an object, we can create an expression using the name of a master item or the label of a measure created in the object.

The **Background color expression** simply references the name of the master item containing the numbers we need. Referencing an existing expression label or master item name instead of repeating the same code can also benefit overall chart performance. This is because Qlik Sense only has to aggregate the values at a base data model level once; thereafter, the output can be reused from the cache memory where needed.

There's more...

When using a **Master items** name in an expression, the syntax checker in the expression editor can show a warning message, **Bad field name**, but don't worry; if the name is correct, it will work.

When referencing a label of an object's measure, the syntax checker works fine.

Creating dynamic charts

To increase the flexibility of a single chart object, you can set it up so that the dimension used is based on what the user wants to see. This is a much more efficient use of space for single sheets, and makes the whole experience much more dynamic.

Getting ready

For the purpose of this recipe, we will make use of the sales information for different fruits, as defined in the script:

1. Create a new Qlik Sense application and call it `QS_DynamicCharts`.
2. Load the following data into the **Data load editor**:

```
Transactions:
Load
 Mod(IterNo(),26)+1 AS Period,
 Pick(Ceil(3*Rand()),'Standard','Premium','Discount') AS
    ProductType,
 Pick(Ceil(6*Rand()),'Apple','Orange','Cherry','Plum','Fig',
    'Pear') AS Category,
 Pick(Ceil(3*Rand()),'Heavy','Medium','Light') AS Weight,
 Pick(Ceil(2*Rand()),'2013','2014') AS Year,
 Round(1000*Rand()*Rand()*Rand()) AS Sales
Autogenerate 20
While Rand()<=0.5 or IterNo()=1;

SET vDimension = 'GetFieldSelections(Dimensions)';

Dimensions:
LOAD * INLINE [
    Dimensions
    Weight
    ProductType
```

```
        Category
    ];
```

How to do it...

1. From the **App overview**, create a new sheet and enter the Edit sheet mode.
2. Add the **Dimensions** field on to the main content pane.
3. Drag a **Bar chart** object on to the content pane.
4. Add the following expression as a measure:

   ```
   Sum(Sales)
   ```

5. Add the following calculated dimension by clicking on the expression button:

   ```
   =Pick(Match($(vDimension),'Weight','ProductType',
       'Category'),Weight,ProductType,Category)
   ```

6. Enter one click of the space bar as the label to make it appear as if there is no dimension label.
7. Exit the editor mode, and select a value in the **Dimensions** field.
8. The final product should resemble the following screenshot:

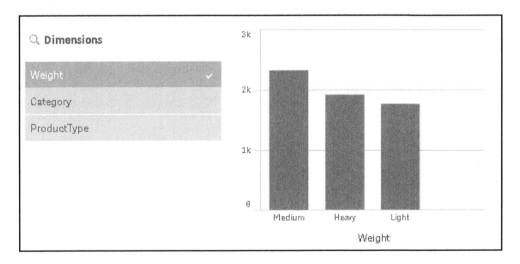

How it works...

In the script loaded at the beginning of the recipe, we set a variable called `vDimension`. The `GetFieldSelections()` function will return the values selected in the field we specify inside the brackets `GetFieldSelections (Dimensions)`. The `Dimensions` field is simply a hardcoded list of specific fields in the data model. The code we wrote in the dimension field of the chart uses this variable value to set the dimension dynamically to whatever value the user picks in the list box we created.

There's more...

If you are running Qlik Sense September/2017 or later, then you can now enter expressions on the Dimension label. If so, enter the following code:

```
=$(vDimension)
```

The result will be as follows:

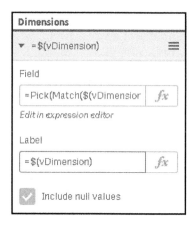

This displays the selected dimension in the dimension title dynamically. If you are running an earlier version of Qlik Sense, simply leave the label blank. After this, I would suggest creating a textbox explaining the chart, which will display whatever the value is, in the associated listbox. You can also use the preceding expression in the explanation textbox.

Other Books You May Enjoy

If you enjoyed this book, you may be interested in these other books by Packt:

Mastering Qlik Sense
Martin Mahler, Juan Ignacio Vitantonio

ISBN: 978-1-78355-402-7

- Understand the importance of self-service analytics and the IKEA-effect
- Explore all the available data modeling techniques and create efficient and optimized data models
- Master security rules and translate permission requirements into security rule logic
- Familiarize yourself with different types of Master Key Item(MKI) and know how and when to use MKI.
- Script and write sophisticated ETL code within Qlik Sense to facilitate all data modeling and data loading techniques
- Get an extensive overview of which APIs are available in Qlik Sense and how to take advantage of a technology with an API
- Develop basic mashup HTML pages and deploy successful mashup projects

Implementing Qlik Sense
Ganapati Hegde, Kaushik Solanki

ISBN: 978-1-78646-044-8

- Understand the importance and expectations of a consultant's role
- Engage with the customer to understand their goals and future objectives
- Design the optimum architecture, using the best practices for the development and implementation of your projects
- Ensure successful adoption using real-life examples to make your learning complete
- Learn about the important stages of a Qlik project's life cycle

Leave a review - let other readers know what you think

Please share your thoughts on this book with others by leaving a review on the site that you bought it from. If you purchased the book from Amazon, please leave us an honest review on this book's Amazon page. This is vital so that other potential readers can see and use your unbiased opinion to make purchasing decisions, we can understand what our customers think about our products, and our authors can see your feedback on the title that they have worked with Packt to create. It will only take a few minutes of your time, but is valuable to other potential customers, our authors, and Packt. Thank you!

Index

A

ABC analysis
  creating 282, 284, 285
Aggr()
  used, for combining set analysis 280, 282
  using, with Rank() 278, 279
alternate states
  using 250, 251, 252
approved sheets
  creating 123, 125

B

bar chart
  performance measure, highlighting 68, 71
Basket Analysis
  intersection, using between sets 246, 249
box plot charts
  used, for measuring statistical data 90, 91
Business Intelligence (BI) 7

C

Calendar fields
  generating, with Declare functions 195, 197
charts
  alternative dimensions, using 163, 165
  alternative measures, using 163, 165
  limitations, applying 154, 157
code
  packaging, in script files 102, 104
colormix1 function
  using 75, 76
command line programs
  executing, within script 118, 119
community sheets
  creating 123, 125
comparison sets

using, in Set Analysis 230, 232
composition 77, 80
Concat() function
  used, for capturing list of field values in Set
    Analysis 241, 242
  used, for displaying string of field values as
    dimension 183, 185
  using, to store multiple field values in single cell
    116, 118
content
  adding, to story 60, 63, 65
  creating, to story 60, 63, 65
cumulative effect
  analyzing, with waterfall chart 91, 93
currency exchange rate calendar
  creating, with Peek() function 204, 207

D

Dashboard Analysis Reporting (DAR) 57
data files
  data, extracting 8, 11, 14, 16
Data model viewer
  data, previewing 28, 33
  Master Library, creating 33, 35, 38, 40
Data model
  associations, viewing 30
  table metadata 31
  viewing 29
data relationships 80, 82
data-manager model viewer
  visual-data preparation, using 44, 48
data
  extracting, form data files 8, 11, 14, 16
  extracting, from databases 8, 11, 14, 16
  extracting, from FTP server 19, 21, 23
  extracting, from web files 16, 18
  extracting, from web services with REST

Connector 23, 26
  previewing, in Data model viewer 28, 33
databases
  data, extracting 8, 11, 14, 16
Declare functions
  used, for generating Calendar fields 195, 197
dimensional value
  latest record read, identifying with Previous()
    function 176, 179
dimensionless bar charts
  creating, in Qlik Sense® 145, 147
disable
  visual-data preparation, using 56
distinct clause
  working with 293, 295, 297
distribution analysis 85, 86
dual() function
  used, for setting sort order of dimensions 214,
    216
dynamic charts
  creating 304, 306

E

Edit mode
  Master Library, using 41
element functions E()
  using, in Set analysis 242, 245
element functions P()
  using, in Set Analysis 242, 245
embedded functions
  using, in Set Analysis 233, 235
embedded sheets
  adding, to story 66, 68
extended interval match
  used, for handling slowly changing dimensions
    170, 172, 175
extensions
  importing, into Qlik Branch 256, 257
  searching, on Qlik Branch 254, 255

F

field values
  persistent colors, associating with script 72, 74
FirstSortedValue() function
  used, for identifying the median in quartile range

193, 194
following
  visual-data preparation, using 51
For each loop
  used, for extracting files from folder 201, 203
  using, to load data from multiple files 114, 116
Fractile() function
  used, for generating quartiles 190, 192
FTP server
  data, extracting 19, 21, 23

I

images
  creating 150, 152, 154
intersection
  using, between sets for Basket Analysis 246,
    249

K

Key Performance Indicators (KPIs) 68
keyboard
  using, for interact 291, 292
  using, for navigate 291, 292
Keyhole Markup Language (KML) 129
KPI object
  using, in Qlik Sense® 138, 140

L

latest record read
  identifying, with Previous() function for
    dimensional value 176, 179
Legacy Mode
  activating, in Qlik Sense® desktop 26, 27
list of field values
  capturing, with Concat() function in Set Analysis
    241, 242

M

Master Library
  creating, from Data model viewer 33, 35, 38, 40
  using, in Edit mode 41, 43
measure names
  using, in object expressions 302, 304
median

identifying, in quartile range with
  FirstSortedValue() function 193, 194
Minstring() function
  used, for calculating age of oldest case in queue
    185, 187
moving annual total (MAT)
  about 197, 200
  setting up 197, 200
multiple tabs
  working with 287, 290, 291

N

nested aggregations
  using 275, 277
NetworkDays() function
  used, for calculating working days in calendar
    month 179, 182

O

object expressions
  measure names, using 302, 304
Open Database Connectivity (ODBC) 9

P

Peek() function
  used, for creating currency exchange rate
    calendar 204, 207
  used, for creating trial balance sheet 208, 211
performance measure
  highlighting, in bar chart 68, 71
persistent colors
  associating, to field values with script 72, 74
Previous() function
  used, for identifying latest record read for
    dimensional value 176, 179
private sheets
  creating 123, 125

Q

Qlik Branch
  extensions, importing 256, 257
  extensions, searching 254, 255
Qlik Management Console (QMC) 122
Qlik Sense

subroutines, using 105, 108
Qlik Sense® application
  publishing, created in Qlik Sense® Desktop 122
  publishing, to Qlik Sense® Cloud 125, 128
Qlik Sense® desktop
  Legacy Mode, activating 26, 27
Qlik Sense®
  dimensionless bar charts, creating 145, 147
  geo maps, creating 129, 134
  KPI object, using 138, 140
QlikView Script File 102
quartiles
  generating, with Fractile() function 190, 192

R

RangeSum() function
  using, to plot cumulative figures in trendline
    charts 188, 189
Rank()
  using, with Aggr() 278, 279
reload extension
  using 262, 264
reload time of application
  optimizing 111, 113
REST Connector
  used, for extracting data from web services 23,
    26

S

Sales reference lines
  versus Target gauge chart reference lines 135,
    137
scatter chart
  data points, navigating 160, 162
script files
  code, packaging 102, 104
script
  command line programs, executing 118, 119
  debugging, efficiently 97, 100, 102
  structuring 96
  used, for associating persistent colors to field
    values 72, 74
search strings
  using, inside set modifier 238, 240
Set Analysis

= sign, using with variables 224, 226
combining, with Aggr() 280, 282
comparison sets, using 230, 232
element functions E(), using 242, 245
element functions P(), using 242, 245
embedded functions, using 233, 235
flags, using 221, 222, 224
list of field values, capturing with Concat()
  function 241, 242
multi-measure expression, creating 236, 238
syntax, cracking 218, 219, 220
used, for point in time 226, 228, 229
set modifier
  search strings, using 238, 240
ShowHide Container extension
  using 267, 271, 273
simple KPI extension
  using 264, 267
single cell
  multiple field values, storing with CONCAT
    function 116, 118
slowly changing dimensions
  handling, with extended interval 170, 172, 175
snapshots
  creating 58, 60
sort order of dimensions
  setting, with dual() function 214, 216
standard deviation (SD)
  reference link 150
statistical data
  measuring, with box plot charts 90, 91
Statistical Process Control (SPC) chart 150
story
  content, adding 60, 63, 65
  content, creating 60, 63, 65
  embedded sheets, adding 66, 68
string of field values
  displaying, with Concat() function as dimension
    183, 185
subfield() function
  used, for splitting field into multiple records 212,
    213
subroutines

using, in Qlik Sense 105, 108

T

Target gauge chart reference lines
  versus Sales reference lines 135, 137
text
  creating 150, 152, 154
thumbnails
  adding 157, 159
treemaps
  creating 142, 144
trendline charts
  reference lines, adding 147, 150
trial balance sheet
  creating, with Peek() function 208, 211

U

UI calculation speed
  optimizing 109, 111

V

value comparison 83, 84
variable extension
  using 258, 261
variables
  managing, in layout 297, 302
  managing, in script 297, 299, 302
  managing, layout 299
visual exploration menu
  using 165, 167
visual-data preparation
  using, on data-manager model viewer 44, 48,
    51, 56
visualizations
  structuring 86, 89

W

waterfall
  using, to analyze cumulative effect 91, 93
web files
  data, extracting 16, 18
web services
  data, extracting with REST Connector 23, 26